path to :Gregor's

ING
WITH NATURE

"From the first paragraph, this masterpiece of a book
weaves a magical spell. Warm as a tropical sunset, fresh as a
woodland glade, Catriona MacGregor's inviting prose lifts
the veil between the material and spiritual worlds—and
transports you to the heart of being found in nature."

—**Dawson Church, PhD**, author of *The Genie in Your Genes*

"Catriona MacGregor's poignant *Partnering with Nature* is a
beautifully wrought synthesis of poetic spirituality and
well-grounded practical fact. Catriona creates an intriguing
tapestry of thoughts and images, weaving together history,
geology, scientific research, and her own profound spiritual
connection with the natural world."

—**Amy Racina**, author of *Angels in the Wilderness*

"Catriona's book *Partnering with Nature* is a gentle yet
somehow startling book, a work of unsuspected beauty, and
generously far-ranging in its scope, considering how much
it encompasses. It is written with the clarity of one who is
consciously living in the web of life and empowered by a
unique and enduring vision."

—**Jim Gilkeson**, author of *A Pilgrim in Your Body*
and *Energy Healing*

# PARTNERING WITH NATURE

## The Wild Path to Reconnecting with the Earth

## Catriona MacGregor

**ATRIA** PAPERBACK
New York London Toronto Sydney

 BEYOND WORDS
Hillsboro, Oregon

**ATRIA** PAPERBACK

A Division of Simon & Schuster, Inc.
1230 Avenue of the Americas
New York, NY 10020

**BEYOND** WORDS

20827 N.W. Cornell Road, Suite 500
Hillsboro, Oregon 97124-9808
503-531-8700 / 503-531-8773 fax
www.beyondword.com

Copyright © 2010 by Catriona MacGregor
Registered logo for Soul Coaching, Celtic symbol © 2010 by Denise Linn
Tree of Life image © Jen Delyth

Managing editor: Lindsay S. Brown
Copyeditor: Gretchen Stelter
Proofreading: Jennifer Weaver-Neist
Design: Devon Smith, Sara Blum
Illustrations: Isis Design
Composition: William H. Brunson Typography Services

First Atria Paperback/Beyond Words paperback edition April 2010

**ATRIA** PAPERBACK and colophon are trademarks of Simon & Schuster, Inc.
Beyond Words Publishing is a division of Simon & Schuster, Inc.

For more information about special discounts for bulk purchases, please contact Simon & Schuster Special Sales at 1-866-506-1949 or business@simonandschuster.com.

The Simon & Schuster Speakers Bureau can bring authors to your live event. For more information or to book an event, contact the Simon & Schuster Speakers Bureau at 1-866-248-3049 or visit our website at www.simonspeakers.com.

Manufactured in the United States of America

10  9  8  7  6  5  4  3  2  1

*Library of Congress Cataloging-in-Publication Data*

MacGregor, Catriona.
    Partnering with nature : the wild path to reconnecting with the Earth / Catriona MacGregor. — 1st Atria Paperback/Beyond Words paperback ed.
       p.  cm.
    Includes bibliographical references.
      1. Nature—Psychological aspects.   2. Whole and parts (Psychology).
3. Gaia hypothesis. 4. Human ecology. I. Title.

    BF353.5.N37 M33   2010
    155.9′1—dc22

                                  2009045599

ISBN  978-1-58270-219-3
ISBN  978-1-4165-9245-7 (ebook)

The corporate mission of Beyond Words Publishing, Inc.: *Inspire to Integrity*

To my family and my ancestors—the MacGregors—
who came to be known as the "Children of the Mists,"
and to all the other wild-eyed lovers of nature who have
gone before and those who are to come

# CONTENTS

Introduction: Partnering with Nature     ix

Part 1: Our Relationship with Nature
  1   Touched by Nature     3
  2   A Feeling Knowing—A Knowing Feeling     11
  3   Banished from the Realm of the Sacred     15

Part 2: The Wisdom of the Wild
  4   Plants As Evolutionary Masters     31
  5   Reading the Signs of Nature     55
  6   The Power of Animals     63
  7   Sacred Places     85

Part 3: Inner Wholeness
  8   The Spiral Dance     103
  9   Vision and Nature Quests     111
 10   Rites of Passage     127
 11   Healing Ourselves through Nature     145
 12   Honoring the Creative Within and Without     157

Part 4: Changing Ourselves, Changing the World
 13   Earth Song     175
 14   Toward a New Global Ethic     187
 15   Reverence for Life     197
 16   Singing the Animals Back to Life     207
 17   The Biggest Love     227
 18   Humanity and Purpose     235

Epilogue: Discovering Joy in Nature     257
Acknowledgments     263
Notes     265
Resources     287

# Introduction

## PARTNERING WITH NATURE

The real voyage of discovery consists not in seeking new landscapes
but in having new eyes.

MARCEL PROUST, French novelist

In this age of scientific triumph, our daily connection with the Earth
has diminished alarmingly. We are cut off from nature, and separate
from the animals and plants that surround us, making us strangers in
our own home. We miss the subtle changes in the wind, the calls of
birds, the smell of the fragrant Earth beneath our feet. We long for the
wonder of seeing the brilliant stars in the night sky and experiencing
the peace that pervades from a deep, tranquil pool of water. We spend
more time indoors than our ancestors did, and this leaves little time
for deep inner journeys or quiet walks in the woods, even though who
we are and what we are—the very root of our identity—is connected
to the Earth. Our spirits need engagement with the natural world;
without this, our souls wither. Though we seek the warmth of relationships, joy, and authenticity, none of these can be found in the
electricity lighting up homes and offices around the world.

Yet we are not alone. Nature is our partner in the truest sense of
the word. The Earth, animals, and plants do more than meet our

daily physical needs; they are our spiritual brothers and sisters. They not only do the obvious—feed us and befriend us—but they also help us reach greater heights of understanding, health, and spirituality. For thousands of years, people have connected with nature to gain greater knowledge and spiritual fulfillment. Nature offers us healing, wisdom, and an opportunity to connect with the sacred. It is a portal to an infinite and timeless realm offering insights into a larger reality that is beyond our day-to-day comprehension. Even today, there are ways that we can become more closely attuned to the natural world, lifting the veil between us and the underlying mystery and beauty of the world.

Partnering with nature means understanding that nature reflects the ultimate creative, compassionate force in the universe. Divinity is not of some other place but is found on Earth: in the gentle wind, the life-giving water, the animals, and the plants all around us.

Partnering with nature means opening up to an ongoing conversation, listening to and learning from everything—from the smallest living being to the Earth Herself. We are not meant to exist in isolation as a species; the path we are meant take is with all other life on Earth.

Partnering with nature means reviving the ways of knowing that we possessed when we lived closer to the rhythm of the Earth while understanding that we have evolved and must continue to evolve these ways. We rely on the wisdom of the ancients while drawing from the new.

Partnering with nature means learning to live simply and joyously within a new global ethic that values the environment.

Partnering with nature means changing our underlying beliefs about our role in relation to nature and other living things.

Partnering with nature means learning new ways of living and working by applying nature's wisdom.

While this book is about how human beings can gain greater wisdom, health, and spiritual enlightenment, it is also about the need for us to address growing environmental problems. We will be able to solve problems, such as global warming, when we gain greater awareness about who and what we are in relation to the Earth and other living creatures. By adopting the ethical construct that all living things are sacred, we can save the Earth.

We need to begin the healing with ourselves. We cannot separate our thoughts and beliefs from what is happening in the world around us because the one creates the other. From the invisible realm of thoughts, beliefs, and feelings comes the world we are creating.

While I have protected the environment through legislation and conservation projects for many years, my focus has broadened over time to include helping people to heal their disconnectedness from nature and ultimately from themselves. It is this disconnection that is the root cause of many of our environmental problems. By building an enduring bridge between humans and the Earth, we heal ourselves as we heal the planet.

Usually, when we speak about protecting the environment, we speak about habitat protection, reducing carbon emissions, and banning toxins. These external acts are absolutely essential, but without a vision for ethical goodness toward all life, the "environmental cause" is unlikely to succeed in the long run.

Is our sole purpose on Earth to gain physical mastery of the world? Are we here to dominate nature and the "lower" animals? I do not think so. Rather, is it our unique ability to connect with the great diversity of life on Earth and ultimately the Creator Herself that is our larger goal.

We humans are like a mirror of the world around us. We have the capacity to tap into the web of existence that underlies the universe and connects every living thing. We are here to unleash the physical, energetic, and spiritual potentialities within us and other species, and to bring greater life, joy, and wisdom to the universe. As a species, we are defined by our capacity to love. Our role on

Earth is to love, appreciate, and serve the great diversity of life as if it were our own life—because it is.

Nature, in its pure, unpolluted state, contains the energetic and spiritual elements that sustain life. Being in touch with the land, the mountains, the sea, and the forest enhances our sense of self and our ability to make wise choices. From this place of clarity, calm, and steadiness, we influence the energies around us for the better. We choose to make a positive contribution to the Earth and other living things.

Healing often begins with the journey to the spirit—the invisible, energetic core that infuses all creation. We gain emotional and physical harmony when we reconnect with the Earth, and this brings us to the door of a spiritual awakening. In ancient traditions around the world, humankind communicates with the Creator through interacting with the animals, birds, and trees. It is through these "messengers" that humankind connects with the sacred to be at one with all creation.

I have had mystical experiences in nature since childhood which have allowed me to learn how to help myself and others to connect with nature to gain healing, knowledge, peace, and joy. The greatest thing that I have learned from nature—the sage—is the simplest: Honor and celebrate the world and sing its praises. Sing the praises of our brothers and sisters on Earth—the animals that we are so fortunate to live among, the plants that sustain us more than we know, and this beautiful planet.

I invite you to see the possibilities for yourself and to view nature with new eyes. My hope is that, by reading this book and gaining a greater awareness of your own connection to nature, you will join me in fostering a new ethic—one that reveres all life on Earth.

# PART I

## Our Relationship with Nature

# 1

## Touched by Nature

Forget not that the Earth delights to feel your bare feet,
and the winds long to play with your hair.

Kahlil Gibran, *The Prophet*

For as long as I can remember, I have been in love with nature and touched by her. The feeling that something magical and significant was right outside my door filled my waking hours. Indoors, I missed the stirring life outdoors—the flitting wings of a dove; the tips of the tall, delicate ears of a hare peeking over the grasses. Outside, time took on a new dimension. I would sit for hours watching a pair of red-winged blackbirds build their nest; or walk lightheartedly through the woods, lost in reverie as the day sped by. In my youth and innocence, I was free to simply be in nature.

My outdoor explorations started early. At the age of four, I recall looking down through rows of shiny, dark green needles at my mother and godmother from near the top of a sixty-foot-tall eastern hemlock. Amazed and aghast, they nervously coaxed me to come down. I recall thinking it odd that they did not share my sense of urgency to return the downy, fallen fledgling robin back to its nest. I carefully placed the tiny bird, with its comical-looking tufts of head feathers and its speckled orange breast, back into the beautifully crafted nest of twigs. Satisfied, I climbed down the tree as ably as a monkey into my mother's outstretched arms.

I realize now that my parents gave me great freedom to dive wholeheartedly into the world of nature. Nature beckoned me to come and explore: to follow the deer path through the mountain laurel with delicate pink and white blossoms; to place my bare feet in a stream of cool water; to run with my arms outstretched, pretending to fly with a flock of mourning doves. I grew up with a compass set toward the wilds, and along the way, I learned many things.

During my first years of school, spending time in a classroom seemed unbearable. I felt so confined sitting on the little swivel chair, wedged into the wooden desk. I would keep my face hidden from the teacher behind a book, while gazing longingly out the window. There was so much life out there, where the red fox was making its nest under leaves; where tiny hummingbirds hovered, their iridescent colors mercurially changing in the glinting sunshine. On weekend mornings, I would rouse myself from sleep and wander to the bottom of our garden. Once there, I would crawl under the verdant boughs of the willow tree canopy, with its long leaves cascading to the ground, and sit on the shade-softened grass. I would sit there for long periods of time with my arms wrapped around my legs, resting my chin upon my knees in happy contemplation.

On frequent forays into the woods, my attentiveness to wild things became a magnet to me. Animals frequently appeared as I ran along the woodland trails into the open meadows or peered into dark thickets of blackberry bushes. I brought home the ones that needed help: the tiny, pink baby sparrows with opaque eyelids whose nest fell from a tree; the orphaned young squirrel that "adopted" me when it climbed up onto my shoulder and stayed there as I walked home; the downy sparrow hawk chick that was tossed from its nest in a storm; and the graceful white swan that had been poisoned. These early experiences of "mothering" brought great joy and also taught me about life and death, and how closely these two realms lie together.

Years later, as an awkward preteen-ager, the complications of human existence became all too apparent. My interests turned to boys, fitting in with my peers, and adjusting to my developing body. I was no longer as easily absorbed by the beauty and mystery of the diversity of life around me as I tried to "adapt." The nickname "Nature Girl" stung then, and I turned away from the beckoning call of the woods (which I recognized again as my greatest sustenance). Then the unthinkable happened.

My father, a gentle and wise soul dedicated to his work as a psychiatrist and to the care of his patients, committed suicide when I was twelve. He had saved many lives while serving in the British Navy as a doctor, but had been seriously injured in the Spanish Civil War when a grenade went off and overturned his jeep. Complications from this head injury haunted him the rest of his life. After leaving the navy and graduating from Cambridge University, he opened a successful medical practice in Edinburgh, Scotland. This is where he first met my mother, Irene. He said that my mother, with her auburn hair, green eyes, and lovely lilting voice, was one of the most beautiful women in all of Edinburgh. They started their family in England and Scotland, and, after the birth of their third daughter, immigrated to the United States, where I became the only American-born member of the family. My father, Joseph, a shy, brilliant man, loved the outdoors, and it was his love of nature that inspired me.

I was devastated by his suicide. The world lost its very coherence. Yet just when my faith in the very fabric of the world was most tested, I had a spiritual awakening in the woods near our home. One early morning, before sunrise, I lay in bed, unable to sleep. Filled with despair, I left the house in the pale light of early dawn. Pulling on a wool sweater to protect myself from the chilled air, I went into the forest behind our home. Standing in a tall, silent grove of maple, oak, and birch trees, tears streaming down my face, a gentle stillness filled me. My hands relaxed and opened, and the ache in my heart lifted and vanished.

In that moment, the place within that grove of trees became as vast and infinite as the universe. The shafts of light through the trees filled each thing they touched with a strange ethereal glory. I was enveloped in what felt like a compassionate embrace from the trees. All time seemed to condense into a few everlasting moments that stretched for an eternity. In that otherworldly sky of leaves and branches, I understood and felt connected to all living beings. I stood on the Earth, on ground dappled with tender golden light, and realized that death is a continuum and a person's soul is immortal. It was as if I could see the invisible threads of life that kept us all held together within a compassionate and wise cosmos. In that moment, I knew that all living beings—no matter how seemingly small or lost— always find their way back home.

I fell asleep amongst the trees, lying on soft, jade-colored moss, under the cover of the green canopy. I slept soundly, and when I awoke, the sun was warm upon my body. I lay quietly beneath the soft shadows of the trees, the full light of day now touching the topmost leaves, which reflected the sun like flakes of quivering fire. I watched a towhee, just inches from my resting arm, scatter delicate leaves with nimble yellow legs. Then, in the distance, I heard the soaring call of a red-tailed hawk, and I longed to return home. I rose, gently brushed off the twigs and leaves that clung to my sweater, and walked back a different person than when I had arrived hours earlier. I was now filled with an understanding of a deep truth: no matter how dark or desperate things may appear, we can find the love and wholeness that always surrounds us at the heart of existence.

This occurrence, and others like it, has filled me with profound gratitude and awe for the wisdom that awaits in the shy stare of a black-eyed doe or the profound silence of a towering redwood. Nature helped me come to a view of the world that I may not have come to on my own.

As an adult, I learned that my experiences in nature have been shared by many people around the globe—probably since humans first walked the face of the Earth. These experiences of touching the sacred on Earth have proven to be a songline—a golden thread weaving meaning through my life.[1] My childhood experiences were followed by others of comparable meaning, beauty, and mystery as I grew to adulthood.

## THE TREE OF LIFE

*I wonder if honeysuckles grow about the gates of heaven . . .*
*I have thinks there will be flowers growing all about. Probably*
*Creator brought the seed from heaven when he did plant the*
*flowers here on Earth. Too, I do think when angels bring babies*
*from heaven to folks that live here below, they do also bring*
*seeds of flowers and do scatter them about. I have thinks that*
*they do this so the babies may hear the voices of loving flowers*
*and grow in the way of Creator.*

—Opal Whiteley (six years old)[2]

Twenty years after my spiritual awakening in the forest, I had largely forgotten that singular experience and never discussed it. I eventually grew up, went to college then law school, got a job, got married, had a son, and so on. Like most people, I was influenced by societal dictates and sought to put aside any "unusual" or unexplainable experiences.

This all changed for me on one dark and moonless night in October, when I arrived home late, again, from the office. The dark clouds moved swiftly against a midnight-blue sky, and I was cautiously walking on a poorly lit, uneven stone path to my house.

 I had a full bag of groceries in my arms and a briefcase hung uncomfortably from my shoulder. It seemed as if my entire body ached from the long day. As I turned the corner to walk through the dark, empty lot next to my house, I saw a soft, glowing light. A golden-white light illuminated the lot warmly, like the delicate rays of the first morning sun.

I stopped and looked around curiously for the source of the light. I peered past the large tree in the center of the lot that had now become quite prominent. To my surprise, the strange light appeared to be emanating from the tree. My mind doubted what my eyes saw. I searched around for a more plausible source of light, yet I could find none. In disbelief, I hurried past the tree to my house, fumbled for the keys to the door, and closed it quickly behind me. With my heart beating rapidly, I could not register what I had just witnessed. No longer tired, I put the groceries on the counter, caught my breath, and slowly opened the door to have another look. Placing only one foot outside, I looked toward the vacant lot, hoping to see only darkness. Instead, the tree illuminated the lot and surrounding buildings as brightly as if the moon had come to rest gently upon the soft grass.

Emerging fully onto the small wooden porch, I stood facing the tree. The tree's light felt warm against the chill of the evening. My cares fell away as a deep peace enveloped me. Looking back upon that experience now, what I recall most was the sense of pure beauty and joy. With that glimpse of an infinitely wise and compassionate universe, I knew that the light was the fire of the tree's divine spirit—the tree's very soul. There are no words to describe that which is known as intimately as a lover and yet remains unfathomable.

After an indeterminate amount of time had passed, I turned away, and went inside the house and upstairs to bed. I lay quietly next to my sleeping husband and fell immediately into a sound sleep.

When I awoke the next morning feeling refreshed, the tree was far from my conscious mind. After taking a shower and dressing, I helped my son get ready for school, made his lunch, and packed it neatly into his lunch box. Hand-in-hand, we walked to his school before I headed back to my car to drive the forty-five minutes to my office.

I returned home earlier than I had the previous day, just as the late afternoon sun was beginning to cast long shadows. I found a parking place near the little town center and walked past the statue of the peaceful Indian with a bow held by his side. I noticed there were a few yellow leaves resting gently on his head—a sign of fall. When the empty lot next to our house came into view, I was stunned.

What I saw was not the beautiful tree that I had communed with less than a day before. Instead, I saw a ghastly two-foot stump surrounded by tiny clumps of wood arbitrarily spewed around the lot. Little, ugly splinters of wood were all that was left of something that had been indescribably beautiful. My sadness was immeasurable. Yet, I also recognized the miracle that had occurred. The tree, knowing of its impending demise, shone forth its inner light, sharing its everlasting soul with the rest of the world as if to say: *Behold, I am more than bark and limbs and leaves and roots. I am eternal beauty and wonder. Celebrate and honor what I am and recognize that we are one and the same, as this marvel exists within yourself as well.*

I was altered by this singular vision. I've had glimpses of this deeper reality throughout my life, but while I understood these experiences to be valuable, I nonetheless had kept them separate from "ordinary" life. To explore that "dream time" in the light of day offered an uncertain future in an unknowable realm. I was reluctant to face a destination beyond my comprehension and travel a path that would lead where I had never been before.

On that fall evening, seemingly separate ways of knowing and being collided in an instant. Nature opened the door of my understanding to assert that the two worlds are one after all. A bridge appeared between the common and the sacred, and I knew that I could no longer keep hallowed, mystical experiences within the deep center of myself. This was a sign to gather up all of the mysterious and enigmatic moments threaded throughout my life and unfurl them in the bright light of day. From that time forward, I began in earnest to go where those golden, sacred threads led me. I knew then that, like the tree, I was but part of a divine mystery, and that my path was intertwined with the path of the tree and other living things.

Being a witness to the tree's soul strengthened a resolve in me to live a new life, to follow a new path. I was fully committed to heralding the message of the tree's soul and, along with it, a message of what the human race is here for and capable of accomplishing. This book was, in part, created on that evening. That moment in time ties us indelibly together: you the reader, the tree, and me. We are here together to bear witness to the beauty, grace, and wisdom in nature; to appreciate and love all of this; and to be loved in return.

Although the experiences that I have had reflect a unique bond with nature, all people have the potential to connect with nature in a deep and abiding way. There are many people who used to live and still do live in touch with the wisdom of the wilds.

# 2

# A Feeling Knowing—
# A Knowing Feeling

As we hurtle into the future, the trappings of modern life isolate us from
the Earth and leave little room for the inward journey . . .
We have forgotten how to watch these signs, how to listen to the
messages in the winds, and how to gain wisdom from the trees . . .
Hence very few people truly understand what forces have
motivated their life or shaped their destiny.

Denise Linn[1]

When our ancestors gazed upon an antelope, a bird, a flower, or the stars, they gazed with the intimate eyes of a lover. They knew and understood the wild things because they spent all of their days and nights in their company. They knew how the sparrow hawk holds her delicate body airborne and immobile in a stalwart wind; they knew what the bobcat feeds her young; and they knew when the salmon would return to their home stream to spawn. They understood these things because their own lives were inextricably intertwined with the lives of the animals and the seasons of the Earth. Their daily contact and reliance on nature brought them tremendous insights about the Earth, about relationships beyond the human sphere, and about life itself.

We can learn to live lives of greater meaning by living closer to nature and understanding that the sacred exists at our fingertips. I don't propose that we throw out our modern conveniences; ancient peoples certainly faced troubles we have successfully managed to overcome with modern technology. But we can learn from people who once lived much closer to the Earth, incorporating their intimate understanding of nature into how we lead our lives and infusing life with greater meaning.

Consider the Evenk, the reindeer people who live in northeast Siberia where temperatures can drop to 96 degrees below zero. In spite of this inhospitable climate, they live and thrive by keeping close to ancient tradition. They mirror the behavior of the animals and form tightly woven relationships with the reindeer to help them survive in extreme conditions. The Evenk rely on the reindeer for most of their needs, using their meat for food, their sinews for string, and their bones for tools.

The reindeer are acclimatized to the cold and have adapted a pattern of migration, traversing large distances to find food and shelter when the cold winters have a hold on northern Siberia. For thousands of years, the Evenk have followed the annual reindeer migration from upper Mongolia to northern Siberia,[2] living in temporary shelters until it is time to migrate once again. Although the Evenk rely upon the reindeer's body for survival, they also believe that they share a spiritual, energetic essence with the reindeer and with the land itself. In the Evenk's world, a compassionate spirit pervades the vast landscape. They call this all-knowing, all-feeling spirit Bayanay. Bayanay is not separate from the people, the animals, or the land, but permeates all in a "field of shared consciousness."[3]

By sharing their physical lives with the reindeer, the Evenk are empowered with greater wisdom about how to live in this region. Similarly, we can learn from other creatures' ways of knowing and experiencing the world. For example, animals have incredible skills and abilities far beyond our ken. Dogs are able to tell the identity of a person who quickly walked by hours earlier by simply sniffing the ground. (Dogs have 20–40 times more smell receptors in their nose than human beings.) Some insects and birds can see wavelengths of light outside humans' visible range. This means certain birds that appear drab to us are seen in radiant colors by other birds.

Many plants and animals are intimately familiar with the larger patterns of nature and the universe. Snow geese, which migrate thousands of miles, can see the magnetic lines of the Earth. If a human being had these animals' abilities, we would consider them superpowers. When we develop a relationship with other living things, we begin to "see" and experience the world in the way that they do. Most important, by escaping the confines of our own consciousness, we come closer to experiencing divinity—a realm not easily entered through ego-driven perception.

The Evenk, whose ancestral lineage goes back to the Neolithic time period (eight thousand to nine thousand years ago), have gained a rich spiritual and healing tradition through a shamanic reliance upon the reindeer's spirit. By seeing the divinity in the animals and the place in which they live, an intrinsically dynamic and intelligent universe is open to them. In the case of Evenk shaman, their soul connection with the reindeer empowers them to see the future, understand the unknowable, heal individuals, and advise the entire community.

When we adopt this way of knowing and being in the world, meaning is instilled into even the smallest daily tasks. When the Evenk's ancestors awoke and left their summer khants, they beheld the endless plains of grasslands, the vast sky overhead, and the powerful bodies of the reindeer; they understood the spiritual and energetic dynamics that exist between them, the reindeer, and the land.

The lives of the Evenk were physically difficult in many ways, often filled with peril from the extreme temperature and the demands of a nomadic life. Yet their spiritual awareness brought richness and depth to their lives, in spite of the hardships of living in a remote and harsh region. Because the Evenk, the reindeer, the sky, and the land are united in the rhythmic dance of life, they are gifted with insights about how to live and how to heal each other, along with an abiding sense of belonging to a world of meaning, power, and beauty.

Many indigenous people have managed to keep an enduring vision of the sacred Earth as a place of beauty and connectedness. Native Americans in Alaska know when the salmon are returning to their home streams because a certain yellow flower that is native to the area first blooms in the spring when the salmon return. The blooming of this flower, which matches the color of the salmon's eyes, is not deemed a mere coincidence but rather a sign of the link between the flower and the salmon, and as a glimpse into the workings of the Great Mystery. This singular occurrence speaks to the underlying unity between all three—the Alaskans, the flowers, and the salmon.

We don't need to migrate with the reindeer or fish for salmon in Alaska to experience sacredness on Earth. We can receive greater meaning, beauty, and wisdom by becoming more knowledgeable about the natural world and ourselves. When we see and experience the sacred in all life, we elevate meaning, honoring the sacred in ourselves.

A key premise of this book is that by deepening our relationship with nature, we deepen our understanding of ourselves. We are not only ensuring greater health and wisdom but, ultimately, we are able to solve seemingly insurmountable global problems. Once humankind mends its broken bonds with nature, it will return to its roots, the Earth, and all other living things.

# 3

## BANISHED FROM THE REALM OF THE SACRED

*Nor will I call out upon the mountains, fountains, or hills,*
*or upon the rivers, which now are subservient to the use of men . . .*
*and to which the blind people once paid divine honor.*

GILDAS, *On the Ruin and Conquest of Britain*[1]

When we humans believe that we are separate from other living things, we lose touch with all life and ultimately ourselves. Yet, early Western philosophers inexorably shaped long-standing beliefs of humans being completely separate from other life and even the Creator. For example, Aristotle denied the possibility of evolution, believing that the universe was fixed in eternity with a Creator that existed *outside* of the Earth. Although many of his scientific and theological views are wholly contrary to what we know and believe today, his ideas wielded great influence.

Hundreds of years after the death of Aristotle, these same beliefs were used to shape a new worldview. These ideas were preserved through time because of the power of the written word. Since only a relative handful of people could read and write in Aristotle's day, the ability to write down one's ideas was a rarified honor that exerted immense influence on people's beliefs and perceptions. The Catholic Church immortalized some of Aristotle's ideas for their own ends. The Church furthered the belief that God existed outside the Earth, and by doing so, made the church priests intermediaries to the one distant God and all-powerful purveyors of divinity on Earth. This singular belief that God exists beyond or outside the Earth, and the insurgence of the most successful monotheistic institution in the history of humankind, shaped a paradigm that led to a disconnection between people and all other species, and ultimately a disconnection between people and God.

Prior to medieval Christianity, and for the majority of humankind's time, the sacred was deemed to exist in a vast variety of forms found on Earth. These living and nonliving intermediaries to the Creator could be found in one's own backyard and yet served as doorways to the divine realm. At that time, "pagans" (a term that does not do justice to the sophistication and breadth of the many cultures and peoples that experienced Earth-based divinity) covered the four corners of the Earth. Pagans or polytheists lived in advanced societies, such as Greece, Rome, and Egypt, as well as in supposedly uncivilized cultures. To polytheists, divinity came equally in feminine, masculine, and even animal forms. For example, the Etruscans and the Greeks worshipped the goddesses Artemis and Aphrodite, and great shrines were made in their honor. The Egyptian Creator was known as Ra, the great god of the Sun, and had the head of a falcon. Epona was the great Roman goddess and protector of horses, and it is hinted that she had a greater role as a guide on the soul's final journey.

A colossal spiritual power shift took place with the establishment of Catholicism. This new religious institution and its representatives gained an elite status in society as sole guardians to the divine. Banished from the realm of the sacred, ordinary people were told that a single God, remote from the Earth, could save their souls—as long as they converted to Christianity.

It is needless to enter upon the absorbing work that during those ages occupied the Church in her mission of civilizing the barbarians who invaded and overturned the old Roman culture ... Small place had it in the intelligence of the child of Nature, just emerging from his woodland home, with his simple habits and his few wants. To teach him the elementary truths of the Christian religion, to subdue the native fierceness of his nature, to accustom him to peaceful pursuits, and above all, to induce him to live up to the Christian standard of morality—this was the primary work of the Church. To this must all else yield.

—Brother Azarias[2]

Ultimately, nature-based spiritual practices were marginalized and destroyed by the new religious order. The brutalities of the Church through inquisitions and witch trials eliminated any lingering remnants of European polytheism.

The lasting effect ... upon the world can only be measured in the lives of the hundreds of thousands of men, women, and even children who suffered and died at the hands of the Inquisitors during the Inquisition ... Its effects were even felt in the New World, where the last gasp of the Inquisition was felt in the English settlements in America (most notably in Salem, Massachusetts, during the Salem Witch Trials).[3]

The Catholic Church also played a key role in bringing about the final collapse of the great Greek and Roman religions and civilizations in Europe. Church officials ordered that their temples, devoted to multiple gods and goddesses, be destroyed and then outlawed or took over their religious ceremonies.

During the Middle Ages, as the Church grew in predominance, it became an extremely wealthy institution, holding vast quantities of gold, silver, and artistic treasures, as well as significant property. In fact, for most of the Middle Ages, the Church represented not only religious but secular authority in much of Europe. As a secular or governmental power, the Church levied taxes, collected fees, and even coined money. In addition, those who were put through inquisition could lose all of their property to the church. Eventually, these materialistic pursuits and emphases also became a focus among the people who were contributing financially to the church. At the same time, they were separated from direct connection to their "God," leaving them little option but to look for deep meaning in their lives through physical pursuits.

Most devastating however, was that once the Church fathers depicted God as appearing in the garb of a grandfatherly, white male, divinity was deemed to flow from this one source instead of from every flower that grew. All other living things that did not resemble the white, masculine God—including women, children, non-Caucasian people, and animals—were demoted in this new heavenly hierarchy.

By declaring humankind alone as being in the image of this interpretation of God, while failing to affirm that sacredness exists in all living things, we severely limited our understanding of divinity, and our ability to receive joy and wisdom that resides in all beings. God did not just create humankind; God created all that is. And while humankind is certainly the pinnacle of "God's" creation, we misuse our role when we misuse and underestimate other life forms.

It is important to understand the significant differences between the actual beliefs and teachings of Jesus and the dogma promoted by religious leaders, who were aligned first and foremost with building an institution. For example, the treatment of women by the representatives of the Church differs greatly from that offered by Jesus's model. Jesus upheld Mary Magdalene as one of his closest and greatest prophets, yet the Catholic Church denied equal status to women and portrayed Mary as a prostitute. Jesus condemned the money-changers at the Temple of Jerusalem, and yet Church leaders shaped the institution of the church to accumulate great material wealth. Of course, the defining difference between Jesus's teaching and that of the church is revealed in the Gospel of Thomas. In the Gospel of Thomas, Jesus preaches that divinity exists in even the most commonplace objects:

> I am the light, which is before all things. It is I who am all things. From me all things came forth, and to me all things extend. Split a piece of wood, and I am there; lift up a stone, and you will find me.[4]

By seeing the sacred on Earth, Jesus' teachings closely mirror the pre-Christian beliefs of pagans and other Earth-based spiritualists.

Earth-based spiritualism, once universal, now primarily survives among small pockets of indigenous peoples. Yet all people can find divinity in their own lives; there are many paths that lead to the Creator. But it is not the specific religious path chosen that brings one closer to the Creator. It is a willingness and commitment to seek and cultivate divinity within oneself.

While the Catholic Church can be blamed for some of our disconnection from nature, spirit, and ultimately ourselves, we cannot blame the Church for our ancient inclination (as far back as Adam and Eve) to see the universe in terms of duality versus oneness. In our manifested reality, duality exists all around us. But the Church played no small part in accentuating the worst aspects of duality by cataloging everything as either evil or good.

There are also many Catholics who have benefited the world in no small measure. More concerned with their own good works than with building an institution, they work tirelessly and compassionately to provide help to those in need.

Nature-based spirituality does not need to be contrary to traditional religious belief systems like Catholicism, as it shares with all religions the commonality of seeking for truth. Nature-based spirituality can be a part of all religious experiences and traditions and yet belong to none, because it transcends dogmas and rigid constructions of meaning.

Today, however, connection to divinity through nature-based spirituality has been largely lost. Over time, our eyes have slowly dimmed to the sacredness here on Earth. By adopting beliefs that are antithetical to experiencing the joy of divine creation here, we banished ourselves from heaven on Earth. Yet our fall from grace might never have taken place within the rhythm and cycles of nature. When we stepped out of rhythm with the Earth, that "falling" became a resolute outcome.

## FALLING IN LINEAR TIME

*That which sings and contemplates in you*
*is still dwelling within the bounds of that first moment*
*which scattered the stars into space*

—Kahlil Gibran[5]

At the dawn of humankind's existence, our sense of time was considerably different than it is today. While we have no written records of how time was experienced by the first humans, we can interpret our ancestors' experience from ancient myths and stories. Like many indigenous peoples today, time was likely conceptualized as occurring in cycles with seasonal events. The world was a place of eternal occurrences. Immortality existed through cycles, events, and processes that were destined to repeat. Pythagoras believed in a cyclical run of time. When one cycle came to an end, after many thousands of years, a new cycle would start from its beginning. He further believed that all the same people that had existed at the beginning of one cycle would return and repeat all of the same actions in a new cycle of time.

Over the centuries, time began to be thought of as running from past events along fixed points on a straight line, like the birth of Jesus to fixed points in the future. Time became linear, moving from point A to point B, with no hope of return. When we chained time and delineated past, present, and future, we gained accuracy. For example, in the 1800s, the United States adopted five time zones to coordinate timekeeping with the running of the railroads. People set their watches to "railroad time," and by 1918, standard time zones were codified into laws. In addition, Daylight Saving Time, an artificial convenience to help the agricultural industry be more efficient, came into being.

Although we gained efficiency and accuracy with linear time, we lost a sense of connection to natural cycles and, with it, the opportunity to renew the world and ourselves. We no longer study the movement of the sun, stars, and moon with apt attention when we can now just glance at a watch on our wrist. With our changing perception of time, we began to refer to occurrences and the past as fixed and unmoving: "What's done is done" or "You cannot change the past." We can take an action we regret in linear time and have that action remain with us an entire lifetime. In cyclical time, however, every New Year and every new day brings the opportunity for starting over.

Linear time is unyielding; cyclical time is forgiving. In cyclical time, we always come back to the beginning, and we always have the promise of ascending to a higher level of evolution. With this return is the chance of renewal. Before "falling" out of step with cyclical time, people envisioned themselves co-creating and co-participating with the universe. They participated in ceremonies, sacred rites, and rituals carried out at times that were prescribed by nature and seasons—not by man. New Year's celebrations, solstice celebrations, and the recognition of the cyclical renewal of all creation were a cornerstone of humankind's psyche prior to linear time. We once kept our eyes keenly fixed upon the heavens and the movements of the sun, the moon, and the planets. We danced to the natural rhythms of nature, rose with the sun, harvested in the autumn, and rejoiced the new Earth that bloomed each spring by recognizing the potential for rebirth in our own lives. Once we started to move along the linear path of time, we lost this rhythm. But in learning to partner with nature, humankind can once again participate in the co-creation of the world and ourselves. When we dance with the rhythm of the universe, we ourselves become sacred.

## You've Got Rhythm: Living in Cyclical Time

*To every thing there is a season,*
*and a time to every purpose under the heaven:*
*A time to be born, and a time to die; a time to plant,*
*and a time to pluck up that which is planted.*

—Ecclesiastes 3:1-8, King James Bible

By sowing in the spring and harvesting in the fall, we are involved in acts that are in alignment with the seasons. If we were to plant in the winter and then try to harvest in the spring, we would not be able to successfully grow food. While this is obvious to us, the physical manifestations of seasons, such as falling leaves, sprouting shoots, rain, and drought, reflect deeper, invisible energetic cycles that cannot be so easily observed. We can gain clues about these deeper cycles by looking at the happenings in the world around us.

For example, spring is both physically and energetically suitable for renewal and birth. By participating in energetic acts of renewal in the spring, we have a more auspicious time of year to start anew. Spring is a time of hope—a time when the short, dark days begin to lengthen and lighten; the time when the cold makes way for the warm breezes and new life.

Just as the physical seasons affect us, the invisible seasons affect us as well. The Mayans documented these "invisible" seasonal variations in their cyclical calendars and noted the influence that they exerted on humankind. These invisible seasons could last a day, a week, a few months, or many thousands of years and are influenced by a variety of factors. For example, the Earth and the planets create invisible frequencies that can affect human beings. One of these invisible forces is called the isoelectric field.

Both the Earth and human bodies radiate isoelectric fields. The human isoelectric field is interlaced with the magnetic field of the Earth, thus, at an energetic level, we are coupled with the Earth. Changes in the Earth's isoelectric field can affect our health (specifically our hormone releases and sleep patterns) and even our dreams. By tuning in to the Earth's isoelectric field, we can better align ourselves to these invisible but powerful cycles. Ignoring these cycles throws us off balance, however. For example, the invention of electric lights allowed people to extend their waking hours into the wee hours of the night, yet many people now have insomnia and other disorders related to being out of sync with the natural cycles of sleep and alertness.

Planets, stars, and even cosmic rays also influence us. The Mayans kept precise records and made accurate predictions based on the movements of the Earth, the planets, and the sun because they understood that they greatly influence the fate of humankind and the Earth. The Mayans created a calendar and an astronomical tracking system that reflected their deep understanding of the dance of cosmos and is far more accurate than our present calendar. They tracked universal cycles, which they believed were 26,000 years in length, divided by "katuns," shorter cycles of 7,200 days. They concluded that all events were initiated and shaped by the cycle of time or the energy season in which they arose.

The Mayan's also believed that humankind was largely subject to these seasons. This is why Montezuma is said to have greeted Cortez, the Spanish conqueror, with a speech that indicated that on that particular day, it was destined and foretold by his Aztec ancestors that such a "great" leader would come and take over the city for himself.

Montezuma is recorded as saying upon seeing Cortez for the first time:

This is what has been told by our rulers, those of whom governed this city, ruled this city. That you would come to ask for your throne, your place, that you would come here. Come to the land, come and rest: take possession of your royal houses, give food to your body.[6]

The final day that is mentioned in the ancient Mayan calendar is December 21, 2012 (the winter solstice). Many Westerners have concluded that this day represents the end of the world; however, this incorrect assumption has been made because our concept of time is different than the Mayans. Since we see time in a linear fashion, the end of a calendar cycle is simply an end, whereas to the Mayans, the end of a 26,000-year cycle is also where a new 26,000-year cycle begins.[7] The fact that the Mayan calendar does not go beyond December 21, 2012 points to two likely reasons: Either the Mayans had not yet interpreted the energetic seasons caused by astrological movements beyond 2012 before their civilization came to an end, or the start of the new 26,000-year cycle is so dramatically different from their own time that they were unable to interpret it.

Just as the Mayan calendar predicted patterns that affected Mayan society, subtle universal patterns influence the best time to undertake actions based on individual karma. Karma refers to the "fruit," or results, of our actions taken during many lifetimes. The actions that we take—even the thoughts that we think—influence one's present and future lives. Hindus believe that the reason we are born at a specific time and place is because of our karma. The configuration of the planets on the date of our birth affects our personality and the unfolding events of our life. According to astrologers, we should not send important communications to others when Mercury (known as the planet of communication) is in retrograde (seeming to move backwards against the night sky from our perspective). However, the very same communication could be successfully received if sent during the time when the planets are in a positive aspect to our actions.

The ancient Chinese treatise the *I Ching*, or *Book of Changes*, works with these invisible, ever-changing seasons or cycles to help people understand when the time is right for them to act. The philosophy that underlies the *I Ching* is that the physical universe is a place of constant movement and flow. When specific actions are undertaken during cycles that support those actions, auspicious results will be obtained. Yet the same action taken at a time of unfavorable conditions will instead lead to some degree of failure. As observed by Carl Jung in his foreword to *The I Ching or Book of Changes*, by Richard Wilhelm and C.F. Bayless:

> The ancient Chinese mind contemplates the cosmos in a way comparable to that of the modern physicist, who cannot deny that his model of the world is a decidedly psychophysical structure. The microphysical event includes the observer just as much as the reality underlying the *I Ching* comprises subjective, i.e., psychic, conditions in the totality of the momentary situation. Just as causality describes the sequence of events, so synchronicity to the Chinese mind deals with the coincidence of events.[8]

The *I Ching* makes these invisible cycles visible for many earnest seekers, which is why it is one of the oldest methods of divination still in use today and makes the cosmic cycles that influence our lives transparent.

While we may have lost pace with cyclical time, there are many simple things that we can do to get back in touch with the vibrant cycles of life that surround us. Adopting practices and rituals in time with seasonal changes is one way. In her beautiful book *Kindling the Celtic Spirit*, Mara Freeman describes several Celtic rituals that are performed during different seasons of the year. For example, Rites of Spring, called *Bealtuinn* by the Scottish, is when the Druids and their ancestors lit fires on the hilltops to call the sun to return to the Earth.

> [E]very fire in the household was put out, and on the hill, the fire for the great bonfires, known as the *need-fire*, was kindled with the wood of nine sacred trees. Only the best men were fit to kindle the sacred fire ... When the fire died down, the embers were thrown among the sprouting crops to protect them, while each household carried some back to kindle a new fire in their hearth.[9]

Spring is one of humankind's most important times for ritual and celebration. The ancient Celtic peoples celebrated what used to be called the "new year" for weeks, usually climaxing on the first new moon after the vernal equinox in March.[10] Our modern New Year's Eve celebration pales in comparison to the great celebrations of ancient days. Caesar moved the celebration of the new year from March to January in 46 BCE for political reasons. By doing so, the new year was prematurely celebrated in the middle of winter—the time of the winter solstice—versus the spring, the season linked to new beginnings. Many people now celebrate Easter with an emphasis on this being a time of new birth, much like the ancients celebrated the new year. Today, of course, Easter is linked to the ultimate rebirth, Christ's rising from the dead.

In ancient times, the new year was when people celebrated the sun coming back to the world, the longer daylight hours, and the many spring births. They celebrated the birth of many of the new animals in the forest that were important to them, like the wild boar, and the birth of their domestic animals, like sheep. On all the important holidays, along with feasting with family and friends, their domestic animals would also

be given an extra meal or special food so that they were included in the celebration.

Ancient cultures also celebrated the past year of successes and came to terms with their losses. With the old behind them, they had the opportunity for renewal. If a person had an unlucky past or ill health, the new year brought the opportunity to start over, and find health and good fortune. The Jewish New Year, *Rosh Hashanah*, is also a time to recall past wrongdoings and then promise to do better in the future. New Year's Eve celebrations around the world are often filled with rituals that denote the release, disintegration, and purification of the past. Fire is a common element used to purify and release the past or the unwanted. In Scotland on *Hogmanay* (New Year's Day), barrels of tar are set afire and then rolled down the streets, symbolizing that the old year is burned up, which allows the new year to begin.

In many cultures, it is believed that one should do on New Year's Day what one would like to have happen for the rest of the year. For example, the giving and receiving of gifts to represent the flow of abundance, and eating fine foods and spending joyful times with friends and family, are all typical examples of this. Understood in this light, the act of making New Year's resolutions reflects the deeper understanding about the potential for new beginnings on this day. By attuning to natural rhythms and seasons, we can become whole within the universe and within ourselves.

# PART 2

## The Wisdom of the Wild

# 4

# PLANTS AS EVOLUTIONARY MASTERS

Very old are the woods;
And the buds that break
Out of the brier's boughs
When March winds wake
So old with their beauty are—
Oh, no man knows
Through what wild centuries
Roves back the rose.

WALTER DE LA MARE, "All That's Past"

Trees appeared on Earth almost 400 million years ago.[1] They reigned over a quiet, still world devoid of the sound of bird wings striking the air or even a single lizard scurrying with its tail zigzagging upon the Earth. This silent but fertile time was critical in the evolution of early land plants and in the shaping of the Earth's atmosphere. Not only have plants been around much longer than other forms of life but, without them, nearly all life on Earth would cease. It was the ancestors of the plants who created an atmosphere that ultimately supported complex life forms.[2] They did this of course by creating oxygen, a product of the process of photosynthesis. Photosynthesis literally means a "synthesis of light," and involves the vibrant combination of glucose from sunlight, carbon dioxide, and water to create a life-giving elixir for the plant, while also producing oxygen as a byproduct. Before plants, oxygen in the atmosphere was a rarity, and without an oxygen-rich environment, life was constrained to simple, one-cell organisms.

When oxygen became prevalent on Earth, its presence initially extinguished more life than it created. The living organisms at that time were anaerobic (living in absence of oxygen), and oxygen was toxic to them. Earth's anaerobic organisms were almost entirely wiped out by what is referred to as the Oxygen Catastrophe. It was indeed a catastrophe for ancient life forms subjected to the new and "poisonous" atmosphere. However, once oxygen became available in a usable form for life, evolution of many new oxygen-dependent species took off rapidly. Without this dramatic increase of oxygen, mammals would never have appeared on the scene. The presence of oxygen on Earth freed up greater amounts of energy, which could then be used by higher-level and more complex life forms. Thus, the life-giving qualities of oxygen resulted in the great diversity and complexity of life on Earth.

In addition, oxygen in the atmosphere blocked harmful ultraviolet radiation from the sun by forming the ozone layer, making the Earth a more hospitable home for mammals. These oxygen-producing ancestors of plants laid the foundation for the evolution of all life that depends upon oxygen for survival, including the human race. And plants today still play a key role as oxygen producers. Not only is oxygen in the atmosphere critical for the majority of life forms on Earth, oxygen is also the second most prevalent substance found in our bodies. When we understand the primary role that plants have played in helping life to evolve on Earth, we begin to see plants in a different light.

According to Michael Pollan, in *The Botany of Desire*, while Homo sapiens was learning to walk on two feet, plants had already perfected photosynthesis, a venture into organic chemistry far beyond the understanding of the human race. Photosynthesis is a significant evolutionary advantage that plants have over mammals. Converting light energy to chemical energy is one of the purest and most adroit ways to harness energy. Compared to plants, the way that human beings obtain life force energy—by eating other life forms, digesting, and excreting wastes—seems a great deal less efficient.

Although plants appear to be passive agents in the environment, they play an incredibly active role in the maintaince and evolution of life on Earth. Without plants, which are the organisms on the "front line" of transforming the light of the sun into energy that can be used by all other forms of life, we would not exist![3]

*Green plants and other photosynthetic organisms use the energy of absorbed visible light to make organic compounds from inorganic compounds. These organic compounds are the starting point for all other biosynthetic pathways.*

—Melvin Calvin and J. A. Bassham[4]

Beyond the miraculous feat of creating a nurturing atmosphere for life as we know it, trees and other plants create ecosystems that provide food and shelter for people, birds, animals, and insects. Trees also provide indirect shelter for life that would perish in an instant if exposed. For example, the presence of trees along a streambed shade the stream water, lowering its temperature, which in turn allows the water to maintain a higher oxygen content. Higher oxygen levels in water can support more water-based life, such as aquatic plants and fish.

But trees do much more than physically provide for living things; trees also create and maintain a range of energetic and spiritual reality on the planet. Trees create enough energy to support their survival for thousands of years. The known oldest tree is 6,000 years old, and the known oldest living tree root system is estimated at over 9,000 years old. The world's tallest tree is a coastal redwood in northern California, which is close to 380 feet tall (taller than the Empire State Building).[5]

Significant amounts of energy are needed to sustain living things of such size and longevity, yet trees produce more energy than they themselves need or benefit from. Trees help to enhance the life-nurturing, energetic reality of the Earth.

# TREES AS ALCHEMISTS:
# THE CELTIC TREE OF LIFE (*CRANN BETHADH*)

*In Celtic creation stories, trees were the ancestors of mankind,
elder beings of wisdom who provided the alphabet, the
calendar, and entrance to the realms of the Gods.*

—Jennifer Emick[6]

The ancient Celts understood that trees maintain the energetic and spiritual balance of the Earth. The Celtic Tree of Life was central to their spiritual beliefs. Trees were such a prominent aspect of Celtic culture that their alphabet was based on trees. The Celtic Ogham alphabet, dating from the fourth century, consists of twenty letters, each named for a different tree believed to be sacred to the Druids.

Children who grew up in a Celtic culture received fundamental instruction on which trees were best for dowsing, food, making weapons, worship, and even which trees were most beloved and frequented by the faeries. Although these beliefs may seem irrelevant to our lives today, our ancestors still influence us greatly. For example, the commonly used word *door* comes from the Celtic word *daur*, meaning oak tree.

The ancient Druids saw trees as portals to the world of spirits and divine unity. Trees were literally doorways to sacred time and divine realms, and certain trees were particularly important to the Celts. For example, alder was used to make whistles, ash and hazel were used for making wands, and hawthorn was used for stimulating psychic dreams. Juniper was used to protect the home and

| | | | | | | | | |
|---|---|---|---|---|---|---|---|
| + | A | ⵢ | G | ⊤ | O | ⲙ | U |
| ⊣ | B | ⊢ | H | ⵙ | P | ⵧ | Z |
| ⊫ | C | ⵿ | I | ⊫ | Q | ✳ | ea |
| ⊨ | D | ⵾ | L | ⵷ | R | ◇ | oi |
| ⲙ | E | ⵝ | M | ⵿ | S | ꟼ | ui |
| ⵳ | F | ⵴ | N | ⊭ | T | ⋈ | ia |

**OGHAM ALPHABET**

hearth, pine was for purifying, rowan was used to carve runes, and yew was used to make handles for daggers and bows.[7] The oak tree was the "King of Trees," and considered by the Druids to be *axis mundi*, the center of the world. An oak tree became a sacred portal that transcended all time and space. There, one could undertake a spiritual pilgrimage to the very center of one's existence. Myths from cultures around the world refer to trees as sacred figures: the Tree of Life, the World Tree, and even the Tree of Knowledge in the Garden of Eden.

Although modern humans understand the vital role nature plays in physical and biological processes, few of us comprehend the sacred dimensions that nature offers in our own backyard. Yet, like the ancient Celts, we still bring trees into our homes at Christmas, even if we have forgotten that this act is rooted in the belief of a tree's healing, protective, and spiritual dimensions. In ancient days, the fir tree was revered as a sacred tree, and this is one reason for our habit of bringing evergreen trees into our home during the holidays. Once there, we decorate it with care and adorn it with lights. These are actions befitting a sacred object. I believe that, at a subconscious level, we understand the significance of what we do, even if we go through these tree-trimming motions unaware of their deeper meaning.

# PARTNERING WITH TREES

*It is fact: man can and does communicate with plant life.*
*Plants are living objects, sensitive, rooted in space. They may be*
*blind, deaf, and dumb in the human sense, but there is no doubt*
*in my mind that they are extremely sensitive instruments for*
*measuring man's emotions. They radiate energy forces that are*
*beneficial to man. One can feel those forces! They feed into one's*
*own force field, which in turn feeds energy back to the plant.*

—Marcel Vogel[8]

Oxygen is the most common component of the Earth's crust and the second most common component of the Earth and its atmosphere. Molecular oxygen that is not trapped in water is unique to the Earth; thus far, no other planet in the universe has been found to contain a life-supporting, oxygen-rich environment like Earth's. Plants—from tiny algae and plankton in the oceans to immense trees in the great forests—continue the production of oxygen that ensures our ongoing survival. While we may be thankful to plants for food, we should also be thankful to plants for our every breath.

We are—or rather our material bodies are—65 percent oxygen.[9] The more highly oxygenated our bodies are, the more likely we are to be healthy. Medical studies conducted in the 1930s, and repeated recently, have found that the more highly oxygenated our body cells are, the less likely we are to get cancer.[10] In 1966, Otto Warburg (who won the Nobel prize for medicine in 1931) made this stunning assertion:

> For cancer, there is only one prime cause. Summarized in a few words, the prime cause of cancer is the replacement of the respiration of oxygen in normal body cells by a fermentation of sugar. All normal body cells meet their energy needs by respiration of oxygen, whereas cancer cells meet their energy needs in great

part by fermentation. All normal body cells are thus obligate aerobes, whereas all cancer cells are partial anaerobes. From the standpoint of the physics and chemistry of life this difference between normal and cancer cells is so great that one can scarcely picture a greater difference. Oxygen gas, the donor of energy in plants and animals, is dethroned in the cancer cells and replaced by an energy yielding reaction of the lowest living forms, namely, a fermentation of glucose.[11]

Warburg studied the impact of oxygen depletion on cells and found, when he grew animal cells under reduced oxygen pressure, that within as little as 48 hours, they became cancerous. In contrast, cells taken from the same sources but exposed to higher levels of oxygen remained healthy. From 1980 through 1990, scientists from the University of Madrid, molecular biologists at the University of Texas, and teams from Harvard and MIT all confirmed Warburg's results. They found that cancer cells thrive in an oxygen-depleted environment and are repelled by highly oxygenated states. Physical activity brings more oxygen into the body, which is, I believe, one rarely noted reason why people who are physically active tend to attract fewer diseases.

Oxygen serves another beneficial purpose besides keeping our bodies healthy. When we have higher levels of oxygen in the cells of our body, we can more readily elevate to a higher spiritual/energetic state of being. In other words, the more highly oxygenated our bodies become, the greater our capacity for spiritual growth. This is why many spiritual practices include breathing techniques that improve the intake of oxygen.

Paramahansa Yogananda, the East Indian guru who introduced Kriya Yoga to the Western world,[12] continued to amaze people after his death; his body did not decompose at a normal rate but remained unchanged for weeks. Yogananda's miracle may be due in part to his highly oxygenated state, achieved from his daily yoga practice and of course his enlightened soul.[13]

## CHAPTER PRACTICE

### Oxygen and the Yogic Breath

Most people tend to breathe shallowly and only into the upper part of their lungs. It is important to breathe fully into the lower lobes of the lungs as well in order to completely oxygenate the body. By doing so on a daily basis, you are helping your body to cleanse the byproducts of metabolism, while providing greater levels of oxygen to your cells, critical for your health and well-being.

Stand, sit, or lie down comfortably (assume whichever posture feels better to you and allows you to do this practice well), and make sure your back and spine are straight.

**Inhale slowly and deeply into your abdomen:**

1. Expand the muscles of your diaphragm (below your chest) to pull the breath deep into your body. As you do so, your abdomen should extend out.

2. As you continue to inhale, feel your ribs expand, starting at the lower ribs.

3. Allow your chest to rise as the air that first filled the larger, lower lobes of your lungs now begins to fill the higher, smaller lobes in the chest area.

4. Hold briefly.

**Exhale fully, expelling the air from your lungs:**

1. First exhale air from your chest area.

2. Let your ribs contract back down.

3. At the end, pull your bellybutton in toward your spine and use the muscles of your diaphragm to squeeze the last bit of air from your lungs.

4. It can help to imagine that you are exhaling the air through the tips of your toes. At the same time you engage in this deep release of oxygen, you make room within yourself to receive.

5. Repeat this full process at least seven times.

You can also take this practice deeper by matching it with physical movements to open the lungs. Lift your arms outwards and over your head as you breathe in (which extends the chest and expands the lungs), hold, and then bend down as you exhale, finally clasping your arms behind your legs to fully release all of the old air from your lungs. Do this only if you are free from back pain or injury. It is obviously best to do these deep-breathing exercises where the air is fresh, pure, and free from pollutants.

Not only do plants support our physical well-being as conveyors of oxygen, plants can also support our energetic well-being. For example, trees act as grounding rods in facilitating the movement of beneficial energy and life force from the sky, which is positively charged (yang), to the Earth, which is negatively charged (yin), and back. Within dynamic columns of light, trees maintain an area of vitalized, life-enhancing energy upon the surface of the Earth. When we sit or stand near trees, we come within range of their dynamic channel of energy. This is why so many people have mystical experiences under, in, or near trees.

While trees and human beings may appear on the surface to be completely dissimilar, we share several important commonalities that make energetic and spiritual experiences possible between us. For example, human beings have hemoglobin, which moves oxygen through our bodies in the life-giving river of blood. Hemoglobin is stunningly similar to a tree's chlorophyll in structure and purpose.

Chlorophyll, an essential component of photosynthesis, helps plants obtain energy from sunlight via its molecules, which absorb light and transfer its energy. Both chlorophyll and hemoglobin bring life force energy into the living system. In addition (and as the diagram below shows), the structures of hemoglobin and chlorophyll are astonishingly similar. The primary difference is that hemoglobin uses iron at the center of the porphyrin ring, while chlorophyll has magnesium at its center. The iron gives us red blood (once exposed to oxygen), and the magnesium gives plants green leaves.[14]

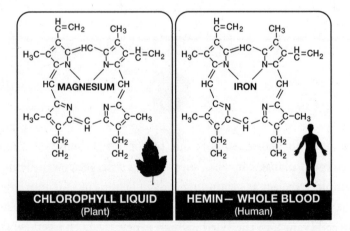

**CHLOROPHYLL LIQUID**
(Plant)

**HEMIN— WHOLE BLOOD**
(Human)

Trees also possess a system that is similar to the human circulatory system. Trees drive sap through internal tubes in much the same way that blood courses through a human body.

Yet, there are also dramatic differences between plants and us. For example, plants are able to create life force energy directly from light. Great yogis have also been able to receive their life force energy directly from the ether, as in the astounding case of Therese Neumann, who did not eat or drink for over a decade. This feat, well beyond most people's abilities, was but one of the "miracles" that Therese Neumann manifested.[15] Trees also free up energy in the environment through the production of oxygen in the atmosphere, while humans use up non-renewable energy and in turn create waste and polluting byproducts. Thus, in many ways, trees are more "advanced" than human beings. Of course, trees and all other living things on Earth lack the exquisite human nervous system, and energetic/spiritual structure of chakras. It is these systems that provide a way for spiritual enlightenment.

Since oxygen and energy are both important to our physical health and spiritual growth, trees are excellent partners in our quest for spiritual development. The Yakuts, Dolgans, and Evenks of Russia, cultures that all practice shamanism, believe that trees are special on Earth because they are the one being that belongs to the three realms: below the Earth (roots), upon the Earth (trunk), and in the sky (branches). The physical reality of the tree reflects its capacity for binding these corresponding spiritual realms together.

Trees help to maintain the homeostasis of the Earth, a process further explained by a theory called "Gaia." Gaia, as defined by James Lovelock, the scientist who developed the hypothesis, is "a complex entity involving the Earth's biosphere, atmosphere, oceans, and soil; the totality constituting a feedback or cybernetic system which seeks an optimal physical and chemical environment for life on this planet."[16]

Lovelock came to this conclusion after an extensive research project for NASA that was seeking life on Mars. He found that Earth has an optimum environment for life not found on any other planet we know of. Lovelock believes that Earth provides a beautifully balanced, homeostatic feedback system created and maintained by the living things that exist here. Of these living systems, plants are clearly one of the most important in maintaining the homeostasis of the Earth.

## CHAPTER PRACTICE

### Tree Affirmation

Now take the yogic breath practice deeper with the help of a tree, and use an affirmation to link the mind and emotions with the actions of your body. This practice is especially energizing when you first wake in the morning.

1.  Go outside or stand by an open window and face a vibrant, healthy tree or plant that provides positive energy to you. (Use the Tree Energy Surfing practice [page 46] to discover which trees and plants have the best energy for you first.)

2.  If you can, stand either near the tree's trunk or within the range of its canopy. Stand tall, with your spine straight, and do a few yogic breaths to warm up. Then, on a deep breath inhalation, lift both arms up and over your head as high as you can. In this open position, inhale fully and affirm, either to yourself or out loud, "I am open to receiving all good." Hold.

3.  Bring your arms down by your side slowly as you now exhale fully, and say or think, "I release all that does not fulfill (or serve) me." As you do this, imagine the breath releasing from the bottom of your feet into the ground.

4.  Repeat this process at least seven times, but feel free to do it more if you so wish.

5.  Finish by sending a blessing of good health and vitality to the tree.

Throughout the day, sitting with your back to a tree can help to ground you, and bring greater clarity and energy. Similarly, if you need energy to help you run or walk, you can reach out and hold a leaf of a tree or vibrant plant to receive a subtle energy boost. People sometimes do this subconsciously as they walk up hills on hiking paths.

Have you heard that that plants can hear? Researchers at the National Institute of Agricultural Science and Technology in Suwon, South Korea, recently discovered two genes in rice that react to sound.[17] Of course, this study supports the far more profound proposition that plants cannot only hear but can actually respond to sound. This may help to explain why people say that their plants grow faster and are healthier when they sing to them.

If you were to ask the great Indian scientist Jagadis Chandra Bose, he would say that plants cannot only hear and respond but that they experience many of the emotions that human beings experience. The results of Bose's many experiments suggested:

Plants have a sensitive nervous system and a varied emotional life. Love, hate, joy, fear, pleasure, pain, excitability, stupor, and countless appropriate responses to stimuli are as universal in plants as in animals.[18]

Plants are a lot more sensitive and capable of picking up things than we usually give them credit for. Trees planted in areas where singing birds live grow faster and more vigorously than trees planted in silent fields.[19] While there are certainly many factors that could influence this outcome, hearing the song of the birds likely strengthens their life systems and encourages their growth.

Cleve Backster, known as the father of the polygraph, proved that a special bond is created between a plant and the person who cares for it. Once attuned to a particular person, plants appeared to be able to stay in touch with that individual, even over long distances.[20] Backster found that when he wired a plant to a sensitive machine that measured the plants "reactions" and compared the plant's reactions to those of its owner, there were some amazing similarities. The plant's electromagnetic graph showed heightened emissions that were similar to the ways a person's body displays a height-ened stress response. For example, when he wired a plant to its caretaker, who was afraid of flying and was about to embark on a flight, he found a direct correlation between the owners stress response taking place thousands of miles away (especially during takeoff and landing) and a simultaneous and sympathetic "stress" responses from her plant. It was as if the plant felt its person's discomfort. In an attempt to isolate what could be helping the plant communicate with its owner, "[Backster] tried to screen a plant by facing it in a Faraday cage as well as in a lead container. Neither shield appeared in any way to block or jam the communication channel linking the plant to the human being."[21]

Plants can do more than simply pick up on their caretakers emotions; they can also respond to specific thoughts and intentions. For example, plants have been shown to grow more quickly when their caretakers send them loving thoughts. Plants also exhibit stunted growth when people hold thoughts of harm toward them or simply neglect them.[22] As Backster's experiments have shown, plants can and do interact with human beings at an energetic or intuitive level. This is one reason why plants are such good partners in developing and attuning one's sensitivity to energy.

It is possible to train yourself to become more sensitive to the invisible world of energy around and within you. By doing so, you can become more adept at sensing whether you are receiving negative or positive energy from other living things, inanimate objects, and even places. The more energetically aware or sensitive you are, the better you avoid people, places, and things that detract from your energy health, while being attracted to people, places, and things that benefit you. The sun's UV rays are invisible, for example, but we can get severe sunburn if we spend too much time in the sun unprotected; similarly, invisible but harmful electromagnetic radiation also presents a danger from overexposure.

Most people are surrounded by harmful EMFs (electromagnetic fields) that come from numerous electrical gadgets, like cell phones, cordless phones, and computers. These EMFs can cause immediate stress responses in people, and long-term exposure can cause health problems and even damage to cellular DNA.

Because everything on Earth—animate and inanimate—is comprised of energy, it is an invaluable skill to be able to discern what things support and revitalize our energy and what things may deplete it. When people are desensitized to energy, they may lose touch with how they are being affected by the energy of others, too. This can lead to that person being in situations, places, or with people that negatively affect them. For example, a person who was raised in a stressful or abusive environment is accustomed to being around energy that is harmful to them. They may continue to be drawn to people, places, and things that bring them negative energy and bad "vibes." When we become more sensitized to the type of energy we are receiving, we can make better choices about who and what we want in our lives.

The following pages offer a simple exercise to help you to develop greater energy sensitivity by partnering with a tree.

## CHAPTER PRACTICE

### Tree Energy Surfing Practice

I refer to this practice as Tree Energy Surfing because it feels like you are "surfing" the tree's energy system with your hands and body.

1. Select a tree in your backyard, a park, or a forest.

2. Stand facing the tree and within an arm's length of it; place your feet together, with the insides of your feet touching each other. Keeping your arms down from the shoulders to your elbows, bend your elbows so that your forearms are parallel to the ground and raise your hands up, with your palms open and facing the tree. Remember to keep your shoulders relaxed. (It is important to have a very relaxed body pose. If you need to stretch or shake out your muscles to loosen up before this practice, please do so.)

3. Stand with your back straight and your eyes staring straight ahead. Take seven long, deep breathes until you feel yourself beginning to relax deeply. Quiet your mind and be in an open state to receive. Become aware of the feeling in your palms, your body, and your head as you receive energy from the tree. This may take a few minutes or more before you begin to sense anything. Just relax and let the tree's energy come to you in its own time. If you are not sensing anything after standing for five minutes or more in this position, you can help to raise the energy flow in your hands by simply rubbing your hands together ten times.

4. After standing quietly for at least five minutes, take stock of any bodily sensations that you may be having. Note if there is any tingling or warmth in your hands or body, or if you find yourself going off balance, being pulled toward the tree, pushed away from the tree, or moving in a subtle circle or figure eight formation. All of these reactions indicate a level of energetic exchange between you and the tree, and they indicate whether the tree is emanating energy that is harmonious or beneficial to your energy frequency.

**Signs of beneficial energy exchange:**

+ Your hands and/or body feel comfortably warmer
+ You feel uplifted, energized, or have greater clarity
+ Your body moves in a subtle figure eight or in a clockwise direction
+ You are pulled toward the tree
+ You feel lighter

**Signs of harmful or depleting energy exchange:**

+ Your hands and body start to get colder
+ You feel nauseous, confused, or saddened
+ Your energy feels pulled down
+ Your body moves in a counterclockwise direction
+ You feel you are being pushed away from the tree

Since each person's energetic signature is unique, every individual will have a different interaction with each individual tree. This means that you may have a positive energy

*continued on page 48*

*continued from page 47*

interaction with a tree, while a different person will have a different experience with the very same tree. You can also have slightly differing reactions to the energy of a tree as your own energy changes over time. Thus, if you have a good or bad reaction, do not assume this will hold true for all other people.

One's sensitivity to energy can be developed with ongoing practice and attention. When you repeat the process with a variety of trees, you gain greater awareness of how different energy fields feel to your body. With all of this work, it is very helpful to maintain a daily meditation practice to grow this awareness of the subtle nature of your being. You can then begin to apply this new skill to identify the type of energy that you receive from people, places, and things.

## THE HEALING POWER OF PLANTS

For thousands of years, humankind has benefited from the healing capacity of plants. Many medicinal remedies are made from plants and many pharmaceutical companies today still rely on plant extracts. Over one hundred pharmaceuticals are derived from plants, including Taxol, an anti-tumor drug from the Pacific yew tree; thymol, from thyme, which is used as an anti-fungal treatment; papaverine, a muscle relaxant from the poppy, (yes, there is some truth to Dorothy of *The Wizard of Oz* falling asleep in the poppy field); and bromelain, which is a anti-inflammatory made from pineapple.

While ancient peoples routinely relied upon plants for their healing properties, Paracelsus, a Swiss botanist born in 1493, was one of the first Europeans to use herbal medicinals. He conducted research on plants and found that they were amazingly effective in treating a variety of human illnesses. Hundreds of years later, Dr. Edward Bach closed the doors on his traditional medical practice to roam the wilds of Wales, seeking to learn all he could about the healing ability of plants from the plants themselves. Following in the footsteps of Paracelsus, he believed that plants radiated energetic frequencies that could elevate and enhance the human energy vibration, and help it become stronger.

Like Paracelsus, Bach found that he could hold the petals or leaves of a plant in his hands and actually feel the quality of the plant's vibration.[23] This allowed him to "listen" to the energetic song of the plant in order to determine which illness the plant could heal. Bach further believed that all illnesses arose from disharmonious, underlying emotions or moods, thus he sought plants that healed the root of emotional distress in order to avert the illness at its source. Today, Bach's famous herbal remedies are known and used around the world. Meanwhile 80 percent of the world's population relies on traditional medicine—largely based on plants—for primary healthcare.

Now plants are even more important to health and healing than they were in the past, since our modern world—our own homes and places of work—has become increasingly toxic from common things, such as cleaning products, paint, carpets, tobacco smoke, and petroleum products. Because newer homes and office buildings are also constructed to be airtight to stop energy loss from heating and air conditioning systems, offending toxins and chemicals are simply recirculated. In addition, newer building materials often contain chemicals that are unhealthy. This has given rise to what is known as sick building syndrome (SBS), a term used by the Environmental Protection Agency to describe buildings that cause illnesses in people who spend time inside them.[24] In fact, this was such a pervasive problem that as early as 1984, the World Health Organization Committee had issued a report suggesting that up to 30 percent of buildings worldwide were making people sick.[25]

Thus, living and working in well-ventilated buildings, and making sure that your home and work environments do not contain toxic materials, is essential to ensuring health and well-being. After you have taken whatever steps you can to detoxify your home (like removing toxic materials), you can then make changes to enhance the indoor environment.

Bringing plants into your home or office is an effective way to clean and purify the air. Plants are amazing natural air cleaners, taking in stuffy air filled with carbon dioxide and pollutants and turning it into healthy oxygen. Through a process of metabolic breakdown, the leaves of certain plants absorb harmful organic chemicals and destroy them. Spider plants excel at this feat. Even formaldehyde, a highly toxic substance, can be metabolized and converted into harmless substances by the humble little spider plant.[26]

---

## CHAPTER PRACTICE

### Bringing the Healing Power of Plants into Your Home and Office

The most important rooms or areas to start with when using plants are those places where you spend the majority of time. Your bedroom and your workspace are two places to start. In your bedroom, place a healthy plant on each side of your bed, preferably on bedside tables. Next, place plants near where you work. For example, put plants right next to your computer if you use the computer a lot. For all of the other rooms in the house, like the living room or kitchen, place two or three plants in the corners, depending upon the size of the room.

---

Some plants that are particularly well suited to purify indoor air are areca palm, red palm, Boston fern, Australian sword fern, rubber plant, weeping fig, bamboo palm, Chinese evergreen, English ivy, gerbera daisy, mass cane/corn plant, pot mum, peace lily, and spider plants.

## PARTNERING WITH PLANTS TO HEAL THE EARTH

*Plants are arguably the single most important group of organisms in shaping the habitats and determining the physical environments that all other species require for survival, and as such, significantly influence total biodiversity richness.*

—Belinda Hawkins, Suzanne Sharrock, and Kay Havens,
*Plants and Climate Change*

As major regulators of the global climate and key players in the carbon cycle, plants should be our number one allies in combating global warming. This is because photosynthesis removes carbon dioxide ($CO_2$), one of the principle greenhouse gases, from the atmosphere. In all, plants consume a whopping 50 percent of the carbon dioxide in the atmosphere.[27] Forests are major carbon sinks that soak up carbon dioxide and store it as biomass and in soils. However, with the rapid destruction of forests, this scenario is changing rapidly. Fewer trees means that there is less carbon dioxide removed from the atmosphere and less oxygen is created. In addition, tropical forest vegetation stores more than two hundred billion tons of carbon globally. Deforestation releases carbon that has been stored in forests and soils into the atmosphere causing 10 to 25 percent of the annual global emissions of carbon dioxide. Consequently, stopping deforestation is undoubtedly one of the most effective ways to reduce greenhouse gases. Yet, up to now, plants have been largely neglected in the climate change debate by most countries—with a few noteworthy exceptions.

Costa Rica is on its way to being the first nation in the world to go completely carbon neutral by 2021. The country is achieving this status by helping its forests to grow. Going carbon neutral means that Costa Rica will absorb and store (in its forests) as much carbon dioxide as the country emits. Costa Rica has been preserving its native rain forests for many years, but in response to global warming, it has increased its forest base by planting over 5 million trees. Forests in Costa Rica now cover more than half the country. This is not only good for the world's atmosphere, it is also good for Costa Rica's great diversity of animals and plants, and even for its economy, which largely relies on eco-tourism. Country officials intend to plant another 8.5 million trees before they are done.[28]

In 2002, the Convention on Biological Diversity recognized the key role that plants play in global climate and created The Global Strategy for Plant Conservation (GSPC) to promote plant diversity around the world. According to the GSPC:

> Plants are universally recognized as a vital part of the world's biological diversity and an essential resource for the planet. In addition to the small number of crop plants used for basic food and fibers, many thousands of wild plants have great economic and cultural importance and potential, providing food, medicine, fuel, clothing, and shelter for vast numbers of people throughout the world. Plants also play a key role in maintaining the planet's basic environmental balance and ecosystem stability, and provide an important component of the habitats for the world's animal life.[29]

A number of countries have already used the GSPC as a foundation for developing their own plant conservation strategies. Along with international efforts to advance forest protection, smaller, regional efforts to increase forestland have been undertaken at the grassroots level. Perhaps the most famous of these community-based initiatives is the Green Belt Movement.

### The Green Belt Movement: Planting Trees in Kenya

Dr. Wangari Muta Maathai of the Nyeri District of Kenya became the first African woman to receive the Nobel Peace Prize for her contribution to sustainable development, democracy, and peace. Among other things, Dr. Wangari Maathai founded The Green Belt Movement (GBM) over thirty years ago in order to stem the serious and interconnected problems of poverty and environmental degradation. Her ingenious and simple solution: plant trees. As a result, more than 40 million trees have been planted to date and hundreds of thousands of women in rural Kenya are no longer living in poverty. Over 30,000 women have been trained in forestry, food processing, beekeeping, and other trades (dependent upon a healthy environment) that help them earn income while preserving their lands and resources. This program is exceptional in bridging human health and welfare to the welfare of forests and the Earth.[30]

---

## CHAPTER PRACTICE

### Plant a Plant

Planting a tree, a shrub, or a flower can be one of the best ways to help the planet, and it is so simple to do. But conduct initial research before planting just any plant. Try to select a plant that is native to the area. You may also want to consider

*continued on page 54*

---

*continued from page 53*

plants that provide shelter or food to other species, or plants that will help to keep your home cooler by providing shade. This is an excellent way homeowners can address moderating the climate indoors, as a plant-covered wall or roof provides ample cooling from the hot sun, reducing the need for artificial air-conditioning. Alternately, you may decide to start a garden so that you can enjoy fresh fruit and vegetables, or plant flowers that provide bees' nectar and beautiful blossoms. Think about what you are trying to achieve and ask people "in the know" in your community (wildlife and native plant specialists, arborists, and others) so that you can make an informed choice.

# 5

# READING THE SIGNS OF NATURE

When a weather change is on the horizon, most folks have their own little ways of being able to tell what's on the way by taking in the signals of nature. Often, these signs are interpreted on the subconscious level, while others are much less subtle, and people tune into those tidbits of information in order to prepare for whatever Mother Nature has planned for them.

DIANA DAWSON, *Weather and Its Lore*

In the early mornings, I often walk with my dog Lia and her two daughters, Bliss and Rose, along the sunny ridges and shady valleys of the foothills of Mount Tamalpais. This is my favorite time of the day, when the sun's golden light seeps over the hillside onto open fields of wild grasses. I pass California bay trees, with their long, slender, pungent dark leaves, and the sweet aroma of yerba buena fills the air as I walk under coast live oak trees. Unlike most other oak trees, California live oaks stay green all year round; their thick, rough leaves have super solar-absorbing abilities, as they have two to three layers of photosynthetic cells. The trees are perfectly adapted to northern California, and their acorns provide food for many of the native species.

One fall morning, while a pair of red-tailed hawks glided high in the sky over the grasslands, I saw an unusual sight. Lying on the brown and red earth of a deer path, was a twisted wing of a red-shouldered hawk. Nearby, a large grouping of its feathers was scattered carelessly on the ground. Further along on the valley floor, I found feathers of a fledgling black-shouldered kite in the shade of a California live oak. I recalled seeing the young kite the previous morning, its beautiful, white feathers glimmering in the sun while it waited for its parents to bring it a meal. Now, all that was left of it was its white feathers, dirtied and strewn upon the dirt.

What had occurred began to take shape in my mind. I saw the great horned owl as it grabbed the beautiful birds with its powerful claws and tore them with its beak. It is unusual for a horned owl to turn upon other birds of prey, as they ordinarily prefer small mammals, such as jackrabbits, cottontails, skunks, meadow voles, and mice. The fact that the owl had turned upon its cousins was a sign to me that the small mammal population might be declining. I went back up to the ridge and saw that the red-tailed hawks were far in the distance, barely a speck in the sky. On the ground, I discovered the vacant burrows of meadow voles and white-footed mice. All of the usual signs of activity like freshly dug soil or even their tiny little footprints were absent. I surmised from these signs that the recent drought was taking a toll on the small mammals and was now reaping consequences further up the food chain.

Sometimes subtle signs like this can indicate seasonal changes or more dramatic shifts. By understanding physical signs around us in nature, we gain greater insight about the natural world. Heeding physical signs can point out important shifts that it benefits us to understand. For example, if we were in better touch with nature, we would have known long ago that our actions were causing global changes. Unfortunately, global warming has progressed today to having a significant impact on thousands of species around the world. A study conducted by Stanford's Institute of International Studies reported on the impact of global warming in Nature:

> Birds are laying eggs earlier than usual, plants are flowering earlier, and mammals are breaking hibernation sooner. Clearly, if

such ecological changes are now being detected when the globe
has warmed by an estimated average of only 1 degree F (0.6° C)
over the past 100 years, then many more far-reaching effects on
species and ecosystems will probably occur by 2100, when temperatures could increase as much as 11 degrees F.[1]

While humans may miss these danger signs, animals tend to be
aware of changes in the environment to a far greater extent. In 373
BCE, historians recorded that animals, including rats, snakes, and
weasels, deserted the Greek city of Helike in droves two days before
a quake devastated the city and killed thousands of people.[2] In
December 26, 2004, an earthquake along the floor of the Indian
Ocean caused a tsunami in Asia and East Africa. Over three hundred thousand people lost their lives, yet few wild animals were
harmed. Why? According to witnesses, many animals were seen to
flee the coast toward the nearest hills the day before (and even just
several hours before) the disaster struck. Biologist and author
Rupert Sheldrake wrote in March 2005:

> According to a villager in Bang Koey, Thailand, a herd of buffalo
> were grazing by the beach when they "suddenly lifted their heads
> and looked out to sea, ears standing upright." They turned and
> stampeded up the hill, followed by bewildered villagers, whose
> lives were thereby saved.[3]

Even domestic animals like cats and dogs may act strangely
before an earthquake by barking, hiding, or running away. Because
of their innate ability to sense disasters, cats and dogs became the
unsung heroes of World War II, proving to be far more reliable
than the alarm in predicting air raids. Nothing can explain these
instances except that the animals somehow knew that a disaster
was coming and escaped to higher ground. Rupert Sheldrake also
noted:

No one knows how some animals sense earthquakes coming. Perhaps they pick up subtle sounds or vibrations in the Earth; maybe they respond to subterranean gases released prior to earthquakes, or react to changes in the Earth's electrical field. They may also sense in advance what is about to happen in a way that lies beyond current scientific understanding, through some kind of presentiment ... With very few exceptions, the ability of animals to anticipate disasters has been ignored by Western scientists, who dismiss stories of animal anticipations as anecdotal or superstitious. By contrast, since the 1970s, in earthquake-prone areas of China, the authorities have encouraged people to report unusual animal behavior, and Chinese scientists have an impressive track record in predicting earthquakes. In several cases, they issued warnings that enabled cities to be evacuated hours before devastating earthquakes struck, saving tens of thousands of lives.[4]

Just thirty years ago, in the small town of Haicheng, China, snakes suddenly appeared everywhere on the ground in the cold of winter. (Snakes normally stay underground in the winter in a semi-hibernation state.) The Chinese found their behavior to be so unusual that they evacuated all of the town's residents. They were just in time to avoid a large earthquake that caused enormous damage. Fortunately, very few people were harmed.[5] Paying attention to our animal partners in order to interpret what is happening in the environment can save human lives.

Many indigenous people predict disaster before it strikes, in part by taking cues from the wildlife around them. According to Dr. V. Raghavendra Rao, director of the Anthropological Survey of India in Calcutta studying this phenomenon, "These tribes live close to nature and are known to heed biological warning signs, like changes in the cries of birds and the behavior patterns of land and marine animals."[6]

Being able to read the physical and biological signs of nature is becoming increasingly important as global warming leads to the creation of many more devasting storms and weather systems worldwide.

## AUGURY AND SYNCHRONICITY

*The term* augury *derives from the official Roman augurs, whose constitutional function was to discover whether or not the gods approved of a proposed course of action. Divinatory signs, or omens, were recognized: such as lightning, thunder, flights and cries of birds, appearance of animals sacred to the gods—the bear (Artemis), wolf (Apollo), eagle (Zeus), serpent (Asclepius), and owl (Minerva), for instance.*

—Encyclopaedia Britannica

Just as our very thoughts influence the world around us, occurrences in nature may reflect our subconscious mind. Carl Jung thought as much. His theory of synchronicity is founded on the belief that there is an observable synchrony between our minds and the phenomenal world outside. Jung referred to this as "meaningful coincidences." In Jung's famous account, a scarab beetle (an Egyptian symbol of rebirth) came through a window in his therapy room at the exact moment that one of his patients was describing a scarab in her dream.

The scarab's unusual entry into Jung's room accentuated the powerful transcendental meaning of the scarab described in the patient's dream. The scarab is a symbol of the sun and an emblem of Egyptian god Khepera. Khepera is a form of the sun god Re, who is depicted as a human with a beetle on his head or with the beetle as his head. His name comes from the Egyptian word *kheprer,* which means "to become." Scarab images were often placed on mummified remains to help them be reborn. In Jung's patient's dream, the scarab reflected a new consciousness developing within his patient that would help her consider a new way of living and being.

Long before Jung, thousands of years ago, people observed natural phenomena to determine whether timing was right for a specific course of action. Augurs in ancient Rome observed the movement of animals and the significance of weather and seasons to be able to advise the actions of people and to interpret future events. Perhaps if Caesar had listened to his augur Spurinna, who warned him to beware the Ides of March, he may have lived to see another day.[7]

Ultimately, if we pay attention to the signs, we are better prepared for significant changes that could impact us as well as future generations. Reading the signs of nature can also provide greater understanding about how in tune our motivations are with the outer world. If we believe in synchronicity, then we must believe in a direct correlation between our thoughts, beliefs, and the tangible world. All of life on Earth exists within us, just as we exist in all life on Earth. Because of this innate tie, occurrences and events in nature reflect both an inner and outer level of reality.

## OBSERVING SIGNS OF NATURE

The Earth speaks to us all—if we care to listen. In *Odyssey of the Heart: Paths to Wholeness Through Feng Shui*, author Deborah Redfern writes about how signs from nature helped to guide her. Deborah had decided to undertake a solo vision quest, but the morning of her quest was cold, and the sky was overcast and foreboding. Deborah began to have second thoughts about conducting the quest and delayed getting ready. While she sat at her kitchen table, comfortably sipping hot tea, a red-tailed hawk flew into her garden and sat in the branches of a tree in full view of her window. Since a red-tailed hawk had never come into her garden before and the arrival of one can indicate rising spiritual energy, Deborah felt that this was a sign for her to follow through with her vision quest. Deborah's quest turned out to be a wonderful and insightful experience. The weather also cleared and the day got considerably warmer.

Afterward, she remembered that the hawk was selected as the first of her spirit animals in a spirit animal reading, and she felt a link between the hawk's appearance and her successful quest.

During vision quests and outdoor pilgrimages, people frequently experience meaningful animal encounters and interpret signs from nature. Ron, a participant in a quest I led several years ago, had a powerful experience with a bobcat.

## Ron's Story

At the time, Ron was being plagued with self-doubt over a recent examination he had taken just before the quest. During the group sharing, Ron let us know that he was anxious because he felt he had not done well on the test. Before the quests, participants receive helpful information to provide guidance during their quest. Many trainings include animal identification and behavior, and spirit animal practices. The following four days after the training, during his quest, Ron actively sought to call in the animal spirits to help him, and they responded with a significant number of "encounters." Here is Ron's version of his meeting with a bobcat:

*The third day, I resumed my routine of meditations, dances, and journaling. Sometime near sundown, I sat down to rest and drink water. After resting for several minutes, I saw some movement in my left peripheral vision. I slowly turned my head and saw a large bobcat stealthily making its way up the dry creek bed toward my sacred circle. Its stripes and spots blended in seamlessly with its surroundings. We locked eyes for about five seconds, and then it slowly turned around me and gracefully made its way back from whence it came. I very much wanted to learn what message nature was providing for me from this most unusual visit, so I closed my eyes and went into meditation to communicate with the bobcat's spirit. It occurred to me that the bobcat appeared to convey that the beauty, serenity, and grace I saw in the bobcat also existed within me. This message was sorely needed considering how my self-esteem had been shaken by the comprehensive examinations.*[8]

Signs from nature can powerfully shape a person's life by providing guidance or insight that we might not find on our own. Signs from nature can speak to "what is" from a scale of understanding beyond our limited human consciousness. Fortunately, Ron passed his examination and is now well on his way to writing his PhD dissertation on transformational learning in organizations.

Deborah and Ron interpreted the meaning of these signs as being significant to their lives in specific ways. It is when external signs resonate at a deep level within our spirit or consciousness that we know a message of truth has been sent and received.

# 6

# THE POWER OF ANIMALS

An animal's eyes have the power to speak a great language.

MARTIN BUBER, nineteenth century
Jewish philosopher from Austria

All living beings are remarkably similar to each other except for the rate at which they resonate—or sing—with life force energy. By working with spirit animals, we go beyond our own limited realm of awareness and cross a distant territory that we might not reach on our own. The sacred is often just a single vibration away. When we join with the frequency of other life, we can find a portal to a divine realm. Thus, animals and plants not only teach us about the world we live in, but they serve as our guides and allies in one of the greatest journeys of all: the spiritual journey.

## SPIRIT OF BOBCAT

*I dreamed last night that a wild cat, with golden eyes
and fur tufts on its ears, came to the door of my house.
I opened the door and let it in, and put some food in a
small bowl on the floor for it. It entered briefly and*

*started to eat, but the domestic cats in the house
came and chased it away.*

—Catriona's diary entry, November 26, 1984

In the dream state, we are free from physical limitations, and this provides a rich landscape for potentialities hidden deep in the subconscious. Sometimes messages come to us from our deeper consciousness through our dreams—messages that might not get through during our waking state. I have made a practice of keeping

track of my dreams and, when possible, recording them soon after they take place.

I wrote the above diary entry long before I ever laid eyes on a bobcat. It was a brief entry and the only one that I had made on that day. I soon forgot about that dream and would have likely forgotten it had I not written it down. I do not recall what meaning, if any, I ascribed to this dream at the time. I know it seemed important in some way, but I would only fully understand the meaning of the dream and the importance of Bobcat in my life many years later. The event that brought the full meaning of the dream to light took place on a bright spring morning in northern California—a place where bobcats still roam.

One February morning, after a particularly fierce storm, I was walking on one of my favorite paths, which began in a narrow valley next to one of my beloved black oak trees. The path continued uphill, under the shady canopy of California bay trees, and then opened up onto a ridge of golden grasslands.

While still in the lower valley, I came upon a large broken branch, two feet in circumference and over fifteen feet long, lying on the ground in the woods. Just a few feet from the broken branch, near a tiny stream channel, the golden eyes of a young bobcat looked out at me. Its yellow eyes, filled with ancient knowledge, were also filled with burning pain. The bobcat, about six months old, was trapped under the tree branch. Coming closer, I could see that it was seriously injured, its hind limbs paralyzed because the limb that had struck it broke its back. I tried to help the bobcat, and asked a passing hiker to call for an animal rescue service. As I waited, I sat quietly nearby, but far enough away so as not to alarm it. For hours, I observed its beautiful tawny markings interspersed with black lines, and sang softly to it. As I looked into its eyes, I felt like I had seen the cat before. The dream of the wild cat with pointed tufts on its ears flashed before my eyes.

This was the cat I had seen in my dream. Now it was lying injured and dying in front of me. Looking deeply into the eyes of the bobcat, it seemed like there was no separation between us. Its short life began to unfold before me as if I were watching a movie from the depths of consciousness. I saw the bobcat nursing from its mother for nine weeks with two siblings and then just one other cub. Next I observed the young bobcat's first successful hunt on its own of a small mouse, and then this image faded into another scene. Now the bobcat was hiding safely in tall grasses from the approaching sound of human footsteps and loud voices. The next scene was of the bobcat drinking cool water from the stream after the first rains fell on the dry land. Finally, I heard the loud crack and the thump of the tree branch upon its body. Tears rolled down my cheeks as I prayed for the bobcat.

The animal rescue service that arrived hours later was unable to save the bobcat. After it died, I deeply mourned the suffering and loss of this magnificent creature. For weeks afterward, I could not shake the sadness that hung over me.

A month and a half after the bobcat's death, on a brilliantly sunny day, I was climbing high on a golden ridge over the valley where I had found the bobcat. The warmth of the sun between my shoulder blades felt healing after what seemed like a long period of hibernation. I heard a startling call and looked up abruptly, expecting to see a red-shouldered hawk overhead. Surprisingly, I saw no hawk, but instead saw a sight that took my breath away. Walking on the hillside just above me, gently moving through tall yellow grasses, was a young Jesus. His hair and face were luminous and glowing from an inner light, and brilliant flashes of sunlight played upon his simple white robe. The edges of his garment blew softly in the wind moving lovingly around him. Standing by his side was the young bobcat, healthy, alive, and magnificently beautiful. They both seemed palpably real and yet ethereal at the same time because of the resplendent aspect of their being. As I watched them, my body suddenly felt as light as air. The entire world seemed to slip away as my awareness centered only on these two seeming apparitions.

This vision of Jesus and the bobcat healed a rift within my psyche between what I learned was the "correct way" to find God and the sacred experiences I had through nature. It was an undeniable sign to me that sacredness comes through all creation. It reminded me too of the fellowship that humankind has with all creation, as reflected in Jesus's teachings and actions. When we care for other living things, we reflect the compassionate heart of creation. We can be our own worst enemies, filled with habits and social customs that drive us away from the divine source. Bobcat's medicine helped to affirm to me that I should trust my experience of divinity, even if it appeared on the surface to be contrary to traditional teachings and societal expectations.

## JOURNEYING WITH THE ANIMALS

Everything in the universe is infused with a compassionate, intelligent spirit. Every person, every animal, and every tree has the capacity to express this intelligence. When we bypass the noise of our daily lives and experience the living flame in all things, we bypass the physical differences that our eyes observe and see the inherent spiritual unity of all things. Humankind communicates with the Creator through interaction with the animals, the birds, and the trees. It is through these messengers that humankind can connect with the sacred and be one with all creation.

> We should understand well that all things are the works of the
> Great Spirit. We should know that He is within all things:
> the trees, the grasses, the rivers, the mountains, and all
> the four-legged animals, and the winged peoples.
>
> —Black Elk, *The Sacred Pipe:*
> *Black Elk's Account of the Seven Rites of the Oglala Sioux*

A spirit animal (sometimes referred to as a "power animal" or "totem") is an energetic/spiritual being that you feel closely associated with, and that can bring guidance and power into your life. This animal represents a spiritual being who brings assistance to those in the physical plane of existence. While physical animals have their own individual spirits, they are all connected to an oversoul, or archetypal being, that represents the species and protects it. When working with a spirit animal, you are working with the oversoul of the species, and your relationship with the archetype can be enhanced by relationships with individuals of the species.

Spirit animals have been recorded throughout history as important guides for humankind. Most cultures—including Egyptians, Native Americans, Hindus, and other cultures too numerous to mention here—recognized the importance of spirit animals. Western culture tends to trivialize animals (wild and domestic), but current scientific research, as well as traditional knowledge, points to animals having greater abilities and powers than generally acknowledged. Our European ancestors understood this wisdom that comes from the animals and trees. While little is written about the religious beliefs of pre-Christian Britain—except for what was recorded by their conquerors, the Normans and Romans—we do know that indigenous people of the British Isles were polytheistic. An English law from 1016, during the time of King Canute, expressly banned the "worship of idols," which included: the sun, the moon, fire or water, springs or stones, and forest trees. From records like these, we can piece together that the ancient Europeans worshipped earth, water, fire, the sun, stone, wood, animals, and an ancient Earth Mother.[1]

Seventy-eight years later, the Council of Auxerre passed an ordinance forbidding people to dress up as a stag or a calf. These historical entries reflect the overriding importance of animals and nature to early concepts of divinity.[2] Eventually, the pull of nature and the call of the animals are stronger than cultural constructs and societal paradigms.

Cultures that have a nature-based spirituality believe in what are called spirit animals, animal allies, or animal helpers. The Celts believed in individual and clan animals. Many of the clan names reflect this on their banners and coats of arms. Our family crest—MacGregor—shows a lion, a unicorn, and an oak tree. Animals and trees are often displayed in a variety of ways, painted on shields and sometimes even tattooed on the body. While modern society does not attend to the power of animals in general, a watered-down version of calling upon an animal for its protection and strength is seen in the many animal mascots used by sports teams, and even those used as state and national emblems. The fact that almost every currency around the world shows images of animals also speaks to the fact that our society still recognizes the inherent power of animals.

The best way to discover the benefits of a spirit animal is through direct experience. By developing your own personal relationship with a spirit animal, you will understand the power or "medicine" that an animal brings you. Just be cautious of the abundance of books and cards that generalize the meaning of spirit animals, however, as these stereotypes are not always true. We need to be careful not to trivialize the depth of meaning held by individual spirit animals so as not to trivialize our own experience.

> *If men would pay more attention for these [animal and plant]*
> *preferences and seek what is best to do in order to make*
> *themselves worthy of that toward which they are so attracted,*
> *they might have dreams which would purify their lives. Let a*
> *man decide upon his favorite animal and make a study of it,*
> *learning its innocent ways. Let him learn to understand*
> *its sounds and motions. The animals want to communicate*
> *with man . . . man must do the greater part in*
> *securing an understanding.*

—Brave Buffalo, Teton Sioux[3]

As explained by Brave Buffalo above, studying the animals that one has an affinity for is an excellent way to prepare for an encounter with its spirit or oversoul. Since many myths, ancient stories, and rituals touch upon authentic shamanic experiences with animals, it is useful to study these prior to embarking on a search for your own spirit animal.

The following is a closer look at Sparrow Hawk, Turkey, Snake, Fox, and Mouse as examples of how animals have been helpful in my life and the lives of people that I know. But use your own experiences as your guide for the true meaning of an animal's spiritual significance in your own life.

## THE SPIRIT OF SPARROW HAWK

When I was eleven years old, I found a baby sparrow hawk that had fallen from its nest. Because it is always best to return infant animals to their mothers, I spent hours unsuccessfully searching for the nest and the parents. Since I never found them and knew the baby was far

too young to survive on its own on the ground, I brought the hungry hawk home to raise. The white, downy chick grew into a striking bird with beautiful markings of slate blue and deep orange. Eventually, the hawk matured and began its first efforts at flight. It flew high into the treetops in the evening, and in the morning, I woke expectantly at dawn to search for it. After calling for it for some time, I would often find it in the high branches of the trees in the woods behind our home.

I remember the first time the hawk spent a night out on its own. After searching anxiously for over an hour, I finally found it at the very top of one of the tallest maple trees deep in the woods, its shiny feathers glistening in the new light above me. As I called to it from the ground, it leaned its head to the side and stared at me with its large, dark eyes as if I were a strange being. Just a single night out under the brilliant stars had brought out the wildness in it. I called my familiar call and waited with bated breath, not knowing what it might choose to do with its awakened "hawk-ness." After some hesitation, it flew down to the ground about eight feet away from me. As I put out my hand expectantly to pick it up, it momentarily lifted its talons in a show of growing independence. I encouraged these independent forays so it could be returned to the wild once it was an adult.

My relationship with Sparrow Hawk was a significant one that shaped my youth in key ways. The timing was also important, as it helped me to define my own independence as I transitioned from childhood to young adulthood. While I cared for the hawk, I believe that I learned more from this intelligent wild creature than it did from me.

When I began to work with animals and gain a greater understanding of their ways, I grew to understand that the sparrow hawk's spirit was reflected in abilities that came naturally to me. Animal allies often reflect potential qualities of our being. By developing our spiritual relationship with an animal, we learn to unleash those qualities, and we all have at least one animal ally that can assist us. As in the case with the sparrow hawk, we may encounter animals in physical form prior to understanding our relationship with their spirit. This is why recalling your real life experiences with animals can be a first step toward discovering your spirit animal and why childhood experiences in particular—when we are still so open to the world around us—can point to important animal allies.

Spirit animals can also come to help people through a guardian, family, clan, or community. For example, I was very fortunate to benefit from the spirit of Turkey at a young age through one of my godmothers, Marjorie. Two magnificent, bronze, life-sized turkeys stood on pillars at the entranceway of her beautiful estate. Many years later, I saw these striking statues as but one sign of her alignment with the spirit of Turkey. This occurred later in my life, when I had learned more about the power of animals and their spirits.

Turkey is a wonderful example of the feminine power of creating positive change through caring and nurturing others. Turkey brings out the best in people by helping them to express generosity of spirit. This is because Turkey understands that all beings are connected.

Marjorie never had children of her own, yet she inspired many people with her generous nature and *joie de vivre*. She gave one of her homes to a family that was struggling to make ends meet, and helped others who struggled financially. She also sent several young people to college who could not afford to go. Beyond her financial support, Marjorie offered sympathy and moral support. Today, I always give support to charities and people that I care about as one small way to let generosity and the spirit of the turkey flow through me. For many years, before I met my life totem, I believed that Turkey was my life spirit animal because of my close relationship with Marjorie.

My experience with my godmother's spirit animal is similar to the experience of Native Americans and other indigenous cultures. Many indigenous people have the protection and help of spirit animals that watch over the entire community. In the case of the Crow people, each member benefits from an association with Crow, though each individual of the tribe can also have his/her own spirit or totem animal(s) that may be different from Crow. Today, a group may link itself to a specific animal as a clan, as a team, or even as a nation or state.

For the Celtic peoples—who also believed in power animals and pilgrimages into nature—dreams and omens help to bring one closer to understanding one's life journey. No matter what method is used, the discovery of an animal spirit guide is always a voyage that leads to greater insight and transformation of self.

## SPIRIT OF TURKEY

Since turkeys spend most of their lives with their feet on the ground, they know many of Earth's greatest secrets. And these secrets can be revealed when one builds a relationship with Turkey's spirit, which became abundantly apparent to me one beautiful September afternoon.

I had just finished swimming in a pond set in the open, surrounded by sloping hillsides. It was a warm, late afternoon, and the sun was beginning to cast long shadows on the ground. I felt very relaxed after my swim, and I was just drying off and wrapping my hair in a towel when I felt I was being watched. I lifted my head and glanced up the farthest slope, where a half-ring of large stones lay in a semicircle on the ground. A large turkey hen was standing silent and alert on top of one of the stones, looking toward me. I stared and felt immediately drawn to look at its left eye. The turkey was a considerable distance away, so I was amazed that I could see its eye so clearly.

As I looked into the turkey's eye, I began to see the world from its point of perception. I became very aware of the tall grasses next to Turkey, the stones at its feet, and the flight of the vulture over its head. I was pulled into a deep trance: my body became lighter than air as my consciousness began to flow toward Turkey's eye. My spirit and awareness seemed like they had gone inside Turkey's eye, and I was now seeing the world entirely from Turkey's perspective. I could see each blade of grass and stone by the turkey—I could even see a small anthill near turkey's feet.

During the time that my consciousness was with Turkey, I began to be able to see light emanating from the Earth in the shape of bows. These light bows appeared like miniature, pure-white rainbows springing from points below the surface of the Earth. It came to me that these light bows are the deepest reality of the seeming physical sphere of the Earth. They are the congealed light with which the physical manifestation of the Earth is held in the mind of the Creator. The light bows give the Earth a seemingly solid existence, while serving as the points at which vital energy and information flow to and from the Earth and the sky realm. Here I was seeing the very essence of what the Earth is made of—pure light. I was overwhelmed at the thought that the seemingly solid ground beneath my feet was nothing more than illumination and recognized that if the Earth was but light, held in the mind of the Creator, then my very body, and all the beings upon the Earth, were also of the same luminous cloth.

I understood that the light and the dynamic of "movement," or bows, hold the Earth in perfect balance between the yang energy coming from the ionosphere and the yin energy coming from the Earth's core.

These light bows are also integrally connected to the Schumann resonance and Earth's rhythmic song. In 1954 German physicist Professor W. O. Schumann made the astonishing discovery that the Earth radiates an electromagnetic resonance, or song, occurring at the frequency of 7.83 hertz. (Over the years, additional resonance frequencies other than the elementary Schumann frequency of 7.83 hertz have been discovered.)[4] Earth's song, as it turns out, plays at the same or similar frequency of the human brain wave, known as alpha wave. Alpha wave brain patterns are associated with meditation and deep inner peace.

Before coming out of the journey into Turkey's eye, I saw a place in the land where the light bows were converging. The place with the most dense convergence of bows was filled with radiant light.

It was not until the following week that I returned to this place. I hiked up the hill and sat cross-legged at the exact spot where I had seen the light bows converging on the land. I initially experienced a wave of intense energy and felt giddy as I entered the circular area, approximately twenty-by-twenty feet in diameter. I sat in the center of the energy circle and soon felt heat rising up my spine and into my hands. As I meditated, I felt the presence of an intelligent force in the land itself. Turkey had shown me a place where I felt like I could hear and speak to the very soul of the Earth.

Without the help of Turkey, I would not have been able to have this vision and find this powerful place on my own. This is but one example of how working with animal allies can help us gain greater awareness of the world around us.

## THEY CHOOSE US

While we cannot always generalize about the ways that spirit animals help us, there are some general rules that universally apply when working with them. Spirit animals choose the person—not the other way around. When I run spirit animal journeys for groups, I sometimes start by asking people in the audience if they believe they already know their spirit animal. Invariably, a few people tell me that they know their spirit animal is Wolf or Eagle or Bear, yet the spirit of these animals may not be closely linked to them. Instead, people may be expressing their ego-based preference for what type of animal they would like to think their spirit animal is. This is why they will select a large, charismatic species that is often admired in our society as strong or powerful. Sometimes people's understanding about animals is not sufficient, and their opinions may be based on cultural misunderstandings about what these animals are really like.

In many cases, one's spirit animal is hidden from the conscious, ego-oriented mind, and the spirit of the animal will not approach until gentler, more intuitive or shamanic processes are employed, such as shamanic journeys, spontaneous visions, or dreams. A person's animal ally can be very different than what a person might expect. For example, David, a large, heavyset man over six feet tall who attended one of my workshops several years ago, raised his hand at the beginning of the workshop to confidently say that he knew that his spirit animal must be a bear.

After our workshop ended and participants had experienced a shamanic spirit animal journey, David patiently waited to speak with me alone. He smilingly told me that a beautiful hummingbird had come to him in his spirit animal journey, and he had experienced great joy because he felt that this was his true spirit animal. I let him know that the hummingbird is considered one of the most powerful spirit animals and is especially highly regarded in South American cultures. In the high Andes of South America, the tiny hummingbird is seen to have power over resurrection and death. While David was very open to accepting this unexpected spirit animal, some people find their spirit animal(s) hard to acknowledge. In fact, a few people may even find their spirit animal repellant at first. This is often because their knowledge of the animal may be tainted by their cultural traditions or belief systems. For example, in societies influenced by Christianity, the snake is one of the most deeply misunderstood and maligned animals.

## SPIRIT OF SNAKE

Linda, a guidance counselor from Seattle, contacted me to get help with discovering her spirit animal. She was convinced it was a cat, since she was so fond of cats and had two cats living with her and her boyfriend. But as we worked together, nothing unusual or significant appeared to link her with some type of cat as her spirit animal. Yet, I soon noticed a distinctive pattern developing; either just before or during a session with Linda, a snake would appear to me. Sometimes these snakes were real snakes—like the one wrapped around the neck of a young man that I ran into downtown ten minutes after talking with Linda—and sometimes they were images of snakes—like the one that was sent in an email that came immediately before a phone call from Linda. These meaningful coincidences indicated to me that Linda's spirit animal was a snake.

I chose not to tell Linda about my hunch so as not to influence her discovery of her spirit animal during her journey. In our fourth week of working together, Linda was ready to conduct a spirit animal journey, and on that journey, she connected strongly with the snake as her totem. According to Linda, "it seemed as if I took on the very essence of being a snake. I no longer had skin but smooth scales. I also felt tremendous power and energy surging through my body, and I stopped the journey short because I felt afraid of what I was becoming and the unusual feelings I was experiencing."

While most people usually enjoy connecting with their spirit animal, Linda's initial experience of connecting with Snake was repugnant to her because snakes have been maligned in our Western culture. Yet in ancient times, snakes were revered. Snake represents a powerful feminine energy often associated with the element of water; Snake has powers of healing and transmutation; and Snake is able to reach deep into the realms where illness and death exist, transforming this energy at its source. Snake is also linked to tremendous energetic and spiritual power. The Goddess Kudalini is also associated with Snake as "coiled" energy that lies dormant at the base of the spine until spiritually awakened. Once awakened the Kudalini energy rises up the spine like the uncoiling of a great snake. Because snake energy is source energy, it can appear to us as dark and foreboding. Like Kali, the Hindu goddess associated with death and destruction, as well as the goddess of time and change, snake energy may be interpreted as dark and violent. Yet this energy refers to annihilation of the ego as well, which is what occurs when one enters the "ultimate reality" or the devine realm.

Snakes have long been used as the symbol of physicians and alchemists. The rod of Asclepius, from early Greek times, symbolizes the healing arts by combining the serpent, which is shedding its skin (a symbol of rebirth and fertility), with the staff, which illustrates Snake's reputation as healer. Snakes are highly respected in India, and their lore and symbolism are highly regarded in that culture. American Indians also see Snake as a representation of fertility and healing.

Ultimately, Linda was conflicted about having Snake as a spirit animal because she was fearful of her own potential as a powerful healer. Rather than encouraging her to become a psychiatrist, which was her dream, Linda's high school guidance counselor told her that, given her grades, she "did not appear to have the aptitude for the profession." She became a high school teacher instead. While she enjoyed working with the teenagers, she always felt like she was missing out on something and that she had not given herself a chance. But she soon became very busy with her own family and teaching career and let this dream lapse.

Connecting with Snake was unsettling to Linda because it meant, if she were to be true to her innate power as a healer, she would be using those abilities best in a healing profession like psychiatry or psychology. In some superficial ways, it would be more comfortable and easier for Linda to just keep on doing what she was already doing versus having to go back to school to get a degree while working. Snake medicine was also uncomfortable for Linda because she got a taste of how significant and powerful her work could be in helping others to become whole. Linda experienced goose bumps on her journey, which were her body's reaction to the tremendous positive force that she had the potential to become if she stepped into her full abilities and took charge of her life.

In some cases, when people encounter new and powerful ways of being, they retract and retreat. This is because change brings a little death to the old ways of being. In Linda's case, as she worked to welcome Snake medicine into her life, opportunities came forward that made it possible for her to reach for her dreams. She began to take evening classes to become a psychologist, and she was also able to cut down to four days a week at her job, leaving her more time each week to study and do her homework. Ultimately, Snake medicine helped Linda begin to work with powerful creative forces coming alive in her life. Even other seemingly unrelated areas of her life began to improve at this time. She noticed significant, positive changes in her relationship with her boyfriend and her mother as she stepped into a role that gave her greater self-confidence and responsibility. Linda is still pursuing her degree and is now working with clients under supervision as part of her training. She is already getting tremendous feedback about the value of her work and her healing presence with people that are fortunate enough to come to her for care.

## SPIRIT OF FOX

Fox is a beneficial ally to many people from different cultures around the world. There are references to Fox medicine helping people take on a different form (or role) with ease (China), obtain great favors from the gods (Egypt), and even travel to the next life (Persia). The Apache also give credit to Fox for bringing fire to humankind.

While there are many interpretations of Fox energy in spirit animal books and cards, none of them really speak to the experiences that I have had with Fox through my shamanic journeys. After a particularly powerful journey with Fox, I was skimming through a book of Finnish legends when I discovered a reference to the Finnish name of the northern lights, *revontulet*, which comes from a Sami, or Lapp, legend. In this legend, it is told that the northern lights are caused by the tail of a fox running along snow-covered fells, striking the snow drifts and sending a trail of sparks into the sky. The word *revontulet* literally means "foxfire." This legend closely matches my understanding and experience of Fox on our journeys together. Fox helps me jump off the edge of the world. In other words, when Fox shows up, I know I will quickly be taken to a realm beyond this world and consciousness. It literally feels as if I am taking a leap of faith and jumping with Fox into another universe.

This is but one example of many where it is shown that we must measure our experiences with the animal spirits as they come to us and not be limited in our experience by generalizations in popular books and cards. This story also highlights another truth: many of the myths and legends that are passed down from generation to generation were actually once experienced in some form (possibly in a shamanic journey) by our ancestors.

## SPIRIT OF MOUSE

*Small, sleek, cowering, timorous beast...*
*I'm truly sorry man's dominion*
*has broken Nature's social union,*
*And justifies that ill opinion*
*Which makes thee startle*
*At me, thy poor, Earth born companion*
*And fellow mortal!*

*But Mouse, you are not alone,*
*In proving foresight may be vain:*
*The best laid schemes of mice and men*
*Go often askew,*
*And leaves us nothing but grief and pain,*
*For promised joy!*

*Still you are blest, compared with me!*
*The present only touches you:*
*But oh! I backward cast my eye,*
*On prospects dreary!*
*And forward, though I cannot see,*
*I guess and fear!*

**Robert Burns, "To a Mouse"[5]**

The physical size of an animal in no way reflects the ultimate strength of its spirit or medicine; the spirit of Mouse can be as powerful as the spirit of Bear. This is an important aspect of spirit animals for people to understand today, in a world where superficial appearances can be taken too seriously.

One of the most powerful yet tiny spirit animals that I work with is Mouse. Behold, the tiny mouse, prey to so many larger animals, and yet it goes through life with purpose and joy. Mouse's great spirit teaches about trust. While it is wary, it does not put its life on hold because of the dangers that may exist around the next corner. Trusting the universe and trusting life are key ingredients for happiness and for making the most out of our lives. Without trust, we will not take the chances that we need to fully express who we are, nor will we appreciate the power of the small.

Sometimes small, temperate steps are the way to great changes. A river forms a wide valley like the Grand Canyon slowly, with small changes to the land over a long period of time. It is also true that even small things in our own lives can have an exponential impact. For example, I find that even if I am only able to meditate for fifteen minutes in one day, the next twenty-three hours and forty-five minutes are more centered and fulfilling than if I did not meditate at all. Think also on how a single kind word that takes but a second to utter can bring someone long lasting joy.

In the realm of the universe, human beings are tiny compared to the larger forces around us. It is only when we tap into the larger energetic and spiritual reality that true greatness can be achieved. In order to be able to tap into that vast field, we must approach it with a humble and trusting stature, as is represented by Mouse medicine. Spirit animals like Mouse can teach us things that we may never learn from another person, in part because of the innate humility of the animals; they are natural teachers because they do not judge.

Discovering one's life spirit animal can bring greater understanding about one's life path. However, simply discovering one's spirit animal without further developing the relationship is a hollow reward. Just as meditating once will not likely create any significant beneficial changes in one's life, simply recognizing a spirit animal once will not likely bring significant long-term benefits. Shapeshifting is one method used in an effort to come to know a spirit animal better, and to even share some of its powers and wisdom.

## SHAPESHIFTING: A WAY TO WISDOM

One summer, my mother gave me a little bronze statue of a mermaid in recognition of my love of swimming. This miniature of the life-size mermaid sculpture in Copenhagen is one of the few possessions that I still have from my childhood because it touches a chord in my psyche. The statue reminds me not just of my affinity for the sea but also of a profound and poignant reality: the statue speaks of

being between two worlds and not fully belonging to either one.

When I was seventeen, I learned the story of the selkie and was enamored by it. At the time, I did not understand its shamanic roots, nor did I know that the selkie story had commonalities with stories worldwide that spoke of the ability of a human to shapeshift and become like an animal. Ancient shamans are said to have had the ability to shapeshift, and since all beings are cut from the same fabric of carbon and oxygen, the possibility that a shaman could become a raven is not so unusual.

Like cracking a secret code, once shamans understood and could replicate the vibrational resonance of another living being, they could become that being. And there were many benefits to shapeshifting: the shaman could experience the world with the senses and abilities of the adopted animal. Some shamans who shapeshifted became so accustomed to their new form that it is said that they lived out the remainder of their life as the animal.

Shapeshifting stories also appear in Western culture. The well-known tale of Merlin and King Arthur has many examples of shapeshifting. Merlin, the wizard, had the ability to shapeshift into a hawk at will. He also taught his disciple, Arthur, to shapeshift into a variety of different animals. Similarly, the mythological selkie, whose story originated in the Orkney Islands of northern Scotland, tells of seals that can take on human form and vice versa. The selkie-folk, as they were known locally in the Orkney, came to be regarded as gentle shapeshifters with the ability to transform from seals into beautiful, lithe humans. Once in human form, the seals would dance on a moon-lit shore or bask on a rock in the sun. In all of the selkie myths, the shapeshifting occurred when a seal cast off its skin to assume human form. Then, instead of a seal, usually a beautiful man or woman could be found standing on the shore.

Shapeshifting is certainly an advanced art that only a small number of people have been able to achieve. Yet, when we enter the energetic, spiritual, and even physical world of another being, we are able to walk with their feet, fly with their feathers, and swim with their fins. A rock, a tree, a person, and a hawk—these are all composed of energy and life force. The only difference between them is the rate and quality of vibration of the energy in each. Ancient shamans had the ability to physically transform into other animate and inanimate beings. (Even animals and plants have the ability to shapeshift—in some cases even taking on human form.) These wise ones learned how to modify the vibration of their "energy strings" to vibrate in resonance with the animal.

Humankind has achieved amazing feats that might not have been possible without gaining from the innate wisdom and experience of the animals. For example, the Polynesians tell of how their ancestors connected with nature and animals to successfully navigate thousands of miles of ocean. As noted by historian John Broomfield,

The Polynesians told of great voyages of exploration undertaken by their ancestors hundreds of years earlier. They explained that their navigators had relied upon an intimate knowledge of star paths, the habits of migratory birds, and the varied patterns of light and motion of ocean waves and currents. Their pilots who guided these ancient voyages had the capacity, they said, to rise in spirit above the masthead to see far beyond the horizon. In crises, when even these skills proved insufficient, guardian spirits might be summoned in the form of birds, fish, dolphins, whales, or sea dragons to point the voyagers to their destinations.[6]

At that time, their sea voyage was as far a journey as the moon is today. The incredible feat of navigating 5,690 miles (4,944 nautical miles) in relatively small crafts could not have been accomplished, according to legend, if it were not for the guardian spirits and ocean-going animals that helped to guide their journey. Some of the chants and prayers used to conjure up the animal spirits are still sung in New Zealand today. Similarly *The Seafarer*, one of the oldest epic poems in the English language, explains how seafaring explorers followed "the whale path" to find their way across the vast ocean. They, too, had found a way to gain knowledge from and perhaps even intertwine their souls with those of the whales to safely navigate the seas.[7]

In the book *The Way of the Human Being*, Calvin Luther Martin tells the story of an Inupiaq Eskimo, Katauq, who claimed that he could have his spirit leave his body to join with the body of a whale. He would then bring his spirit back and let the people know the whale's habits and even the whale's perspective on individuals in his community.

By understanding the experience of other living things and entering their world, we can learn where the gray whales go to birth their young, how migrating birds see the electromagnetic fields of the Earth, or how a mother wood duck selects her nest. This ancient way of knowing is becoming more important as global environmental problems arise. This way of knowing can present us with a way to gently unlock the secrets we need to help us heal the Earth and ourselves.

# 7

# SACRED PLACES

For thousands of years, we have been taught to focus on the words that were given, rather than the place in which they were given. The actual mountain, we are told, is unimportant. Why would religious leaders negate such an important factor of the Mount Sinai experience? ... Is it possible that we lost a crucial part of the revelation when we left the mountain behind?

JAMIE KORNGOLD, *God in the Wilderness*

$\int$ ach of us has ties to specific places on the Earth. Human souls are intertwined with the land: the places where we grow up, the places where we have memorable experiences, and the places we frequent.

Places that are used for spiritual practices like outdoor shrines, places of worship, and places of spiritual occurrences build up and retain an energetic field that can remain in the land. People coming to these special sites may sense a profound peace or even experience a spiritual awakening. Many of the places that animals and people unconsciously choose for spiritual focal points are aligned with existing positive energy. However, places can also become sacred because of human- or animal-initiated events.

A stone labyrinth thirty feet in diameter lies on a peaceful hillside surrounded by high ridges and deep valleys. On clear days, the San Francisco skyline can be seen in the distance. Two local residents created the labyrinth here seven years ago, and now it lies under the open sky, formed of small stones in a spiral path interspersed with grass and wildflowers. The labyrinth has become a place for people to engage in meditative and spiritual practices, and in the center, people leave offerings, such as flowers, beautiful stones, coins, or tiny written notes filled with their wishes and prayers.

The labyrinth lies near but not directly on a powerful line of land-based energy. The physical attributes of the hillside influenced the people who created it as much as the energetic attributes of the land. This is why the labyrinth lies directly on top of the hill with the best 360-degree view and is about 120 feet away from a powerful line of land energy. Over the years, people have infused the labyrinth with their energy and intentions, which has built up its energetic resonance over time. This is because people can weave their energy and intention into the fabric of the land.

Places in the land can also be negatively affected by people's actions, becoming spiritually and energetically polluted. This is why people who are highly sensitive to energy have difficulty being in places where terrible occurrences took place. War sites, concentration camps, and prisons are all prime examples of places that build up negative energy. (Eight years ago I took a tour of Alcatraz prison, which is now open for public visits. Even though I was there only a short time, less than two hours, I was overcome with feelings of anxiousness and nausea.) Even simple arguments and conflicts may be held in the land, or in people's homes or places of work. It is almost as if the harsh words and actions hang in the air and seep into the soil, the walls of a dwelling. These places may feel disturbed for some time afterward or until they are cleared. (These places are also greatly affected by repeated exposures to either negative energies or positive energies.)

Because of this energetic link, relationships between specific people and places on Earth can and do develop. Many native peoples observe this intimate relationship with the Earth. According to Lakota Chief Luther Standing Bear:

The Lakota ... loved the Earth and all things of the Earth, the attachment growing with age. The old people came literally to love the soil, and they sat or reclined on the ground with a feeling of being close to a mothering power. It was good for the skin to touch the Earth, and the old people liked to remove their moccasins and walk with bare feet on the sacred Earth. Their tipis were built upon the Earth and their altars were made of earth. The soil was soothing, strengthening, cleansing, and healing. That is why the old Indian still sits upon the Earth instead of propping himself up and away from its life-giving forces. For him, to sit or lie upon the ground is to be able to think more deeply and to feel more keenly; he can see more clearly into the mysteries of life and come closer in kinship to other lives about him.[1]

Special relationships with the land are often formed in childhood, and these links between places and individual souls can be forged so strongly that they remain after death and into the rebirth of the soul in a new body. When one encounters déjà vu in a specific place, it may trigger a long-forgotten memory from early childhood or a past life. This explains why people who experience past lives frequently see and/or feel the place where they were in previous lifetimes.

## MOUNT TAMALPAIS: SLEEPING DRAGON IN THE MOUNTAIN

*As darkness recedes, the robin hesitatingly starts its song. The awakening California towhee calls a repetitive one-note "teek" and a Bewick's wren begins its own variations on a theme ...*
*One can hear these sounds because the streets are not yet singing the song of tires on pavement. But in the eighteenth century, an Indian hunter waiting for bird to walk into a trap*

*or a Coast Miwok woman quietly weaving a basket
could have heard even the whir of butterfly wings.*

Betty Goerke, *Chief Marin: Leader, Rebel, and Legend*

Mount Tamalpais, with its graceful slopes that conjure up images of a reclining woman, rises from the Marin coastal range just twenty miles north of San Francisco. Mount Tamalpais was a sacred mountain to the Coast Miwok Indians, who lived in this area for over 10,000 years. They believed that there was a sleeping power within the mountain. Like a sleeping dragon, Mount Tamalpais may be the site of a blind thrust fault.[2] Thus it may indeed be a focal point of dramatic shifting of the Earth in the future.[3]

In its quiet state, as it has been for several hundreds of years, it allows more subtle movements in the Earth to take place, unleashing slower bursts of energy feeding the creative energy of many in this region.

The mountain has symbolized a sacred place for many people from all walks of life. Made famous in Matthew Davis and Michael Farrell Scott's *Opening the Mountain*,[4] Mount Tamalpais became the sacred center of walking as spiritual exercise. The act of walking meditation is like moving through a three-dimensional mandala where one becomes a part of the sacredness of the place.

Today, Mount Tamalpais and the surrounding Golden Gate National Recreation Area, comprising over 115 square miles, have been protected, so the mountain is almost entirely free from development or industry—an incredible feat given its proximity to San Francisco. As such, the mountain is one of the largest preserved places adjacent to an American city.

For those of us who live and work in the small towns in the foothills of the mountain, the mountain is omnipresent. Whether commuting to San Francisco, hiking the many paths and trails in the area, or visiting a friend living in the foothills, we can always see Mount Tamalpais. The mountain's all-pervading presence is a serene yet powerful force in our lives. As the mountain penetrates the blue of the sky above, so it penetrates our very consciousness.

## GLOBAL SACRED SITES

There are places on Earth that are significant to many people and are acknowledged as sacred by even the earliest inhabitants. These sacred sites are found throughout the world and can be associated with naturally occurring landforms, springs, and rivers.

The Ganges is a sacred river that winds 1,500 miles over northern India, from the Himalaya Mountains to the Indian Ocean. On the banks of the Ganges River, also referred to locally as the sacred goddess Ganga Ma, faithful followers can be found cleansing themselves. This cleansing is a sacred act that has the power to wipe away sins and omissions. The river also aids the journey of the deceased on their way to heaven.

Another of the world's most well-known sacred sites is Machu Picchu in the upper Amazon basin. Machu Picchu is the sacred mountain where a famous Inca temple was constructed in the mid-1400s. Legend says that touching the forehead to a special stone there, called the *Intihuatana*, opens one's vision to the spirit world. Intihuatana stones were destroyed by the Spaniards to break the spirit of native peoples, who believed in the power of the stones. Luckily, due to Machu Picchu's remoteness, it was never discovered by the Spaniards, and the Intihuatana stone remains in its original place. Like Stonehenge, another one of Machu Picchu's primary functions was that of an astronomical observatory. The Intihuatana stone, or "Hitching Post of the Sun," was used to pinpoint the location of the sun during the equinox.[5]

While some sacred sites are left in their natural state, like Ayers Rock in Australia, many sacred sites such as Chartres Cathedral, are enhanced by manmade structures. In some cases, outside conquerors and leaders of opposing religions purposely selected natural sacred sites of the indigenous population to use as their own places of worship. They would destroy the original statues and relics and then replace them with their own relics and architecture.

Chartres Cathedral in France, a holy shrine built in the Middle Ages, sits upon holy ground that was a destination for spiritual seekers long before the Cathedral was built. The Druids held sacred rites in the oak forest groves and underground grottoes there. According to legend, powerful spiritual energy emanates from the Earth at Chartres. Some of Chartres's modern day pilgrims believe that the cathedral's crypt is connected to a sacred, underground spring that has spared the cathedral from destructive forces, such as fires, the Reformation, the French Revolution, and two world wars. Today, the site draws over 1.5 million people a year.

> The name Chartres comes from Carnutes, a Druid tribe that lived in the region. It is stated in Roman records that it was the forest of the Carnutes where all the Druids of Gaul would gather once a year. Some believe that the precise location was here, deep beneath the present cathedral; that there was a cave, which symbolized the realm of the Mother Goddess.[6]

## LEY LINES: PATHS OF POWER

It was Alfred Watkins, who lived in England in the early 1900s, who first rediscovered ley lines. Ley lines are powerful paths of invisible energy upon the surface of the Earth that tend to run in straight lines. It is told that his vision of ley lines first came to him in a trance-like state, or what has been referred to as a "flood of ancestral memory." During the vision, Watkins saw a "map" of energy lines, and understood that all of the ancient and sacred sites (known to him) ran in a straight line along these energy pathways. Watkins later conducted surveys to confirm and document his vision, and he found that the ancient sites did indeed lie in straight lines across the landscape where he had seen the lines of energy.[7]

While the discovery of ley lines seemed like new knowledge to Watkins, ancient shamans were able to view and travel along these energetic pathways in trance states. Shamans believed that these external lines of energy on the Earth were linked to inner visions or energy maps within the human mind. For example, the Kogi Indians can see the routes that shamans take during shamanic journeys in the spirit world. The Kogi live in a remote region in the mountains in northern Colombia. They are believed to be descendants of the Tairona civilization (AD 1000) who escaped into the mountains when the Spaniards invaded their region. The Kogi have retained many of the ways and beliefs of their ancient ancestors for over five hundred years. The Kogi Indians believe that some of the straight roads that they use are physical manifestations of spirit routes. They also have a "map stone" that shows many lines that crisscross, which they say are representations of spirit paths.[8]

> The original nature of the straight landscape line appears to have been symbolic of spirit travel, of journeying in the other-world of spirits, of the ancestors, which in shamanic terms was simply another level or dimension of the physical landscape... Within the context of soul flight, straightness lends itself to an extra dimension of symbolism, for flight is the straight way over the land—we say "as the crow flies" or "as straight as an arrow," using the very metaphors used by shamanic tradition itself. The lines, in essence, were the markings of a spiritual geography— geography of the mind superimposed on the physical landscape. The mapping of ecstasy.[9]

Watkins's spontaneous knowledge of ley lines and the Kogi's ability to map invisible energy routes are achieved by accessing an inner vision that all human beings have access to in certain states of consciousness. Sadly, this ability is now dormant in most people since we do not exercise or acknowledge this inner knowing. However, there are ways to become more in tune with the patterns of the land and energy of the Earth.

## STEP ONE:
## CREATE A MAP OF YOUR OUTER LANDSCAPE

Creating a map is a powerful way to focus your attention on a region and the things within it, thereby supplying greater awareness of your outer and inner landscape. Remember that your inner and outer landscapes have both physical and energetic features, and when you move through the outer landscape, you are also moving through subtle energy fields, bringing your energy to different places in the environment.

I used to create habitat maps for wilderness areas and private properties to assist with the management of wild animals. These maps indicated habitat types (wetlands, uplands, meadows, shrub land, forest land, streams, ponds, and so on), and what was needed by way of trees, plants, and water to support specific species. I was surprised at how quickly the habitat and plant species changed every twenty to forty feet or so. Sometimes you only notice these quick changes in the landscape when you focus your attention by making a map.

1.  First, determine the scope of the area you would like to map. This could be as small as your yard or a neighborhood park, or as large as your county or state park if you have time to travel.

2.  Make a list of the things you would like to become more aware of. For example, you may want to map plant

species, animals, walking paths, rivers, or sacred sites like labyrinths or churches. You may also want to map subtle energy. For example, are there certain places where you feel peaceful, energized, or safe? Or are there areas where good or bad things tend to happen, like frequent accidents?

First define what you intend to focus on in your map. Once you have decided this, create a map key using simple symbols to represent each thing. For example, for a tree you may want to use a stick tree; for a river, three wavy lines. For different types of energy experiences, you may want to have a light bulb that appears either empty, half full, or full of light. Or you may simply want to use words for how you feel in specific areas.

3. Next, take several sheets of large paper, some pencils, and a few erasers, and go explore the area you are mapping. Preferably explore on foot or by bicycle, but you can go by car if it is a large area (as long as you get out at key spots you wish to map). As you go along, mark in on your draft maps the key symbols, comparative distances, and locations of the things you are visiting.

4. If you are marking energy in the land, be attentive to the energy you feel as you move through different places will be documented on your map. Energetic characteristics can influence your thoughts, your emotions, and your body. For example, are there specific places where you feel lighter, more carefree, while other areas make you feel anxious? Does your body feel warm and relaxed or chilled and stiff while you sit or stand in different

*continued on page 94*

*continued from page 93*

places in the environment? Paying attention to these subtle clues can help to identify the energy characteristics of the land.

5. After you are done with your first walk-through and have penciled in some key symbols on your draft map, return home to create a final map. You may also decide that you want to take several walk-throughs before completing a final version.

   Get a very large sheet of paper or poster board and draw the outline and border of your map, including familiar things like roads and buildings. Then enter what you've chosen to document with the corresponding key symbol. You may also want to color-code your keys if you are tracking several things.

6. When you are done, place your map on a wall where you can view it, and note any patterns or trends that pop out at you.

7. Soon after making it, seek to dream about your map. Encouraging dreams to reveal information about the landscape that is not available to you in a waking state (such as the type of energy in different areas) can unleash new discoveries about otherwise invisible or hidden knowledge. You can do this by looking intently at your map before you fall asleep at night, asking for a dream that will reveal information to you.

8. Next time you walk through the area that you have mapped, try to visualize where you are on the map that you have drawn. Continue to do this for forty days. You will be amazed at how your spatial connection to the

place you have mapped has grown significantly. When we strengthen our understanding of a place on the Earth, we also deepen our overall ability to read the land and understand where we are in physical space.

9. You may also want to show yourself moving in the map by using different colors to indicate well-used paths. Some say that when we move from place to place we are helping the Earth to connect its energy together—as if human beings act like acupuncture needles. Remember that your map is documenting a living, changing place; mapping is a powerful way to connect to a place on Earth, and to notice patterns and trends that you would not ordinarily see. It also fulfills a deep, unmet longing to develop a sense of place and belonging.

One of the things that I love about this simple map-making exercise is how it can powerfully reshape our lives. Most people today suffer from a serious sense of "placeless-ness" since they move so often and spend so little time outdoors in their environment. When we lack a sense of place, we can feel inauthentic and aimless.

Everyone needs a strong foundation—a base—for his or her life. Family, friends, and community are a key part of that foundation, but the land is also an important underpinning from which our life grows. While this map-making exercise cannot replace the incredible ground-edness of someone who lives in an area where his or her ancestors have lived for hundreds of years, it can help you to establish a new and stronger base for your own life, no matter how many times you have moved. If reclaiming the place as your own is important to you, you may also want to give your own names to trees and other natural features in your area. For example, Opal Whiteley, a child author, used to refer to a spring near her home as the "singing creek where the willows grow."

There are also powerful places on the Earth that feel like a welcome home to everyone. These special places contain an energetic reality that can positively influence most people—no matter where they were born.

## STONEHENGE: PLACE OF POWER AND HEALING

Stonehenge, which is older than ancient Greece, is estimated to have taken more than thirty million hours of labor to create. Why would a culture exert such a huge effort to bring these enormous stones together? Surely, if the sole purpose of Stonehenge was astronomical observation (Stonehenge is aligned with the midsummer sunrise, the midwinter sunset, and the journey of the moon in the sky), that function could have been successfully achieved by using smaller or different stones. Instead, the stones themselves also have great significance.[10] Myths of old hint that the stones are powerful conveyors of health. In the famous myth of King Arthur, Merlin tells King Aurelius:

> Laugh not so lightly, King, for not lightly are these words spoken. For in these stones are a mystery and a healing virtue against many ailments . . . for they did wash the stones and pour forth the water into the baths, whereby they that were sick were made whole. Moreover, they did mix confections of herbs with the water, whereby they that were wounded had healing, for not a stone is there that lacketh in virtue of leechcraft.[11]

As mentioned previously, mythical stories are often based on truth. Layamon, a thirteenth century British poet, also speaks of the healing quality of Stonehenge:

The stones are great/And magic power they have
Men that are sick/Fare to that stone
And they wash that stone
And with that water/Bathe away their sickness.[12]

Since one individual healing stone of Stonehenge would likely be more than enough for the healing of a human being, why did the ancients go to the effort of bringing so many of these stones to this one location? We may find the answer by turning to the example of the Kogi.

The Kogi call themselves the Elder Brothers of the human race and us (supposedly "civilized" people) the Younger Brothers. They are convinced that they are acting as intermediaries between humankind and creation by holding the world in balance through their shamanic beliefs and practices. They live in an isolated region of the world, called Sierra Nevada de Santa Marta, which to the Kogi is the Heart of the World. They believe that they can have a greater energetic and spiritual influence on the universe from this place.[13] As author Paul Devereux explains:

Traditional Kogi religion is closely related to Kogi ideas about the structure and functioning of the Universe, and Kogi cosmology is ... a model for survival in that it molds individual behavior into a plan of actions or avoidances that are oriented toward the maintenance of a viable equilibrium between Man's demands and Nature's resources. In this manner, the individual and society at large must both carry the burden of great responsibilities, which, in the Kogi view, extend not only to their society but also to the whole of mankind.[14]

Similarly, I believe that the ancient people who created Stonehenge viewed the island of Britain as an important, energetic, and sacred place. Stonehenge then was no less than a divine center that served as a focal point for energetic and spiritual work concerning the entire universe, while acting as a bridge between mundane and sacred reality. The fact that Britain lies on an important planetary ley line no doubt supports this assumption that to the ancient people who constructed Stonehenge, it was the "center of the world."

The ancients decided to create Stonehenge as a dynamic portal to the very center of the universe. The chosen stones contain crystalline material that attracts and conducts electromagnetism from the ground and the atmosphere. Through Stonehenge, the ancients no doubt saw themselves as helping to maintain the harmonic balance of the Earth, while gaining access to higher levels of energy and spirit. I believe the creators of Stonehenge created it not only for its beneficial healing effects and its well known astronomical capacity, but to help maintain the harmony and balance of the Earth Herself. Stonehenge was a way for humankind to contribute to the very well-being of the planet.

---

## STEP TWO:
## IDENTIFYING YOUR PLACES OF POWER

We all have a place or places on Earth where we feel supported, strong, or inspired. Often these are places that we find when we are children and have more time to play and explore outdoors. They may also be places that we have found as adults during a time of reflection—where we may have gained awareness or had an *ah-ha* moment, or where we may have felt awe.

1. Write down or, better yet, draw your special place of power on a piece of paper. Then use short phrases or adjectives to describe what it feels like to be in this place.

---

When done, put down your pen and paper, and sit or stand comfortably with your spine straight.

2. Take seven deep yogic breaths, relax, and imagine that you are now in this place. What does it feel like, what does it look like?

3. Spend at least five to fifteen minutes imagining that place in your mind (or if it is still near to you, go there in person), and notice how your body feels when you are there. Make this experience of being there in person as real as you can. Then call for the strength of the place to fill your being. You may notice that you are sitting or standing taller, with your chest forward and shoulders back.

4. At night, right before falling asleep, ask to be taken to that special place in your dreams.

Ultimately, by connecting with the land around us, we gain a greater inner cohesiveness in our lives. By going to sacred places, we come a little closer to discovering wholeness in ourselves. A journey to a sacred place may be a few miles or many thousands of miles, but the road we travel is the same road traveled by all life on Earth. This is because all living things arise from the same divine place, and the spiral is the sacred road that we travel together.

# PART 3

## Inner Wholeness

# 8

# THE SPIRAL DANCE

If you would understand the Invisible, look carefully at the Visible.

TALMUD

One sunny June morning, more than a decade after my experience with the sacred tree, I stood on a high ridge overlooking four rounded hills covered with golden grasses. The bright hillsides were dotted with groves of coastal live oak, coyote brush, and California bay trees. The gentle wind, filled with the delicate freshness of the Pacific Ocean twenty miles away, cooled the back of my neck. A small flock of western bluebirds flitted above the tips of the grasses. As I watched them land on the ground in a small, sociable grouping, a brilliant shimmer of silver caught my eye. Looking up, I saw an osprey about three hundred feet above my head. With its long, tapered wings and gleaming body, it looked like a cross suspended in the sky. Held securely in its strong talons was a newly caught fish. The brilliant silver flashes were the reflection of the sun's rays on the fish's gleaming, still-wet scales.

The fish was moving its tail back and forth as if swimming, its valiant head forward with its eyes staring into the great innocence of the sky. For an instant, I felt pity for it; however, the osprey did not carry the fish in a straight line to its nest, but flew in a slow-moving spiral of expanding circles. It gave the fish a majestic ride over the green and gold hillsides, over the doe and her two spotted fawns, over the long-eared hare standing up on restless hind legs, and over the wonderstruck woman and her dog.

In that moment, the osprey's act seemed no less grand than if I was witnessing firsthand the discovery of the Holy Grail. The "sacred vessel," now held aloft so triumphantly, shone its brilliant silvery light into my soul. My consciousness was instantly lifted beyond the every-day to a vision of a grander sphere. My spirit soared with the osprey and the fish, and my perception shifted as I now saw what the fish saw: the body of the Earth revealed. It was a marvel so far beyond the fish's oceanic dreams, and so far beyond my own experience, that I, like the fish, entered a previously unimaginable place. On that morn-ing, the Creator and master alchemist transformed me as I witnessed that spiral flight.

The osprey continued to fly in expanding circles around for over twenty minutes while I stood entranced on the ridge below. During this time, the image and meaning of the spiral was integrated into every cell of my body. As I made my way home, the impression of the spiral stayed embedded in my mind. It seemed that everything I looked at—each blade of grass, each tree branch, and even the trees' very trunks—rose up from the ground as joyous spirals before my very eyes. I felt the dynamic motion of the spiral move as a gentle yet powerful force upon the Earth. It was as if I had seen the wizard behind the curtain—the magic that gracefully weaves itself through all existence.

> *One of the chief beauties of a spiral ... is that it is not merely*
> *an explanation of the past, but it is also a prophesy of the*
> *future; and while it defines and illuminates what has already*
> *happened, it is also leading constantly to new discoveries.*
>
> —Theodore Andrea Cook[1]

The spiral is one of the most powerful and beautiful patterns in nature. Spirals are everywhere, from luminous spiral galaxies ablaze in dazzling colors to the tiny spirals at the tips of our fingers. The spiral is simultaneously a structure and a movement. As a dynamic movement, the spiral can be creative beyond measure or devastatingly destructive, as exhibited by tornados or tsunamis. As structure or design, spirals are the form that animate and inanimate things take. The fact that the spiral form is found throughout the great diversity of life and beyond speaks strongly of an underlying unity in the universe, shared among all creation.

Human movement, at its best, follows a spiral pattern. Movements that manifest the spiral energy within us are more powerful and graceful than movements that are not in alignment with this inner spiral pattern. Aikido (a Japanese martial art) takes ultimate advantage of the grace and power that exists within the spiral movement. Even the pitch of a professional baseball player uses the same dynamic movement to throw a fastball. Many great works of art similarly depict the human body in a subtle spiral or helix position, known since Greek times as an S-Curve. In fact, most classical sculptures depict their human figures posed in an S-Curve.

Plants grow in slow-moving spirals toward the heavens, water spins in spiral and circular shapes within ponds and streams, and flowers and snail shells have a spiral pattern of growth. Even our very bones grow in spirals. While spirals may go unnoticed by our conscious mind, we are subconsciously aware of the naturally occurring symmetry that is all around and pleasing to us. This is why we so often seek to replicate symmetry and balance in things that we create, and why we feel more comfortable and relaxed in an environment which reflects balanced proportion. Spirals and other naturally occurring, proportionate patterns nurture an inner balance and harmony within our very being. This is one reason why we enjoy the beauty and harmony of nature. Being in nature helps to establish an equilibrium within our body and mind.

It is the spiral that connects us to every other life form on Earth: the blueprint for all life on Earth exists in a spiral! Deoxyribonucleic acid (DNA), which contains the genetic instructions needed to create the components for cells, proteins, and RNA (ribonucleic acid) molecules of life forms, is shaped like a spiral.[2] Thus, the spiral is the very fundamental expression of movement and shape of life, and within the spiral exist the deepest secrets of creation.

The predominance of the spiral in the physical world is echoed in the invisible, energetic, and spiritual worlds; spirit and energy also move in a spiral. Since the spiral is the intrinsic pattern of creation from which all things grow and evolve, spirals are frequently displayed in ancient drawings, sculptures, and other works of art found around the world. It is also found at many sacred places worldwide. For example, the spiral is a favorite sacred symbol of the Maori in New Zealand; it is also found in sacred uses in Africa, and its form is carved into the ancient rocks at Newgrange, Ireland. Neolithic peoples understood the power and prevalence of this living symbol, and they captured its essence in their designs, and in their rituals and spiritual gatherings. People from many cultures wished to depict the dance of the universe through the power, symmetry, and beauty of the spiral.[3]

Ancient cultures knew that the spiral was the expression of their link to the rest of life and even the larger cosmos. The spiral itself is infinite, which links it to the Creator (who is also infinite), and yet the spiral is also found throughout the universe in all "limited" life forms. Thus the spiral, in effect, is capable of going from the physical realm of the material world to the world of spirit, and ultimately the birthplace of all creation. The spiral unites us with all life, with the Creator, and ultimately with our deepest selves.

The spiral dance that we observe in nature also takes place within our own psyche. Many creation stories have cyclical or spiral patterns, reflecting that human psychological and spiritual growth follow a spiral path. Don Beck and Chris Cowan introduced the Spiral Dynamics theory of human development.[4] They believe that human nature is constantly enlarging as it adapts to the outside world and that there is an ongoing internal learning that takes place because of this interaction between the world and inner psyche. As we "transcend" psychologically and spiritually, we build upon previous value systems much in the way that a tree grows around its central core: ever-expanding outward and upward, the inner rings of its being serving as a foundation for growth. Like a tree, once a person grows in their psychological development, it becomes a part of the inner core of their being. This inner growth then supports future evolution and transformation.

> Maybe the evolutionary sequence really is from matter to body to mind to soul to spirit, each transcending and including, each with a greater depth and greater consciousness and wider embrace. And in the highest reaches of evolution, maybe, just maybe, an individual's consciousness does indeed touch infinity—a total embrace of the entire Cosmos—a cosmic consciousness that is Spirit awakened to its own true nature.
>
> —Ken Wilber[5]

Just as our psychological growth comes about through a spiral evolution, so does our spiritual understanding. When we move into a sacred place within our being, our spirit can rise like a spiraling snake. Kundalini energy rises from its resting place at the base of the spine and climbs up through all of the chakras. This is why understanding movement is critical to understanding not only matter but the energy that underlies all matter, for without movement there is nothing, and the movement—the dance—of the universe is the spiral dance. When we attune ourselves to this subtle dance of creation, we enter a sacred realm—we find our own Holy Grail.

Ultimately, the spiral within all things shows us that our path is the path of all life—a path of evolution, unfolding, and transformation. The spiral is the vibrant, golden thread that weaves all living things together.

## INDRA'S NET: THE FABRIC OF THE UNIVERSE

As Wordsworth wrote in his Ode: "Intimations of Immortality," we came to this Earth "trailing clouds of glory" from the Creator. Other beings, animate and inanimate, come to this Earth trailing those same clouds of glory; they simply arrive with different physical forms and anatomical attributes. The Master Creator uses the same biological building blocks to make the vast diversity of life forms.

For hundreds of years, scientists searched for the one unified force that underlies all creation. They finally discovered it in the tiny realm of quantum reality. Initially, they never expected that this quantum force influenced the larger world that we see and experience with our five senses. We now know that this subtle but all-encompassing force not only influences the world at large, it may be the single greatest power that we will ever know. It is a repository for all of the fields in the universe. Physicists call this great, invisible realm the zero-point field because it is the ground zero from which everything arises. It is the great void; it is the cauldron of creation from which everything comes into being. It is Indra's net:[6]

> Far away in the heavenly abode of the great god Indra, there is a wonderful net ... that stretches out indefinitely in all directions. A single glittering jewel hangs at the net's every note, and since the net itself is infinite in dimension, the jewels are infinite in number. There hang the jewels, glittering like stars of the first magnitude, a wonderful sight to behold.[7]

No matter what it is called, this invisible realm is nothing less than the source of all life and all creation. And it is this unifying source of creation that exists in all things that can call each life back to wholeness and to the Creator Herself.

> *If the zero-point field [is] included in our conception of the most fundamental nature of matter . . . the very underpinning of our universe [is] a heaving sea of energy—one vast quantum field . . . Everything [is] connected to everything else like some invisible web.*
>
> —Lynne McTaggart, *The Field* [8]

Within this great field, all animate and inanimate things arise and take shape as they gain "life coherence." Life coherence refers to the individuality of each being that is created with intention and a specific frequency or song. This intention frequency gathers condensed energy (matter) to form an individualized being out of the infinite field of undifferentiated possibility. The "song" becomes a human being, or a raven, or a coyote, depending upon the quality and characteristics of intent and its frequency. Each unique being contains this seed of intent directly from the divine mother, the Creator, the source of all life.

Once born in the world, all living things swim within the ocean of energy from whence they came. This sea of energy exists around and within us in every moment, and it is the source of some of the unexplainable phenomena of our physical world. Physicists now understand what mystics have known for centuries: acts such as levitation and telepathy are the result of the human mind being able to tap into the sea of energy via altered states of consciousness. Ironically, the physical aspects of the universe—those things that we see, feel, and experience with our direct senses and believe to be "real"—are but a tiny fraction of the true universe. In place of something solid, only light, frequency, and movement exist. Because our bodies are 99.999 percent non-matter (the atoms or matter within us are comprised of largely open or empty space just like the space around us and in other living things), we are able to connect with this vast field of energy around us. We can leave our own narrow harbor of being and sail into the boundless sea of potentiality and consciousness.

# 9

## VISION AND NATURE QUESTS

*A quest of any kind is a heroic journey. It is a rite of passage that carries you
to an inner place of silence and majesty, and encourages you to live life
more courageously and genuinely.*

DENISE LINN, *Quest*

For centuries, people have embarked on rites of passage in nature to
gain awareness of the sacred realms and of greater self-knowledge.
Spiritual journeys into nature can provide greater life direction and
harmony. These archetypal passages, or quests, into nature are powerful acts that can change a person's life profoundly. This is why so
many myths and stories around the world have the hero's quest as a
central theme.

Native Americans conducted vision quests (a term coined by
an American anthropologist) in which a young boy would go into
the wilderness alone to find life direction and prophecies. Native
American quests usually lasted a number of days, and helped
young boys on their path to becoming a man and a respected
member of the tribal community. These quest experiences were
often physically demanding and required the initiate to fast and
sacrifice in some way. If he was lucky, a great vision would be
granted that would help the boy or his people, which is certainly

the case of the prophetic vision of Chief Plenty Coups of the Crow nation.

In the spring of 1850, when Chief Plenty Coups was nine years old, the Crow people (also known as *Absaroke*) arrived at their annual spring gathering place, the Land of the Shining Mountains. (Today, these mountains are the Beartooth Mountains in the state of Montana. The area is one of the few places on Earth where grizzly bears still roam, surrounded by the fragile beauty of the place and other animals, such as golden eagles, moose, mule deer, mountain goats, pikas, bighorn sheep, and, of course, crows.) By 1850, the Crow people, along with the many other Native American tribes, were facing their greatest challenge: what to do since the European settlers were staking a permanent claim on their homeland. These were dark and confusing times, and this was a turning point for the Crow.

Plenty Coups had conducted his first vision quest that spring. At the age of nine, he spent several days and nights in the wilderness alone, calling for a vision. What he received was powerful, filled with prophecy. He witnessed what seemed to be the impossible: the disappearance of all of the millions of buffalo that roamed the plains. He told of how these great, brawling beasts spilled from the Earth until they were gone:

> Everywhere I looked, great herds of buffalo were going in every direction, and still others without number were pouring out of the hole in the ground to travel on the wide plains. When at last they ceased coming out of the hole in the ground, all were gone—all! There was not one in sight anywhere, even out on the plains...

[After the buffalo had vanished,] out of the hole in the ground came bulls and cows and calves past counting. These, like the others, scattered and spread on the plains. But they stopped in small bands and began to eat the grass. Many lay down, not as a buffalo does but differently, and many were spotted ... And the bulls bellowed differently too—not deep and far-sounding like the bulls of the buffalo but sharper and yet weaker in my ears ... They were not buffalo. These were strange animals from another world. Finally, [I] saw a great storm combined of the winds from each of the four directions. The storm was fierce and dark, and was heading towards a great forest. It ravaged the forest and knocked down every single tree but one. In the lone standing tree sat a tiny chickadee.

[Then I heard a voice:] "In that tree is the lodge of the Chickadee. He is least in strength but strongest of mind among his kind. He is willing to work for wisdom. The Chickadee person is a good listener. Nothing escapes his ears, which he has sharpened by constant use ... He gains success and avoids failure by learning how others succeeded or failed, and without great trouble to himself ... Develop your body, but do not neglect your mind, Plenty Coups. It is the mind that leads a man to power, not strength of the body."[1]

When Chief Plenty Coups returned from his quest, the elders helped him interpret the meaning of the prophetic vision. They decided the vision was a prophecy that the buffalo would vanish from the plains, and in their place new animals—domestic cows— would appear.

They further advised that the four winds that created the storm represented the Europeans and their allies who would fight against the Native Americans, felling each tribe like a cut tree. They believed that the dream was a prophesy for their people to listen and learn from this catastrophic event, and not to make war on the

Europeans. Then they would be like the one tree standing after the storm.

The Crow people could be left standing if they watched and learned from the mistakes of others like the chickadee. Plenty Coups's prophetic vision convinced the tribe's elders to cooperate with the Europeans. In the end, the Crow tribe was protected from some of the worst military actions Europeans used against other tribes. The Crow were also one of the few Native American nations to remain on a portion of their ancestral homeland, just as the little chickadee was left with his lodge in the one standing tree.[2] By asking for guidance and calling for a vision, it became possible for Plenty Coups to access an all-knowing field of wisdom and discern future events.

There have been many great leaders and sages from different cultures, and religious persuasions—including Buddhism, Hinduism, and Taoism—who have been able to discern future events. However, they have all understood that they receive this knowledge from a source greater than themselves. This sage way of perceiving and living in the world is not dependent on race or religious background, and can be encouraged by connecting with the larger energy field of the Earth and the animals.

A modern day quest into nature can be a powerful experience. While some Native Americans continue to practice vision quests specific to their cultural understanding, every culture on Earth has nature-based rituals, sometimes referred to as pilgrimages, walkabouts, or retreats. I often refer to the quests that I conduct as "vision and nature quests," since modern Westerners are often out of touch with simply experiencing nature firsthand. These quests are non-denominational and rely upon methods and practices primarily from

Celtic, shamanistic, and Taoist roots, as well as on guidance from the resident animals and plants, and the land itself.

For many beleaguered and busy people, a quest may simply present an opportunity to spend contemplative time alone in nature as a salve for the stresses of modern life. In other cases, people partake in a quest as a way of soul seeking, while others embark on a quest as a way to deal with important life passages, such as death, divorce, or changes of career. Some simply conduct quests to rejuvenate and renew their spirits, and find greater understanding about their life path. As people unwind in nature, new revelations about their lives and the universe come to the surface. Thus, modern day quests are ideal ways to:

- relax
- find inner peace and balance
- find the answers in one's heart
- tap into one's dreams and visions
- connect deeply with nature
- face one's fears and step into courage
- deepen one's meditation practice or learn to meditate
- communicate with animal totems and spirit helpers
- be at one with the Creator/the universe and oneself

## VISION AND NATURE QUESTS: A STEP TOWARD DISCOVERING YOUR LIFE'S PURPOSE

Nature is one of the best venues for accessing our deepest selves. We now know that, in a deep state of relaxation or meditation, the electromagnetic frequency of the brain attunes to the electromagnetic field of the Earth. The Earth's primary harmonic resonance has been measured at 7.83 cycles per second or 7.83 hertz (Hz).

The frequency of the electrical activity of the brain during periods of meditation is also around 7.83 hertz. This is not a coincidence but one of the many reasons why we feel so rejuvenated and inspired in nature.[3]

There are many other ways in which nature helps us get closer to the core of our being. In nature, we are surrounded by the creative, living world; natural patterns and movements stimulate our consciousness and imagination. This is why some of the greatest discoveries and inventions have occurred while observing nature. Isaac Newton had a creative leap of imagination when he observed a falling apple, which led to his famous discovery of the law of gravity. In 1502, Leonardo da Vinci studied the flight of birds and invented flying machines by copying the design and functionality of a bird's wing. By observing original creation, we can receive a spark of imagination to learn how to best mimic natural laws and properties that better our lives, portray beauty, or envision a new way of living and being.

When we spend time in nature, free of the distractions of daily life, we break out of outdated modes of thought and behavior. Part of this has to do with leaving behind the known, habitual, domesticated world and opening your heart to wildness. In her book *Kindling the Celtic Spirit*, author Mara Freeman explains this phenomenon beautifully in a poem:

> *If you sit still long enough*
> *On the forest floor*
> *The universe will approach you*
> *Like a shy animal.*
>
> *Breathe softly and don't move:*
> *If encouraged it will nuzzle your open hand.*
>
> *Open more!*
> *Open your heart, your head, and your soul*
> *All doors all bars*

*That catch and trap and bind*
*The wild and dreaming beast*
*That sleeps*
*In you.*[4]

From the peace that nature offers, we can experience the gentle movements of the animals, the slight changes in the wind, and the subtle shift in the light as the day progresses.

Without interruptions like ringing phones and schedules, our thoughts go further: we hear the usually silent inner voice. Spending time in nature and learning from animals and plants can also inspire us to express ourselves fully and authentically. Karen, a participant in a nature quest, provided an example of how this happened for her:

*As I sat in my sacred circle deep in the forest on the third day of my quest, I heard something so exquisitely beautiful. It was a lilting and sweet song of a bird. A glorious being was singing its heart out, and as I searched the branches of the oak trees that shaded me, I saw the beautiful bird with its head tilted and its throat stretched fully in its gorgeous song.*

*Between the branches, the sky was [a] brilliant, crystal-clear blue, and as I listened, I came fully into the moment. I felt I was in the presence of a being expressing its pure, true self without any self-consciousness, hesitation, or fear. There was a boldness and beauty in his song and his actions. I wanted so much to be like that bird—to live my life boldly and beautifully—and it was in that moment that I decided to change my life.*

In nature, we are removed from societal constructs, so we do not need to wear a mask or meet the expectations of others. We can freely connect with the pure essence of who we are.

## CONDUCTING A QUEST OR
## PILGRIMAGE INTO NATURE

*My deep wish going into the nature quest was to experience
myself in nature, free of the distractions of daily life.
I discovered a reservoir of inner strength, clarity,
and fearlessness that I can now easily access in my
day-to-day life ... There is no doubt that the nature
quest is one of the most daring, rejuvenating,
and transformative practices I've ever done
and I am profoundly grateful
for the experience.*

—Alice, spring 2005 nature quest participant

Experiencing a nature quest is a unique physical, emotional, and spiritual adventure offering many inherent benefits, such as getting in touch with one's inner rhythm. A quest can also provide the impetus that people need to take the first steps toward living a life in tune with their inner desires. Sarah, another nature quest participant, shared some of the benefits that she obtained during her quest with me:

> *I now feel like I have a direction to go when I get back home, which is HUGE for me. I have felt totally lost lately. I do not think that that lost feeling is going to be so prominent when I return home.*
>
> *I gained clarity and insight, and I feel more grounded, focused, and centered. I also feel more rested and not as frazzled. I feel more in sync with nature, which I am hoping will make me more aware of signs and synchronicities that are presented to me.*

By conducting a quest, we abandon—if even for a short time—the hectic pace of life that keeps us from being in touch with what matters most to us. The presence of the animals and plants can also have a profound effect on our experience during a quest. According to Jason:

> *One highlight was having the coyote approach my circle; nothing like that had ever happened to me before. Part of the wonderfulness of it was the simple beauty of the animal—its eyes, its delicate muzzle, those toothpick legs, and its seemingly playful nature. But another part was finding a segment of my reality exposed as false. It was a joy being surprised by the world, thinking I knew what was possible between a coyote and a person, and finding myself wrong.*

These unusual experiences can keep us motivated to explore deeper aspects of ourselves, like guiding signs along a path. They give us hope that the world is indeed filled with meaning. And between these signs, we need to cultivate our growing awareness about who and what we are by daily practices like meditation and prayer.

Quest participants can also experience answers to long-asked questions and/or the healing of old hurts that they might not have achieved on their own. For example, Janine experienced powerful insights that helped her heal her troubled relationships with her husband and family. During her quest, she connected powerfully with the spirit of her godfather, who had died that day many years earlier. Through dreams and visions, she experienced a release of guilt that was binding her to negative ways of approaching her current relationships.

Similarly, Tom, another quest participant, was able to break through obstacles in his relationship with his mother by connecting with childhood memories that came to the surface in the stillness of the scared circle.

*Sitting in my sacred circle, I was visited by childhood memories I did not know that I had. They came one after another with great clarity. I ended up being so moved by them that I wrote a letter to my mother in my journal that I feel very good about—it's a letter that I think will bring her some happiness.*

Some people undertake quests to find answers about the meaning of their lives. Mark, a middle manager in a large company, found that for him, the quest was an opportunity to connect with a sense of purpose.

*The confusion and uncertainty that has hung over me like a fog for so long has lifted. It is almost like I was able to have the "glasses" that I always needed to be able to see the world and myself for what is truly there. It felt like I had left my body behind and gone to the spirit realm. There I was able to ask the Creator: "Why am I here now?" I received answers that will enable me to live a more authentic life, in harmony with my deepest heart.*

Steve, a computer tech consultant and a frustrated playwright, was able to connect with his passion in life. He related that the nature quest helped him to "rediscover a piece of my authentic self that has been suppressed, and for that I am eternally grateful."

A quest can provide a safe and nurturing environment for people to identify and overcome limiting beliefs and habits. The beauty of a nature quest is that the experience meets us where we are.

## THE QUEST LOCATION: THE CENTER OF THE WORLD

Places in the land where people feel supported, healed, and strengthened are best for quest experiences. Like finding a place to live, location is key to the quest experience. I find locations for quests that have a large diversity of wildlife and are energetically healing. Sometimes a quest participant's affinity for specific types of habitat—mountains, seashores, forests, rolling hills, or flat plains—is also important to take into consideration.

Quests always begin in a base camp with the quest leader. This is where the quest leader stays and where quest participants gather to become acclimated to their surroundings; to share stories, experiences, and meals; and to receive training in different practices, like meditation, energy sensitivity, spirit animal journeys, and how to create a sacred circle. The sacred circle is where quest participants will spend part of their quest in solitude and contemplation.

Sacred circles are actual circles that one intentionally creates upon the Earth. The term "wheel" is sometimes used instead of circle to depict the flowing movement of this space. The sacred wheel or circle becomes the center of the world for quest participants.

A sacred circle can be in the middle of the woods, near a stream, in a field, on top of a mountain, or in a quiet valley. Once one is alone within the sacred circle, there is no need to respond or react to anyone else, but instead witness the recurring cycles of the day, the rising and setting sun, the circling stars, the changes in the moon, and the activities of the animals all around. One begins to attain a natural rhythm. Being at the center of the circle—the center of the world for the duration of the quest—ultimately brings one to the center of oneself.

There can be times when there is a strong yearning to leave the circle. We are so used to avoiding or ignoring our inner voice when we are bombarded by distractions, like an email or a friend stopping by. This is why it can feel odd or even uncomfortable to be left alone with nothing but our thoughts and feelings for long stretches of time. It is important to stay through this uncomfortable or awkward stage and remain in the circle. When we reach the other side of our limited thoughts or feelings, we can experience great freedom.

Through the pre-quest practices and the sacred circle, participants are helped to work directly with the four primary elements to obtain inner balance and cohesiveness. Working with the elements—air, water, fire, and earth—we can actively participate in balancing these forces within ourselves.

---

## CHAPTER PRACTICE

### Balancing the Four Elements Within

This is one of my favorite practices to help balance the four directions/elements. This practice can be done in as little as a few minutes or much longer, depending upon the need. It also works both inside or outside, but I believe that conducting this practice outside, surrounded by nature, is more powerful. To begin, you will need a compass to determine east, south, west, and north and to then select a place where you feel empowered and will not be disturbed. I often select the tops of hills or mountains so that I have a wide-open view of each direction.

Next, imagine that you are standing in the center of a circle. If you wish to create a real circle with natural objects found in the location, all the better. Once in your circle, you will turn your body clockwise to each of the four directions:

#### Air

1. First, face due east. East represents the element of air and the season of spring. It conjures up inspiration and new beginnings. While facing east, recall all the times that new ideas or concepts have come into your life. Does inspiration come easily to you? How does it feel to be in an inspirational place of new beginnings? Some

---

people get energized in this state and never want to leave it, simply going from one new idea to another. Others are locked into taking up the ideas and inspirations of other people versus nurturing their own ideas. Where do you fall in this range?

After contemplating the different qualities of the east and the element of air, invite the power of this direction and element into your life. This may be a generalized request or a specific request such as *let new ideas flow to me freely*. You may imagine feeling the wind or air filling you with inspiration. It is helpful to combine any request that you make with the feeling that you already have what you are asking for. What does it feel like to be inspired with a new idea? Energized? Motivated to start something new?

### Water

2. Then, turn to the south. South represents the element of water and the season of summer. South is the direction of emotions, where ideas and concepts interact first with our emotional body. How do you handle ideas and concepts that flow to you? Do you find yourself nurturing them, reacting to them, or simply shutting down? South is also the direction from which intuition flows. Do you have an active "feeling" side; do you trust your senses and hunches or do you shut them down? While facing south, consider your openness to ideas and intuitions. Intuition is where ideas and inspiration, which are close to being pure energy, begin to meet feelings and emotions, which are moving toward manifestation within you. Do you feel

*continued on page 124*

*continued from page 123*

in touch with your feelings? Do you let feelings flow through you or do you tend to block or deny your emotional self? Think back on the experiences of your life through this lens of perception. Would people say that you are approachable, warm, and friendly, or reserved and remote from others? Do you end up in situations or with people that do not support you because you are not paying attention to what your feelings are telling you about them? Or are you usually drawn to people, places, and things that help you?

These are just a few qualities that may express the element of water and the direction of south. After you have contemplated the meaning and characteristics of the element of water, invite the power of water into your life. Again, this can be a generalized request or a specific request such as *let me be more in touch with my emotions and their meaning in order to help guide my decisions.* Invite in the feeling that you might have if you were feeling your emotions freely and they were guiding you to places and people that supported you.

### Fire

3. Next, turn to face west. West represents fire, passion, and transformation. West represents the season of fall, when physical manifestation has taken root—when the idea has reached the stage of being born into the world. Are you a person of action or passivity? Do you like to take charge and get things done, or would you prefer to contemplate and examine all the ins and outs of an action before moving forward? How many times in your

life have you started new projects, ventures, or creations that still exist in the world? Have you taken any risks in life, or have you let others lead the way while you continue to do the same things you have always done? Do you consider yourself committed to a significant project or work, or do you simply chug along in boring tasks because you fear failure? In a group, are you always the naysayer who says it cannot be done, or are you the one out on an edge, asking for people to reach a new level?

Invite in the power of fire and the direction of the west into your life. Imagine what it feels like when you are passionate about what you are doing. Perhaps recall a time in your past when you were working happily on a project or at a job, or simply having an adventure. Bring that feeling in now and imagine that you feel that passion in this moment. Feel the warmth of the flames of passion fill your body and spirit.

### Earth

4.  Finally, turn to face north. North represents the element of Earth and the season of winter. North is most often associated with introspection and wisdom—when we become the observer of our past actions and consider what we have reaped. Do you take time to review your accomplishments and determine the overall impact? Do you take the time to understand the world, changes, or trends that have occurred or may be occurring? Have you taken into consideration how your actions have affected your relationship with others and the quality of those relationships? Do you tend to spend a lot of time

*continued on page 126*

*continued from page 125*

in contemplation, like a wise sage, providing advice to others but not yourself, or do you avoid going too deep when considering the impact of your own actions? Do you feel frustrated when others question or ask you to evaluate where you are now before taking further action, or do you welcome this assessment as a way of avoiding future mistakes or unneeded risks?

Invite in the power of Earth and the north into your life. What does it feel like when you quietly contemplate? Imagine that you are peacefully contemplating in this moment as you call in the wisdom of the Earth to ground your being.

5. When you are done asking for guidance and have invited the four elements into your life, say a short prayer asking for a balancing of these forces in your life to bring greater harmony, power, and wisdom. Recognize that life's harmonies are all around you at all times.

# 10

## RITES OF PASSAGE

"Initiation means beginning the revelation of one's true self."

MIRCEA ELIADE, *Rites and Symbols of Initiation:*
*The Mysteries of Birth and Rebirth*

Conducting a nature quest, discovering your spirit animal, or simply committing to a nature-based ritual can provide passage from one way of being to another. Rights of passage are particularly important for teenagers. It is on the verge of adulthood that defining our identity and role in the world is of the utmost importance. This is why so many cultures around the world emphasize adolescent rites of passage and incorporate some type of ceremony to recognize this important transition. These rituals delineate the departure from childhood and the coming into adulthood. In some cases, the rituals define the young person's future role in the community.

In indigenous societies, young women often begin their rite of passage at the time of their first menses. Some of their initiation rituals include being isolated from the tribe by staying in a dark cave, the hollow of a tree, or a hut without windows or light. This enclosure serves as both a tomb, for the ritualized "death" of the former child, and a womb for the birth of the new woman. The initiation ritual is of extreme importance, not just in the life of the initiate but for the future well-being of the tribe and culture.

[E]ach daughter represents the psychic as well as genetic womb of the tribe. Each represents the well of ancestral memories and the creative crucible from which the future will come.[1]

Today, some "modern" cultures still recognize this important time in a young person's life, notably the Jewish bar mitzvah and bat mitzvah, which are two of my favorite celebrations. In many cases, however, young people go through adolescence without any kind of communal recognition of this important passage. Yet the need to experience a rite of passage is so strong within our human psyche that it will take place even if it is not carefully planned by the community. Often, a youth's teenage peers take on a dominant role in leading a "rite of passage" in the case of sororities and gangs. This is why it is so important for adults in the community not to abdicate their role in recognizing and assisting youth through this important time in their life.

Rites of passage can also help adults transition from one phase or role in their life to the next. Since people are living so much longer today, we may reinvent ourselves many times in one lifetime. Going through a series of initiations can result in a positive progression toward greater fulfillment of our true nature. Before embarking on any conscious change of direction or transformation, setting an intention is very important.

## WHERE INTENT GOES, ENERGY FLOWS

Your intentions can dramatically affect physical reality. Human beings' ability to shape the world through intention is one of our greatest gifts from the Creator. Used masterfully, intention becomes a guiding light on your journey to fulfilling your true purpose in life. This is because, when we set an intention in motion, the universe has a tendency to align with that intention. When we share our intention with another person, like a family member, friend, colleague, coach, or nature quest leader, the intent is greatly amplified, bringing greater likelihood of its fulfillment. The shared intention of two people is three times as likely to occur as with one person because energetic power is not linear and generates greater strength with the addition of more people. This is why I ask all people who come to me for nature-based practices to create a letter of intent for our work together. I also recommend that participants share their intent with supportive people in their lives. By building a network of support for their intent, they are putting a powerful team together on their behalf.

Overall, a letter of intent serves four useful purposes:

1. Creating an intent statement focuses our desired direction.

2. By declaring our intent on paper, we are taking the first step to manifest our intentions. Just as an architect always starts with a drawing or architectural plan, we can start with a written intention.

3. By manifesting our intent in written form, we can share it with others who can help us amplify the power of our intent.

4. Setting a positive intention is also very important to forging good karma.

Karma (Sanskrit for "action" and "work") refers to the cause and effect of one's thoughts and actions on the world. Bad or "unskillful" actions tend to lead to bad karma, while good and/ or skillful actions tend to lead to good karma. Karma also connects our desires and dreams with the future. The things we desire have an opportunity to manifest in the world. If they do not manifest in our lifetime, there is a likelihood that we will reincarnate to manifest any unmet longings.

When it comes to karma, it is the quality of the root intention rather than the outward appearance of the action that determines its effect in the karmic cycle. This is because larger forces can influence an individual's karma. For example, if you throw a ball on a windy day, the wind will influence the direction, speed, and ultimate distance of that ball. Similarly, you may have intent to help someone, but you may not be able to manifest that intent because of intervening outside events. For example, our society's understanding of the importance of intent is mirrored in our criminal justice system, where often the intent that one holds affects the level of crime and punishment, such as the crimes of first-, second-, and third-degree murder. Each degree is tied to a level of intent.

Everyone is subject to larger forces that can and do influence individual intent, yet everyone has complete control over their own intentions. Thus, holding positive intentions will lead to better karma even if that intent is not met in this lifetime.

Because intent is so important, we always work with the power of intent when we conduct vision quests. Here is a sampling of some intent statements from vision quest participants:

*My intention for the quest is to release my heart to love deeply and accept love gratefully, to renew my creativity and allow it to flow in my work, to renew my playfulness and how I relate to others, and to be more like a tree, pulling energy from the sky and putting out life-giving energy.*

*My intention: To find peace within myself. To overcome my fear of isolation and embrace what comes to me when I am alone. To bring my relationship with others into right alignment—especially my husband and in-laws. To connect with my ancestors and helping spirits.*

*Through this quest, I would like to explore my hidden talents and passions, and tap into my creativity in a career that supports me. Letting go of perceptions and thoughts that stop me from achieving my creative potential, and finding a path that energizes me and provides a sense of flow and fulfillment.*

*My intention is to understand my old patterns so I can let go of what no longer works for me and continue to move forward.*

*What I want the most is complete and total love for and of myself. With that profound love would come many other wonderful qualities, like total self-acceptance and belief in my self-worth. I would not hesitate to express myself and share my gifts with others.*

*I wish to utilize the powers of the natural world to open my spiritual channel to the universe. From the safe place in my heart, where animals and elements exist, I want to bring forth my true voice, truest essence, greatest given strengths, and my purpose on this planet.*

## CHAPTER PRACTICE

### Creating Your Own Intent Statement and Vision Seed Collage

You can start setting intentions for every aspect of your life today. You can set an intention for the next year, the next month, the next day, or even the next hour. Intent statements can be made verbally (out loud or to yourself), written down, or even explored through the use of visual images in a collage. By making a visible record of our intent we are already making it manifest in the world in much the same way that an altar or sacred circle becomes a real place that

*continued on page 132*

131

*continued from page 131*

connects our spirit to the larger universe. By writing something down, or better yet, creating a collage using visual images, we are bringing form to something that was formless, giving substance to our beliefs and dreams.

Here are some simple steps for creating an intent statement and a collage that expresses that intent:

1.  Focus on what you want and make sure you express your intent clearly, in as much detail as possible.

2.  After writing your intent statement, take out a sheet of paper and write (in present tense) as if you already have the result you are seeking.

3.  Spend time gathering images and words that have meaning for you and relate or advance your intent (this may take place in one day or a week). Use photos or images from old greeting cards, magazines, or other sources and cut out the images and words that attract you. I usually get a large manila envelope and write my brief intent statement on it. I then gather images as I find them and place them in the envelope until I am ready to use them.

4.  When you are ready to make your collage, pick up a large poster board or other large collage base, a glue stick, scissors, colorful pens or crayons, and even glitter glue (or any other creative-art material).

5.  Set aside time to create your collage when you can relax and focus just on the collage. Consider putting on some music that you like, as music can activate creativity and let intuitive understandings flow.

6. Now spread out the images and words on the poster board. It is often useful to put an image of yourself in the middle of the collage with the other images around it. Arrange the images and words until you feel they are in the "right" place. You may also want to add your own words or drawings in colored pens or crayons. Once everything is where it belongs, glue it all in place.

7. After your collage is completed, put it in a place where you can see it several times a day. You may also want to frame your collage or shrink it and carry it with you (most copy centers can do this for you). Trust that the universe will help you realize your intent, and then let go of the timing and the exact form of the outcome.

## OVERCOMING FEAR: CONNECTING TO COURAGE

*A fear named is a fear tamed.*

—Denise Linn, "Facing Your Fears: Life, Death, Aging . . ."

The word "courage" originates from the Middle English *corage*, from the Latin word *cor*, which means "heart." I believe that we cannot have courage without being connected to our heart, or core. Strengthened by our core, we gain the mental and ethical strength to follow our beliefs and overcome obstacles in our path. For example, it can be a challenge to break free of work that does not suit us because of the demands of making a living to keep a roof over our head and food on the table. But if we don't go deep within to allow the negative emotions to be fully considered and released, we may never get a handle on them. Fear of facing negative feelings drives people to overwork, take drugs or alcohol, or simply ignore the feelings completely. Yet, when we sit quietly and explore the emotions and bodily sensations that are associated with the discomfort of fear, we are able get to the heart of the fear and dismantle it.

Once we face our fears and evaluate them for what they really are, we can learn from them and learn how to overcome them. Surprisingly, when we do this—when we actually face our fears—they tend to disappear. This is because most of our fears are perceptional illusions without a real basis in the manifest world. One of the benefits of a vision quest is that the experience helps you to defeat these small fears. When we put our fears into perspective, we become stronger with the realization that we are capable of more than we imagined.

Steven explained the fears that he experienced during his vision quest in 2004:

*My greatest challenge was conquering my fear. My fear of the unknown. My fear of experiencing a worst-case scenario. My fear of what I might uncover about myself while sitting alone for three days. There were moments before the quest that I considered backing out, but I knew I would regret that decision the rest of my life, so I pushed through and conquered my fears.*

Prior to their quests, participants are also asked to begin to identify and name their fears. Sharing this information with others and thinking about these fears from an objective perspective is helpful.

But we need not embark on a quest to overcome fear. Sometimes we can begin with small, daily acts, like taking a different route to work, wearing different clothing, or taking the initiative to say something to someone that we have wanted to for a long time but never had the nerve. As we successfully journey into the boundary of our fears, we may find that they are not such a big deal after all and break free of them for good.

Fear is a highly destructive force when it keeps people from growing. Each of us suffers from unnecessary fears to some degree. This may range from simple feelings of not being worthy or being rejected by others, to fears of actual physical harm, abandonment, illness, or even death. The most common reaction to fear is to flee or freeze, but sometimes this is not the best way to handle fear in our life—especially when that fear is in reaction to a perception of the world or self that is not true.

While there are certain fears that are needed because they help to appropriately guide our actions such as avoiding a dark alley or a dangerous person, many of the fears that we hold are not real and are detrimental to our well-being. For example, we may stay at a dead-end job or in an empty relationship for fear of not being able to transition to a better position or a happier relationship. If we can name our fear and come to understand it, we can stop our baseless fears from dominating our life.

## CHAPTER PRACTICE

### Overcoming Fear

This practice presents one way to get an objective look at your fears, thereby allowing you to make choices free from unfounded fears.

Begin by thinking of one thing that you would really like to be doing in your life right now but have been putting off. For example, would you like to travel or start a business, family, or creative project? When you're ready, get two different

continued on page 136

*continued from page 135*

colored pens or pencils and some paper, and proceed with the following steps:

1.  Using your dominant hand (the right hand, for most people), write down at the top of a sheet of paper the one thing you would like to be doing now.

2.  Then write down all of the reasons that you are not acting on your dream. Review your list of reasons and think deeply about how these excuses may be related to underlying fears.

3.  List the underlying fears with that same pen or pencil. Then rate these fears on a scale of 1–6, with 1 being a highly probable outcome that your fears will come true and 6 being a highly unlikely outcome that your fears will come true.

4.  Now, with your nondominant hand, write on another sheet of paper how you will manage to overcome the reasoning and the underlying fears that are holding you back.

5.  Finally, go back and review your initial list. Do you still feel the same way about the fears? Rate each fear again from 1–6 in the same color of pen or pencil that you used with your nondominant hand. Note where you may have a different result from the first time around.

Usually, one or more of the fears listed are removed from the list as being unlikely. This is because we may at first give fears more prominence than they deserve, and when they are examined closer, we see that they are not valid.

This exercise can be done each time you consider a new direction or change. It is an excellent way to decipher the probability or unlikelihood of your fears becoming reality so that you are better equipped to decide what to do in a given situation.

## DREAM

*You may say I'm a dreamer, but I'm not the only one,*
*I hope someday you will join us, and the world will live as one.*

—John Lennon, "Imagine"

The lyrics from the song "Imagine," by John Lennon, referred to his dream for total peace on the planet, yet the lyrics have a dual meaning. When we enter the dream state each night, realms that are usually closed are open to us. In the realm of dreams, we can gain deep insight into others and ourselves. We may even experience incredible events not possible in waking life, or even see the future unfold.

Everyone dreams at night for approximately three hours during a standard eight-hour rest. Our deepest, most meaningful dreams tend to happen during the rapid eye movement, or REM, cycle of sleep. The REM state is ripe for entering larger realms of consciousness and moving beyond the confines of the body. While dreaming, we are more open to the larger flux of the universe and can tap into information and perception otherwise unavailable to us. Solutions to scientific problems, works of creative genius, and simple answers to daily questions may unfold in dreams.

Dr. Otto Loewi, the 1936 Nobel Prize winner in physiology, received a critical piece of information in a dream, leading to his discovery of how to trace the chemical transmission of nerve impulses:

> I awoke, turned on the light, and jotted down a few notes on a tiny slip of paper. Then I fell asleep again. It occurred to me at six o'clock in the morning that during the night I had written down something most important, but I was unable to decipher the scrawl. The next night, at three o'clock, the idea returned. It was the design of an experiment to determine whether or not the hypothesis of chemical transmission . . . was correct.[2]

The popular song "Yesterday," by Paul McCartney, was also inspired by a dream. According to McCartney:

> I woke up with a lovely tune in my head. I thought, "That's great, I wonder what that is?" I liked the melody a lot, but because I'd dreamed it, I couldn't believe I'd written it. I thought, "No, I've never written anything like this before." But I had the tune, which was the most magic[al] thing.[3]

Some cultures highlight the importance of dreams and make their interpretation part of their daily routine. When we pay attention to our dreams, they tend to become particularly potent and filled with meaning. It is even possible to engender greater awareness about our dreams and to control them. Controlling our dreams is referred to as lucid dreaming, which usually works like this: We are fast asleep in the REM state, and there is a dream experience unfolding before us. While we are fully in the dream, all of a sudden we become aware that we are not only in the dream but that we are dreaming the dream itself.

The Senoi, indigenous peoples who dwell in the mountains of Malaysia, teach their children at an early age to recall and relate their dreams, and even to affect the outcome of their dreams. Their culture embraces and uses lucid dreaming on a daily basis, believing that specific dream outcomes are better than others and that dreamers should proactively seek to gain a beneficial outcome in their dream. For example, if you meet a kindly character in your dream, you should seek to obtain a gift from her or him. By obtaining a gift, the power of influence of that helping being can be brought forward into waking life. In the case of a fearful dream encounter with a hostile being, one must turn and face the opponent, not run. The Senoi believe that this simple act of bravery will help the dreamer to overcome challenges and meet rivals in real life.[4] You can similarly benefit from shaping your dreams, and this is best done when you are able to conduct lucid dreaming.

During nature quests, participants may become aware of having unusual or significant dreams. Claire, one of my vision quest participants, dreamed that she was riding on a wild horse, but it got away from her and ran off. The horse is a powerful symbol to Claire, who participated in the quest to help her find her life's purpose.

Horses have been important animal helpers to humankind both physically and spiritually throughout history. When we align ourselves with Horse medicine, we have a powerful ally helping us to move forward. Claire's dream of a wild horse was an auspicious sign, since she was able to ride the wild horse. This indicated that she was able to get in touch with the powerful movement of her inner calling. Since Claire lost the horse and felt that it belonged to someone else, the dream also spoke of the need for Claire to gain greater self-confidence and mastery, so she could stay with the horse and continue to travel through life with her passion. By working toward capturing the wild horse in her dream and staying with it, Claire would be empowered by the spirit of Horse to find her way to her passion.

While many quest participants spend much of their time peacefully and quietly in meditation or deep thought, creative ideas sometimes come with such tremendous force that participants find themselves creating on the spot in their sacred circles. This happened to Shaun, a fall 2005 nature quest participant whose burst of creativity was precipitated by a dream. Shaun had a powerful dream that came as a colorful vision on his first night in his sacred circle. In his dream, he observed what seemed to be an ancient ritualistic ceremony, with figures in elaborate, colorful headpieces dancing to music. As we discussed the possible meaning of the dream and the feelings that the image evoked, Shaun gained greater understanding about the dream. He even remembered a few bars of the beautiful melody and chords of the dream music. Shaun believed that his dream was a celebratory announcement of something wonderful to come into his life.

Shaun worked as a medical technician but had secretly wanted to compose music all his life. Years earlier, after working his day job (or night job, because he sometimes filled night shifts), he would spend time working on musical compositions, but never finished them. Over time, he lacked energy and incentive to apply himself to creating his music, and instead would come home and turn on the television. It had been over three years since he had made an effort to get back to working on the composition. However, after having this dream and hearing the beautiful sounds, it was like a creative cork came out of the bottle. That morning, a powerful surge of inspiration filled Shaun, and he soon got to work on a new composition. He worked steadily for the next three days and nights, from the first light of morning till evening when he could no longer see marks on the paper. Within three days, he had completed his musical composition!

Sometimes dreams allow a person to decipher hidden meaning and potentialities in their lives or the lives of others. Dreams have helped me considerably in my own life, and I often record my dreams in a dream journal. One of my favorite prophetic dreams is the one that foretold my marriage. At the time, I had just broken up with a man that I was in love with but who could not commit to our relationship. After many years of first being friends and then lovers, I was convinced that we were soul mates, but our relationship was not meant to be. I was heartbroken.

After a few weeks of feeling sorry for myself, I intended to revive my enthusiasm for relationships and men in general. One quiet Sunday afternoon, I put on some classical music, turned off the phone, and gathered pictures of all of the men in my life that I have loved in some way. I had a picture of my father, boyfriends, and male friends that I had come to know and care for over the years. I arranged these photos on a large sheet of poster board and then drew around them with beautiful, rainbow-colored pencils. Next to each photograph, I wrote what I loved most about that particular man and summarized his beneficial qualities in a few simple words, like affectionate, intelligent, great sense of humor, understanding, adventurer, fun to be with, and so on. I also conjured up the emotional feelings that the qualities elicited as I focused on each man. It was an incredibly uplifting exercise, and I felt like a weight had been lifted from my shoulders.

I thought that my collage therapy had done its job well in shifting my negative attitude to a positive one, but a week later, I received an incredible bonus gift: a prophetic dream that spoke of a beautiful relationship to come. Through an extraordinary vision, I got a glimpse of the coming relationship with my future husband. In the dream, I found myself floating peacefully in dark space that seemed to stretch for infinity. Everything in the dream was on an enormous scale. Beautiful bands of colorful, luminous rings of light—as large as the rings of Saturn—hung gently suspended in space. Each beautiful color conveyed a specific feeling of the relationship to come. For example, the pink ring felt filled with love, the green color was filled with the integrity and honesty of the relationship, the blue the intellectual match, and the yellow ring the feeling of seeing the world with my partner with a sense of fun and adventure. As I felt and viewed the beautiful rings that simultaneously conveyed feelings with each color, I heard a powerful voice say, "You will soon experience this balanced relationship in your life."

It was one of the most prophetic dreams that I have ever had, as it announced the coming of one of the most important relationships in my life. I was also struck by how the sense of hearing, feeling, and vision all seemed to be interconnected and working in unison. I knew, too, that the collage was directly linked to the dream. (Today I use collage therapy with the people I work with.) Two weeks later, I met my future husband, Paul, in downtown Philadelphia. Within six months, we were living together, and within a year, we were married. We have been happily married for nineteen years.

While dreams can play an important part in our lives, there are times when dreams never arise from the depth of the unconscious. This does not mean that people are not benefiting from their dreams, as everyone dreams every night, but perhaps the timing is not ripe for the message of the dream to rise into conscious awareness. I believe, however, that even when we are not aware of our dreams, they do help us in our waking lives. This is why I train people in dream recall, which helps capture dreams, record them, and then interpret their meaning.

## CHAPTER PRACTICE

### Capture and Record Your Dreams

Your sleeping hours are filled with wondrous adventures and fabulous meetings with amazing beings. This is because when you are asleep you are able to access an astral realm that exists at a higher frequency than the material world we live in when awake.[5] Besides providing insight about our consciousness and possibly the future, dreams also help us to experience whatever we desire in our dreams. It is a very extraordinary and powerful experience.

There are ways to help you capture your dreams so that you can record them and bring them into your conscious life. Sometimes, the meaning of a dream will be apparent right away. Other times, it can take weeks, months, or even years for the meaning of the dream to come to light.

Here are a few steps to capturing and recording your dreams:

+ Before you go to sleep at night, affirm several times your intent to recall and capture your dreams. You can also ask for a dream to assist you in some way.

+ Make sure that you have a journal and a pencil within easy reach of where you sleep. (Easy reach means that you should be able to reach it in the dark without having to move your head or body.) Go to sleep as usual.

+ Anytime you awake from a dream, it is very important NOT to move your body, especially your head. For example, if your head is lying facing up, do not turn it to the side.

+ See if you can recall the dream details that you were having before you awoke. If you can, stay in the same position, and repeat the happenings and detailed

continued on page 144

*continued from page 143*

events in your mind several times. What took place, who was there, where were you? What things or places were around you?

+ Then reach for your journal and pencil, and begin to write down the dream. If it is dark in the room, do not turn on the light; just write as best as you can by using your fingers to guide you on where to write.

+ After you are done writing down your dream, you may go back to sleep if it is in the middle of the night or get up for the day if it is morning.

+ When you are fully awake, go back and re-record what you wrote so that you can read it better. Fill in any details from the dream that you may have missed, even if these details seem nonsensical to you. While you may not understand your dream as you record it, there is a high likelihood that you will go back to that dream at a later date and understand it perfectly.

# 11

## HEALING OURSELVES
## THROUGH NATURE

Nature can and does provide a sense of harmony and peace.

DORA VAN GELDER KUNZ, *The Personal Aura*

Recall the exhilaration you experience when hearing the powerful surf and watching the rhythmic flow of the sea. Recall the joy you feel when the first colorful flowers appear in your garden after a long winter. Simple pleasures? Perhaps. Short-lived? No. Nature is a force for the good in our lives, and these simple pleasures can be expanded to transform your life.

Nature is restorative and offers a healing balm for the soul. Walking in nature, playing in nature, and simply viewing nature are beneficial to human health and well-being. For example, even brief exposure to natural scenes reduces stress, and views of natural scenes, through a window or otherwise, can help people heal more quickly. Consequently, a cure-all for emotional and physical ills may be no farther than our own backyard.

In a study covered in the March 2001 issue of the *American Journal of Preventive Medicine*, Mother Nature is depicted as the cure-all for many ills. According to Howard Frumkin, MD, author of the article, and chairman of environmental and occupational health at Emory University:

> Although this is not hard-core medical advice, I think we can advise people to enjoy nature. There are a lot of indications that contact with nature, either walking in the wilderness, gardening, or having a pet, makes people feel better and can minimize the effects of disease. It stands to reason that cancer patients may benefit a lot from some of those kinds of contact.[1]

Two-time Pulitzer Prize–winner and Harvard University professor Dr. Edward O. Wilson, who wrote the commentary for Frumkin's study, believes that environmentalism is a necessity, not a luxury. Wilson's belief in the health connection between people and nature echoes the findings of the great Greek physician Hippocrates.

Hippocrates viewed health as a state of equilibrium between the organism and its environment. As outlined in the Hippocratic treatise, *On Airs, Waters, and Places*, disease results from an imbalance in the natural state of the body within the environmental complex of physical and social factors that affect the life of the person as a whole. According to Hippocrates:

> Whoever wishes to investigate medicine properly should proceed thus: in the first place so consider the seasons of the year and what the effects each of them produces, for they are not all alike ... We must also consider the qualities of the waters. And when one comes into a city as a stranger, he ought to consider its situation, how it lies to the winds and the rising of the sun ... These things one ought to consider and [do so] attentively.[2]

This is a totally contrary view to a traditional Western medical approach, where disease is traced to a single external agent and can be "cured" with a single, artificially created drug. Yet all living organisms—plants, animals, people, and their habitats—share properties of health. Health crosses the artificial boundaries between the human and nonhuman, the physical and invisible. This new paradigm of health is drawing people today closer to the natural world and holistic thinking.

Nature has been thought of as a cure-all even in the Westernized societies that tend to be addicted to prescription drugs. In the 1880s, thousands of wealthy hay fever sufferers fled the cities in August to clean-air resorts in the wilderness of the White Mountains in New Hampshire and the Adirondacks in upper New York state. Some of the more famous health seekers included Daniel Webster and literary figures such as Helen Hunt Jackson and Grace Greenwood. Perhaps the most famous person to claim the rejuvenating effects of nature is President Theodore Roosevelt. Roosevelt was sickly and vulnerable as a child, but as an adult he found health at his remote Elkhorn Ranch, where he spent his days on horseback and his nights in a simple log cabin under the wide-open sky.

Nature can be rejuvenating and healing. There are places in nature that enhance energy flow in and around the human body. For example, rivers and oceans, mountains, and even pine forests are particularly restorative and healthful for people. Just being in these places brings greater mental clarity and physical vigor.

## THE BENEFICIAL EFFECTS OF NEGATIVE IONS

One of the reasons for this phenomenon is that in certain dynamic places on Earth—like waterfalls and oceans—negative ions are abundantly present. Negative ions are electrically charged atoms generated in specific places like waterfalls when falling water breaks up into small droplets. In the process, electrons (negatively charged parts of an atom) are knocked loose from the water molecules and then combine with oxygen atoms in the air to create negative air ions. Most outdoor places on Earth contain 1,200 to 4,000 negative ions per cubic centimeter (about the size of a sugar cube). However, at Yosemite Falls, there are over 100,000 negative ions per cubic centimeter in the area near where the water interacts with the land.[3]

> Negative ions promote alpha brain waves and increase brain wave amplitude, which translates to a higher awareness level. Those ion-induced alpha waves spread from the occupational areas to the parietal and temporal, and even reach the frontal lobes, spreading evenly across the right and left brain hemispheres. All of this creates an overall clear and calming effect, benefiting meditation and concentration.[4]

Once released into the atmosphere, negative air ions are easily inhaled into the lungs and absorbed into the bloodstream. There, negative ions can have significant positive effects on health. Negative ions have been found to alleviate depression and stress, and to boost energy.[5] They also produce biochemical reactions that increase levels of serotonin, creating feelings of elation and high spirits. This is likely one of the "unconscious" reasons why so many people like to experience their honeymoon by Niagara Falls (over 50,000 honeymooners visit annually).[6] Niagara Falls, where 5.5 billion gallons of water spill over the edge of the largest fall every hour, is a veritable behemoth when it comes to making negative ions. Pine forests also contain high levels of negative ions, as do forests of other native and healthy trees. Overall, water and plants create over 50 percent of the negative ions produced naturally on Earth.[7] This is one reason why trees and clean water are so critical to our well-being and help us to feel so good!

One of the leading scientists who studied the effects of negative ions, Dr. Igho Kornbleuh, from the University of Pennsylvania's Graduate Hospital, administered negative-ion treatments to hundreds of patients suffering from hay fever and bronchial asthma.

Two-thirds of the patients experienced partial or total relief from their symptoms. According to one of the doctors applying the negative-ion treatment:

> [Patients] come in sneezing, eyes watering, noses itching, worn out from lack of sleep, so miserable they can hardly walk. Fifteen minutes in front of the negative-ion machine and they feel so much better they don't want to leave.[8]

In 1959 Dr. Kornbleuh took the healing effects of negative ions even further when he treated a group of 138 burn victims at Northeastern General Hospital. Burns tend to inflict the most agonizing pain, and yet over 50 percent of the patients that were treated with negative ions suffered significantly less pain and discomfort, while healing more quickly and thoroughly. The astounding results of this study convinced the hospital staff to subsequently equip its postoperative wards with negative-ion generators.[9]

Negative ions help our bodies heal by accelerating the delivery of oxygen to our cells. Some researchers believe that negative air ions may also positively stimulate cells that regulate our bodies' resistance to disease. Yet, not all ions are good. In polluted areas and indoor areas that do not have optimum ventilation, negative ions may drop to as low as 100 per cubic centimeter, leaving positive ions in much greater amounts. When the air is filled with a larger number of positive ions, people tend to be negatively affected emotionally and physically. An overabundance of positive ions has also been shown to cause depression, tiredness, and irritability. Jan Stolwijk, of the World Health Organization, stated that "There is probably more damage done to human health by indoor air pollution than by outdoor pollution." Most people spend 70 to 80 percent of their time indoors![10]

Hospital admissions, suicides, and crime caused by emotional unrest tend to increase when winds that contain a high percentage of positive ions blow into an area. People also complain about ailments like irritability, tension, migraines, nausea, and even difficulty breathing from bad air—air that is filled with positive ions. The effects of an excessive amount of positive ions can so greatly influence human behavior that people may do things that they might not ordinarily do.

While negative ions have been thoroughly documented as having beneficial impacts on human health and well-being, there are other ways that we benefit from nature.

## NATURE AS A HEALING CATALYST

Nature is a catalyst for transformative shifts in energy, light, emotion, health, and spirit. Everything and everyone participates in the universal field of energy and light that contains a feeling-based awareness. The energies of the whole field affect us, as do the singular energies of others. The unifying field around us contains far more than negative or positive ions; it contains the very fuel for life and vitality, and an emotion-based awareness. This intelligent-compassionate field exists outside of us as well as within every living organism on Earth. When we are in harmony with it, we are able to tap into the ever-abundant stores of health, energy, and light that exist there. Powerful interactions of this feeling-knowing-healing energy are taking place all the time between people, between species, and between people and the Earth. Our bodies also serve as channels, moving energy from within to outside our bodies while receiving energy from the great field that surrounds us.

Like layers on an onion, we encompass many layers of being, with each layer connected to the other and ultimately to the universe. Our physical, mental, and emotional well-being is a layer where our spiritual self connects. Energetically, the simplest way to picture the human body is as a being with three layers or levels: the physical layer of the body, the astral layer which surrounds the body, and the causal layer outside the astral body that connects directly to the larger energy field around us.

Taoists identified eight separate layers of the body:

1. Physical Body

2. Chi Body: Exists within your physical body as well as outside of your body, this is the body where acupuncture has an effect. (I believe that this level of the body contains both physical and energetic qualities.)

3. Emotional Body: Exists within but also outside your physical body. (I believe that this relates to the astral body.)

4. Mental Body: This layer of the body is a step between the astral and causal levels.

5. Psychic Energy Body: This layer is the next step between the astral and causal levels.

6. Causal Body

7. Body of Individuality: Contains the "seed intent" formed at our creation. (I believe one of the most beautiful gifts from the Creator is individuality.)

8. Body of the Tao (I believe that this is the same as the Creator or the Field.)[11]

When all of these layers work together in harmony, we have health and strength, and a solid foundation upon which to achieve self-actualization and spiritual growth. Thus, as the layers of the body reveal, spiritual harmony is not separate from our physical well-being and vice versa.

In a state of imbalance, people isolate themselves from the surrounding field of energy and healing (the body of the Tao or a state of divinity). This happens because people's energy binds up inside them and not because they purposefully choose to do so. When we are ill or out of balance, the energy flow from the field can be slowed or blocked, leading to swirls of energetic debris that get stuck. Thus, the commonly used term of "being stuck" is quite accurate. Whirlpools of clogged energy cause continual emotional and psychic blocks that can eventually lead to physical pain and illness.

One of the effects of being out of sync with the rest of the universe is getting trapped in specific thoughts and emotional patterns that do not serve us. If you have ever gone over and over something in your mind with feelings of anxiety or worry, you may have experienced this energetic blockage. This problem is accentuated in Western societies when we emphasize "fixing" emotional pain and confusion through reason alone. This explains the past popularity of Freudian therapy or talk therapy, but these methods fall short of solving the underlying problem. Analytical investigation and discussion are not capable of addressing the holistic needs of our being.

When we are healthy, our bodies have a vibrant liveliness, harmony, and flow. When we are unhealthy, the energy flow becomes tight and blocked, throwing us out of balance. Nature-based practices balance the energetic body by encouraging the flow of healthful energy and the dissolution of blocked energy. For instance, there are places on the Earth—points of power—where we can receive a large amount of beneficial, cleansing energy. We can also receive healing energy from inanimate natural objects and forces, such as stones, pools of water, trees, and naturally occurring phenomena including wind and rain. Stonehenge, for example, is a place of powerful healing because of its congregation of healing stones that radiate powerful healing energy.

This may be a permanent solution or a temporary one, depending on how ingrained the negative energy pattern is and how ready an individual is to change. Fortunately, human health, well-being, and spiritual growth can also be addressed through the modality of light.

## THE BODY OF LIGHT

Biophotons are photons of light emitted from the cells of living beings. They are weak electromagnetic waves in the light spectrum. All living cells of plants, animals, and human beings emit biophotons that cannot be seen by the naked eye but can be measured by special equipment. Human cells emit biophotons at the quantum level at varying rates. Healthy cells tend to have lower emissions of biophotons, emitting light in highly coherent patterns. In addition, healthy people tend to have a rhythmic emission rate that changes seasonally, with biological peaks occurring at 7, 14, 32, 80, and 270 days. A healthy body emits biophotons in congruence with the orbit of the Earth, and with the rhythm of night and day. Thus, the human body has an ongoing, internal "light clock" that keeps time with the spheres.[12]

When we are in ill health or on our way to becoming ill, our cells begin to emit too much light, almost like a candle that is burning too quickly, which brings new meaning to the expression "feeling burnt out." Healthy people, on the other hand, tend to burn or emit biophotons at a level that is closer to the harmonious and constantly renewing level of the larger field.[13] Thus, the electromagnetic frequency at which cells vibrate reflects varying frequencies depending upon the health of the individual. This slow-burn state, or delicate emissions state, of being allows a person to be in greater coherence with the healing energy and light of the field.

Nature, animals, and trees are potent conductors of biophotons since all living things emit and exchange biophotons. Connecting with living beings and places in nature is healing, harmonizing, and rejuvenating, bringing us to a state of equilibrium and even joy, no matter how out of balance we are. When we place ourselves in nature, there always exists the opportunity for inspiration and joy. Once there, we can receive the beneficial energy found in the land, the elements, the animals, the plants, and the living Earth, away from the distractions of daily routines.

## Richard's Story

Richard, a Londoner, had been terribly depressed for many years and had been on antidepressants for two years. By all outward appearances, Richard was highly successful, with a six-figure salary and a wife and family, but he was filled with despair. No calamity had shaken his world to make him so; it was just the numbing effect of years of ignoring his inner calling.

Richard's initiative in going on a nature quest was to take a bold step toward finding a fulfilling life for himself. Richard had reached a point where he was ready to break out of old patterns that were holding him back. He was a perfect candidate for a nature quest, which would give him the space to gain clarity on what was most important to him.

Richard arrived at the nature quest location in northern California on a clear and cool April day. After our gathering circle and sharing stories about why people were embarking on the quest and what they were hoping to experience, we went for a walk through a stately oak and spruce forest. That evening, after experiencing a shamanic journey, we settled in for the night in our sleeping bags under the starry sky.

The next day, after our breakfast and sacred circle practices, quest participants went off on their own to find their individual quest locations, where they would be spending the next three days and nights on their own.

That morning, Richard seemed anxious, and he frequently glanced at his watch, obviously finding it a challenge to shift into a slower pace of "quest time." I asked him to try to go without his watch for the duration of the quest so he could get more in touch with the natural rhythm of the passage of time around him. He agreed, and that night, alone in his sacred circle, Richard had a powerful dream.

Richard dreamed he was a young boy sitting at a tall table. He felt anticipatory, as if he was about to begin something, but then he recalled he needed colored pencils. He looked for the pencils in different desk drawers but could not find any. Richard said that a large portion of his dream was about him looking for the pencils and feeling frustrated or lost when he could not find them. Finally, he remembered that he had a basement, and he went down to look. There, he found a box filled with crayons and strange feathers that also made colorful marks in every color of the rainbow. The colors were so beautiful they filled his heart with joy; he said it seemed like he could inhale the colors. He awoke from his dream in the silent peaceful night, next to a blue oak tree, and looked out between the branches at the sparkling stars, laughing out loud.

For the duration of the quest, Richard sat peacefully in his sacred circle, listening to the leaves rustling in the wind and watching the sky change from the orange blaze of sunrise to the deep dark night. He welcomed the occasional appearance of animals, including three turkeys, a small flock of western bluebirds, and a horned owl. Over the next three days, his love of drawing came back like a flood from a far-off and forgotten territory.

Once back in London, Richard added a small studio to the back of his family's large home and stocked it with the tools of an artist: paper, canvas, paints, and colored pencils of every hue. When I followed up with him six months later, he had just completed the studio and was spending time just being creative a few hours every weekend, as well as an hour or two a couple of evenings a week. He told me that he hadn't had a single bout of depression since his nature quest and since committing to his artistic passions. The quest experience helped Richard reconnect to what gives him life—to what some would say is his very soul.

## CHAPTER PRACTICE

### Conduct a Vision Quest or Nature Retreat

It may be time for you to conduct a vision quest or nature pilgrimage to help you align with your inner vision, or to simply reconnect with nature. You can conduct a quest with a group or by yourself. If you are going to do a solo quest, I highly recommend Denise Linn's book *Quest* as your guidebook. I also lead quests and nature-based outings throughout the year for individuals and groups worldwide (see page 288 in the resources section).

# 12

## HONORING THE CREATIVE
## WITHIN AND WITHOUT

Anyone, then, who knows the good he ought to do and doesn't do it, sins.

JAMES 4:17, KING JAMES BIBLE

Everything is born with the seed of its full potential. Just as a tiny acorn has the potential to grow into a great oak tree, human beings have the potential to become their greatest selves. They do so by fully expressing the core of who they are. Creativity is the graceful force that coaxes all things into being and then remains at the ready to help them grow toward their greatest potential.

When we express our unique nature through work, we grow creatively. We then manifest the original, creative seed of our true being that is planted within us. When we thwart this growth by pursuing harmful occupations or failing to express our innate nature, the seed of our potential shrivels. We commit the terrible "sin of omission," as evidenced by this startling statement attributed to Jesus, from the Gnostic Gospel of Thomas:

If you bring forth what is within you,
what you bring forth will save you.

If you do not bring forth what is within you,
what you do not bring forth will destroy you.[1]

Similarly, Buddha's Noble Eightfold Path, which is considered the way to end suffering, includes "right livelihood." Right livelihood means earning one's living in a righteous way. Two things should guide us in our occupation: what we need (not desire), and what expresses our inner goodness and innate talents. Buddha also said that one should never take on an occupation solely for money or wealth.[2]

Living authentically—by expressing the truth of who we are through our actions—is perhaps the single most important thing that we can do. This means that our work, our relationships, and our choices should reflect the inner spark that we came into the world with. We need to listen to the yearnings of our soul.

Denise Linn, an internationally recognized healer, author, and speaker of Cherokee descent, defines the soul as "the central or integral part of something, or its vital core . . . It is that place within each of us that is infinite, eternal, and universal."[3] Our own souls are divinely inspired, and if followed, can lead us to a life that feels authentic, balanced, and beautiful. But if we journey far from the core of who we are, our lives become painful and incomplete. Pieces of our souls can be lost bit by tiny bit through simple, everyday actions. Compromising our values by doing a job we hate, getting into debt, putting up with things and people in our lives we would be better without, and, perhaps worst of all, failing to do what matters to us most can lead to soul loss. These small, daily actions off course may not seem significant in themselves, but, like a boat at sea that turns just a few degrees off course till it is lost, they are.

One of my quest participants, Glenn, a physician, put it this way:

*My parents emphasized that the object of life was to be important—to attend the most prestigious schools, to have a prestigious occupation (such as doctor or lawyer), to be highly regarded by one's peers, to earn a substantial six figure income, and so on. To win their love and approval, I absorbed this whole line of thinking, but it made me feel sad, lonely, and imprisoned.*

Into his mid-forties, Glenn followed his parents' concepts about living a good life and being a good son. He became a doctor, made a six-figure salary, and lived in a large home with his beautiful wife and four children. Yet over the years, Glenn's moderate drinking escalated to where he was experiencing heavy bouts of drinking that left him debilitated and ashamed. By the time Glenn embarked on his nature quest, he had already given up drinking, and was ready emotionally and spiritually to make room in his life to find his life's passion.

At first, Glenn questioned whether he could make a successful career change at his "late" age, but the next time we spoke, he shared a George Eliot quote he had found: "You're never too old to be what you might have been." There is great biological support for this statement. Stress places pressure on the cells and the body, leading to illnesses, premature death, and aging. Stress weakens our immune systems and our body's ability to ward off illness. Stress has been specifically linked to being the underlying cause for cardiovascular disease; cancer; gastrointestinal issues; and skin, neurological, and emotional disorders; as well as a host of disorders linked to immune system disturbances, ranging from the common cold and herpes, to arthritis and even AIDS.

In addition to the physical ailments associated with stress, there are many emotional, psychological, and spiritual problems. For example, by the year 2020, depression is projected to be the world's second-most disabling disease, after heart disease. While the use of antidepressant medication has skyrocketed (Americans spend $800 million a year on antidepressants alone), depression rates continue to rise. This is because depression is an offshoot of a deeper, unmet longing that cannot be cured by drugs.

Our modern lifestyle comes at a steep cost. Disconnection from nature leads to physical, emotional, and spiritual disorders. It also causes us to become perpetrators of acts that lead to the destruction and diminishment of other life, and ultimately the destruction and diminishment of ourselves. Yet, if we lead an authentic life filled with moments of joy and fulfillment, we will not only be healthier but that we will ultimately live longer. Thus, following one's passion may be the real fountain of youth.

Glenn's story is like the story of many people who come to me for quests and coaching. It can be easy to lose track of what matters to us, especially when well-meaning loved ones and family members encourage us to pursue an alternative route. They are, in turn, reflecting larger cultural and societal values and systems that influence them. For many generations, Western society has highlighted the importance of material wealth and external accomplishment over spiritual growth and emotional well-being, losing track of what really makes people happy: freedom, fulfilling relationships, and creativity.

This does not mean that all material wealth is bad—far from it. If Mahatma Gandhi did not have his financial supporters and donors, he would not have been as effective in his campaigns to liberate India and the Indian people. He used his wealth and resources to care for his family and to help him create a cultural shift in his country that he was passionate about. Once we focus on essential needs like freedom and being in harmonious relationships with other living things, the resources we need become available.

While our souls may be eternal, our individual lives are fleeting. That is why it is so important to start living one's passion today, not tomorrow. The freedom people seek comes from expressing one's authentic self. We likely experienced greater freedom when we were younger because, as children, we believed that it was okay to fill our waking hours with joyful activities that we felt drawn to. Yet, as adults, we are usually persuaded to put away those interests to pursue presumably more suitable, "realistic" pursuits. In reality, we are meant to become self-actualized so that we, in turn, can help others through direct acts of kindness, compassion, and generosity. We become the best role models by simply living our dreams.

It is easy to take our abilities and interests for granted because they come so easily to us. Yet the very things that drew our attention when we were children are linked to the things that we love and could be doing happily as adults. Imagine what the world would be like if everyone pursued their innate interests and developed careers that expressed those interests.

Each of us knows of at least one person who is the embodiment of living one's passion. Their eyes sparkle, and they are infused with energy and enthusiasm. Living life with passion means living life to its fullest every day. Living with passion provides an extra edge to persevere with what matters most, even in the face of challenging situations. Living with passion means not letting obstacles stand between you and your dreams. To live passionately is to trust in your choices. From trust in self comes profound authenticity and freedom. When we negate ourselves by not expressing our innate being, we destroy ourselves emotionally, physically, and spiritually. We are also more likely to destroy the rest of creation around us. Thus, the pollution and environmental degradation that we have caused on Earth reflects a sickness in our very own souls. When we instead honor ourselves and nurture the seed of potentiality there, we honor all life. When we express our work through our soul consciousness, we find that we conduct ourselves upon the Earth in a life-affirming way. And when we serve that soulful part of ourselves through work, we become willing and able to serve others.

I see the growth of job- and stress-related illness around the globe as a symptom of one of the greatest creative and spiritual crises that humankind has ever faced; I see our failure to manifest our creative potential as being directly linked to our failure to honor the rest of creation. How we express ourselves through our actions, especially through our work, is central to our evolution and the evolution of other living things.

## DISCOVERING WISDOM AND PEACE IN NATURE

As I sit here writing this chapter, I am listening to the repetitive but welcome sound of the first rain of the season. The rain releases the fragrant smell of the Earth into the sky. In the late morning, the mists sit low on the hillsides like mysterious silver veils over the redwoods, eucalyptus, and live oak trees, hinting at the beauty that silently resides below. Flocks of midnight black crows and ravens call to one another from their tall perches. Their *caw, caw* chorus echoes across the valley. Just twenty miles from the Pacific Ocean, Mount Tamalpais gently rises out of coastal redwood forests, while two vultures float masterfully within feet of our living room window. They fly effortlessly toward the northeast, with broad outstretched wings gently lifted by the rising warm currents of air. Their flying displays grace and ease, which beckons a mood of peace and quiet reflection.

It is moments like these that nature speaks to me the most—when the edges between consciousness and the outer world melt away and I am filled with the sky, the tall grasses, and the wind. Our very identity is shaped by our relationship with nature. When we take the time to learn about the natural world around us, we also learn about ourselves. While it is favorable to grow up in a culture that honors nature, the Earth speaks to all who care to listen. This explains how far-flung human societies—separated by deep oceans, tall mountain ranges, and thousands of miles—share similar, nature-based spiritual beliefs and stories of creation. These stories existed long before the internet, telephones, planes, or automobiles connected us across vast distances. We learned directly from the Earth Herself how to live and how to be human. Though we've lost contact with Her, She is always there to guide us back home once again.

Today, the image of Earth viewed from space—as a beautiful blue and green orb beneath swirls of white clouds—has been seen around the world. This singular image has had a breathtaking impact on our understanding of our home planet, at once beautiful beyond measure in the vastness of space. Simply viewing the "vision" of Earth was so profound that astronauts experienced a spontaneous spiritual awakening. Frank Borman, commander of the first space crew to travel beyond Earth's orbit, radioed back a message after peering at the planet from thousands of miles away, quoting Genesis 1:1: "In the beginning, God created the heavens and the Earth." Astronaut Ed Mitchell also experienced a similar spiritual awakening as the space shuttle soared far above Earth:

> It was then, while staring out of the window, that Ed experienced the strangest feeling he could ever have: a feeling of connectedness, as if all the planets and all the people of all time were attached by some invisible web.[4]

What Frank and Ed experienced—as did many other astronauts—is what ancient peoples experienced without having to leave the planet: nature and Earth Herself are reflections of an intelligent divine being. Nature is a portal to spiritual communion with the divine source, the Great Mother, and this portal is open to everyone regardless of religious training or inclination.[5]

## NATURE: DOOR TO THE DIVINE

Animals and plants not only teach us about the world we live in, they serve as our guides and allies in one of the greatest journeys of all—the spiritual journey. Ancient mystical and spiritual leaders like Yogis, shamans, and Druids understood that, by accessing the energetic and spiritual life force within other living things, they could gain entry to a realm far beyond their ordinary ken. They were then able to mediate between the Creator and human society in order to heal illness and disease, and to access an all-knowing, all-compassionate field. Shamans, Yogis, and mystics are made and defined by their ability to communicate with the Creator on an ongoing basis.

The defining difference then between a priest of a traditional religious institution and a mystic or shaman is in what constitutes their experience (and thus their authority) with the divine. As first noted by Joseph Campbell, "the priest is the socially initiated, ceremonially inducted member of a recognized religious organization, where he holds a certain rank and functions as the tenant of an office that was held by others before him, while the shaman is one who has gained a certain power of his own."[6]

Priests and nuns may become ordained by pursuing a course of study and by following specific rules of conduct, but they may never experience divinity directly. This does not mean that they may not contribute significantly to bettering humanity. There are many priests and nuns who have followed an ordained institutional path and have had direct sacred experiences. Therese Neumann is an excellent example of this. She was a devout Christian who became an enlightened saint. On a weekly basis she would experience the "passion" of Christ and bleed from—stigmata—the same locations as those of Jesus' wounds. By receiving energy directly from the ether, she was able to live without food. She showed the world that it is indeed possible to live by the "word of God" alone.[7]

Those who sought and reached communion with the Creator through mystical or shamanistic means predate *all* institutionalized religions and have historical roots dating back to the Neolithic period. They often relied upon nature and helpful spirits (or guardians) in the form of animals, plants, or animal-like beings found in their physical and spiritual realm.

Great spiritual leaders like Buddha, Moses, and Jesus all experienced divinity in nature: Buddha gained enlightenment under a fig tree (the tree became known as the Bo tree, short for *Bodhi* or enlightenment, and the place was later named the "Immovable Spot"), Jesus spent forty days and forty nights in the wilderness, and Moses had direct communication with God through a burning bush.

Today, we are relearning that the individual soul is but a reflection of the harmony and divinity around us in nature. The profound symmetry of the universe is present in the very structure of our being. We enter a hallowed space when we engage with the sacred in many forms of life and/or enter places of power on the Earth.

## THE SACRED CIRCLE: HONORING THE FOUR DIRECTIONS

*The Circle has healing power ... The Sacred Circle is designed to create unity. The Hoop of Life is also a circle. On this hoop, there is a place for every species, every race, every tree, and every plant. It is this completeness of Life that must be respected in order to bring about health on this planet.*

—Dave Chief, Oglala Lakota[8]

For thousands of years, people have looked at the stars and followed the rising of the sun and moon in order to determine their position in the universe. To the ancients, knowing one's place in the universe and where one stood with respect to the four directions provided clues to finding the entryway to the center of the world— the doorway to the realm of spirit. They identified places on Earth suited for accessing sacred realms (like caves) and sought to enhance these places by balancing the power of the four primary elements/directions. For example, Stonehenge and other ancient megalithic structures were built to identify and mark the celestial movements and directions.

The ancients recognized four primary directions—east, south, west, and north—as having specific energetic/spiritual qualities; together, these four directions made up the great unity. Greek philospher Empedocles also believed that earth, air, fire, and water were the roots of all things. In his *Tetrasomia*, or *Doctrine of the Four Elements*, he described these elements not only as physical manifestations but also as spiritual essences. Plato also recognized four primary elements as being the foundation of the universe or the larger whole, which he called "ether."[9] He believed that these four elements are inviolable (can never be changed), and this is why he considered them to be primary.

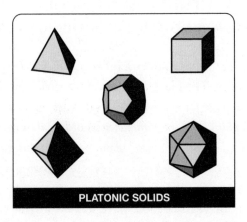

**PLATONIC SOLIDS**

The four elements, along with the "ether" which is a combination of all four, came to be depicted by Plato as physical shapes called Platonic solids. These solids are strikingly similar to Buddhist gravestone images. For example, Buddhist gravestone images also use a cube for earth, a sphere for water, and a pyramid for fire.

As Plato depicted in his understanding of the cosmos, the four elements (or four directions) reflect the four primary aspects of the cosmos, or the great unity. These qualities can manifest as physical forms or be interpreted with energetic and spiritual characteristics. The four have been described as energy qualities, primary elements or directions, shapes, colors, animals, and even seasons, based on the interpretations of people from different cultures, and there are abundant cases of similar interpretations. For example, Black Elk, a Sioux shaman, used the same colors to describe the four directions as those used by the Chinese and the Greeks.

Famous Swiss psychiatrist Carl Jung researched personality characteristics over many years after seeing thousands of patients. During this time, Jung identified and named the trends or types of personality characteristics that existed within all people. Jung determined that there are four main aspects or characteristics of a person's personality, and that these four aspects reflect sixteen major personality types.[10] He also believed that each of these four characteristics had a significant range of manifestation within each person. While each individual had the potential to reach the full range of all four qualities, they had tendencies to utilize just one range of the four. Empedocles also believed that individuals tended to have one or more elements predominate in their personalities. He determined that those individuals who have equal or near equal proportions of the four elements are the most balanced and have the highest clarity of perception.[11]

Thus, it should be no surprise that we can learn to work with the four primary elements to bring greater balance into our lives. Denise Linn uses the four primary elements in her healing and spiritual work, believing that activating and purifying each of these elements can lead to great inner clarity and healing of the body and mind. I have adopted many of her interpretations of the "medicine" of the four directions, as well as her interpretation of their use in the sacred circle, or "medicine wheel," that I use on vision quests.[12]

The sacred circle practice is one of the simplest and most concrete ways to work with the four directions and their four primary elements. When we work within a sacred circle, we not only acknowledge and honor each of these important forces, we invite them to help us become more balanced and empowered. This is because sacred circles honor and maintain the regenerative energies specific to an actual cosmic position in time, space, and significance. Each "wheel" lies upon the Earth in the place in which it was created as well as upon the outer cosmos reaching into infinity. From this sacred circle upon the Earth, we tap into the forces of the four primary elements at the same time that we tap into the vast invisible realm beyond our everyday knowledge.

## CHAPTER PRACTICE

### Creating a Sacred Circle

You can create a sacred circle in your own backyard or in a place in nature that you like to frequent. You can even create a sacred circle indoors. Here are the steps to follow:

1. First, a sacred circle should be on a flat surface, protected from high wind and sun, and away from hazards and natural distractions, like broken limbs overhead, fire ants, damp ground, or an animal or human path. It is always best to make sure that the area you choose for your circle is large enough to lie down in. Once you locate a place that appears ideal, you may decide to stand, sit, or lay still in the center to quietly get in touch with the energy of the place. If the location also "feels" good to you (see the tree surfing exercise on page 46 for clues to when you may be receiving positive versus negative energies), claim it for your sacred circle. Then use a compass to discern where the four directions lie on your

circle. Mark each direction, starting with east and moving clockwise around the circle to mark south, west, and finally north.

2.  Before finding your sacred circle location or soon afterward, gather five objects, four of which you will place on the perimeter of the circle to represent the four directions, and one for the center, or the ether. If you are outdoors, it is best to select objects like stones, shells, feathers, leaves, and fallen branches located in the vicinity of your sacred circle. Sometimes quest participants bring objects with them from home for this purpose. For example, Diane, a psychiatrist, brought a small, beautifully carved stone statue of a bear. She felt closely aligned with the energy of the bear and wished to have Bear energy to support her during her quest. She chose to place her bear in the south of her sacred circle to give her strength and protection. The objects that you use are less important than the feelings and associations that are envoked by them.

3.  Before you begin to lay your objects down on the sacred circle, you may want to first declare your intention for the sacred circle. For example, you can offer a prayer such as this:

    *Fill this place with peace, love, wisdom, and power.*
    *Make it a safe and sacred place where I honor*
    *myself and the world around me, giving thanks to*
    *the four directions: east, south, west, and north.*
    *May I find balance, peace and insight within this*
    *sacred circle.*

*continued on page 170*

*continued from page 169*

Make sure that the words you use have meaning for you. Then convey your intention out loud and powerfully three times, then in a whisper three times, and then to yourself three times.

4.  Next, place your chosen objects on the circle's perimeter according to the direction that suites them each best. For example, you might put a feather in the eastern part of the circle to represent air, a bowl of water in the southern part of the circle to represent water, a candle in the west for fire, and a crystal in the north for Earth. You always begin in the east and then move clockwise, as this lays out positive energy in the spiral movement direction.

5.  When you are done laying out the objects and/or perimeter of your sacred circle (note that some people choose to place objects completely around the circumference of their sacred circle to make a physical perimeter), place the center object.[13] The center of the circle represents the place of all things—the zero-point field, the Tao, or simply the sacred place of divinity within each of us.

6.  Once your circle is completed, enter the circle from the east (which is the same way that you leave the circle). You may want to conduct a ceremony to sanctify the circle and yourself.[14] Dried sage and tobacco are two excellent plants to use for this purpose, as the smoke from each is known for its cleansing properties.

Another way to call upon the four elements is to recite powerful sayings and prayers to conjure up the powerful support of the elements. For example, Saint Patrick successfully invoked a sacred prayer referred to as his "breastplate" to protect him.[15] Inspired by Saint Patrick, I have created the prayer below, which you can use.

---

## CHAPTER PRACTICE

### Calling Upon the Four Elements

This prayer is best recited at sunrise or as soon as you get up. Stand with your spine straight and face east. Breathe deeply and fully until your heart rate is slow and steady, and you are relaxed. Then say the following words from deep within your chest, with feeling and conviction:

*I rise today*
*In power's strength invoking the unity that*
*Underlies all things*
*Believing in goodness*
*Thankful for Nature*
*Praising the World*
*Of Creator's Creation*

*I rise today*
*In the power of love*
*In the power of freedom*
*In the power of wisdom*

*continued on page 172*

---

*continued from page 171*

*I rise today*
*In heaven's might*
*In sun's radiance*
*In moon's luminance*
*In fire's purity*
*In lightning's brightness*
*In wind's swiftness*
*In sea's depth*
*In Earth's stability*
*In rock's solidity*
*In river's flow*
*In sky's clarity*
*In rainbow's promise*

*I rise today*
*In power's strength invoking the unity that*
*Underlies all things*
*Believing in goodness*
*Thankful for Nature*
*Praising the World of*
*Creator's Creation*

# PART 4

## Changing Ourselves, Changing the World

# 13

# Earth Song

Earth voices are glad voices, and the Earth-songs come up from
the ground through the plants; and in their flowering, and in the days
before these days are come, they do tell Earth songs to the wind.
And the wind in her goings does whisper them to folks to print
for other folks, so other folks have the knowing of Earth's songs.

Opal Whiteley (six years old),
*The Singing Creek Where the Willows Grow*

Everything on Earth is held within a nurturing and harmonious
resonance that provides the optimum environment for life. This
harmonious resonance can be expressed as a song—a song that wills
all life into being and evolution. It is a rhythm that dances all things
into existence. Scientists call it the Schumann resonance. I call it
Earth Song.

Gaia, the great mother, sings a song to us, like a mother who
sings a nursery song to her children. Her song is one of life, a tune
that calls all beings back to coherence and evolution. According to
Hinduism, the whole universe started from the sound of *Om*. Like
*Om*, a frequency or song that holds entire creation together, Earth
has its own chord within this larger song. This chord is Earth Song
and can be measured by 7.83 hertz.[1, 2]

This Earth resonance is caused by the balanced exchange
between the negative, feminine energy of the Earth, and the positive,
masculine energy of the atmosphere. Electrical charges from lightning

in the ionosphere create the positive counterbalance to the Earth's negative, feminine aspect. The "feminine" conductive surface of the Earth and the "masculine" outer boundary of the ionosphere generate a resonance frequency that not only penetrates the surface of the Earth but becomes amplified into enormous standing waves of energy and sound. These waves then maintain a constant state of harmonics at the layer of the Earth and atmosphere that is conducive to life.[3]

Like the Earth, the human brain generates electromagnetic frequencies. Each of these frequencies has different characteristics and allows us to operate in different modes of consciousness. We know today that there are at least five dominant wave frequencies that are created by our brain:

1. Gamma waves (30–100 Hz) occur during simultaneous processing of information from different brain areas such as memory, learning abilities, integrated thoughts, or information-rich task processing.

2. Beta waves (12–30 Hz) occur during our normal, waking state of consciousness when we are doing things in the world. Beta frequency is fast and present when we are alert or anxious, or when we are engaged in problem solving, judgment, decision-making, information processing, and focus.

3. Alpha waves (7–12 Hz) occur during dreaming and light meditation. Alpha waves can cycle globally across the entire cortex area of the brain. This induces deep relaxation. Alpha waves are set at the same frequency as Earth Song.

4. Theta waves (4–7 Hz) occur most often in sleep but also during the deepest states of meditation and thought. In theta, our senses are withdrawn from the external world and focused on

the internal mindscape. Theta waves are associated with gurus and exploration of the deeper realms of existence.

5. Delta waves (0–4 Hz) are the slowest brain waves with the highest amplitude. They occur in the deepest meditation and in dreamless sleep.[4]

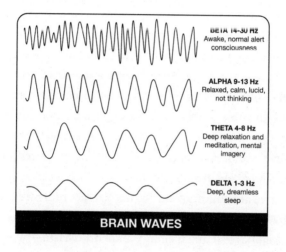

BETA 14-30 Hz
Awake, normal alert consciousness

ALPHA 9-13 Hz
Relaxed, calm, lucid, not thinking

THETA 4-8 Hz
Deep relaxation and meditation, mental imagery

DELTA 1-3 Hz
Deep, dreamless sleep

**BRAIN WAVES**

Research overwhelmingly indicates that in alpha state (and theta state for many people), which is the same frequency as Earth's Song, people tend to experience deep relaxation and a feeling of well-being. In addition, many healing and intuitive abilities are enhanced when we are in alpha state. For example, in alpha state, people have been able to heal themselves and others, to communicate over great distances, and to even conduct remote viewing (which is the ability to see with one's mind's eye places as far as halfway across the world). It is in alpha state that we often receive intuitive messages and understanding.

Alpha is the doorway to deeper ways of being and spiritual enlightenment. When alpha waves cascade throughout a person's cortex, the person becomes calm and centered yet highly alert and aware of all that is around them. Alpha state is a state of peak mind/body/spirit integration for the simple reason that, in this state, the mind achieves overriding coherence between the inner world and outer world. This holistic integration is reflected within the brain itself, as alpha waves engage both sides of the brain versus being confined to one area, as is the case with beta waves.

The whole brain integration that comes about during alpha states can be observed in simple, everyday occurrences. Have you ever lost something only to have it turn up a few days later in a moment of *ah-ha* remembrance? The likelihood is that you lost the object when you were operating in beta state for an extended period of time, possibly even experiencing low levels of stress, and then, when you were able to relax into an alpha state, you could more easily access the knowledge of where the object was located. Alpha waves boost memory capacity and leave us more receptive to the larger energetic field around us.

When we are children, our brains operate more frequently in an alpha state, especially for children five and under.[5] This is one reason why children have so much energy and enthusiasm—why they exercise more, engage in more exploration and creativity, and stay in a state of wonder. It is only as we mature that our brain begins to spend more and more time in the beta brain wave state of heightened activity and fast speed. As adults, we regain this more open and wondrous experience of the world by allowing our brains to spend more time in alpha mode.

In alpha state, we can gain deep insights about the world that are not otherwise available. By tapping into this global channel—global since it is the frequency used by the Earth and other living things—we can receive knowledge that is ordinarily beyond our ken. Information and ideas flow more freely to and from different life systems, just as information and images can flow from your iPod or camera when it is synced with your computer. As Lewis B. Hainsworth puts it:

The frequencies of naturally occurring electromagnetic signals, circulating in the electrically resonant cavity bounded by the Earth and the ionosphere, have governed or determined the "evolution" or development of the frequencies of operation of the principal human brain wave signals.[6]

When we vibrate at the same frequency as the Earth, we are in sync with the Earth and other life forms, and are able to communicate freely across this "channel." This is why animals and people can communicate with each other over great distances. Like using a cosmic radio, living beings can tune into the Earth Song frequency to find each other and communicate. People who are highly intuitive or who can easily relate to other living beings such as horse whisperers or animal communicators are likely able to access alpha state easily. Great psychics and healers also operate from the alpha frequency when receiving intuitive information or when relaying healing energy.

Yet today, most human beings have fallen out of rhythm with Earth Song. We spend an inordinate amount of time in beta states of mind and tend to rely on this state—the logical analytical state—for solving everything. While beta state is valuable for periods of intense concentration and calculation, it is unhealthy when one stays in it for too long.

I believe that we face epidemic proportions of Alzheimer's in part because people spend too much of their lives in beta wave states. Excessive beta states can cause breakdowns in the brain's ability to function cohesively. This also explains why Alzheimer's is so prevalent in high-income countries, where many more people work at jobs that involve analytically intensive work that requires long intervals of beta brain wave activity.[7]

Essentially, too much beta brain wave activity literally starves our brains of oxygen. Yet, when we access alpha states, we nourish our brains with oxygen, as well as with the nurturing world of energy and spirit that surrounds us. Early stages of Alzheimer's can be slowed and even reversed by meditation and harmonizing one's overall brain function under the influence of alpha brain waves.[8]

One way to get back in touch with Earth Song is to get back into rhythm with the Earth. When we fall out of rhythm with the natural internal and external cycles, we lose our inner integrity and balance, leaving ourselves open to illness. We all commonly experience this when we stay up later at night and throw off our internal rhythm, feeling tired and lethargic the next day. This is why paying attention to one's internal rhythm and aligning this rhythm with that of the world around us can set the stage for optimum health and awareness. (Note: It can be very helpful to "fall" out of rhythm with cyclical time of the manifest world when delving deep into shamanic practices, but that is a topic best left to another book.)

Earth Songs or frequencies are subject to a universal, cyclical (and perhaps spiral) rhythm that changes diurnally, seasonally, and with variations in solar activity. [9]

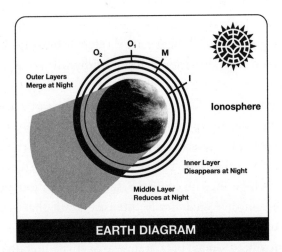

**EARTH DIAGRAM**

You can see from this diagram that the sun does not ionize the atmosphere on the dark side of the Earth, and some of the layers of the ionosphere disappear until the next sunrise.

These cyclical rhythms mirror the rhythms of the human body's internal clock. Each of us carries a rhythmic song inside that is created by the oscillating energy waves that occur within our bodies and extend outward. Our bodies also have a daily rhythm, known as the circadian rhythm, that is linked closely to the sun and the moon. Many people associate this rhythm with the sun's light, yet the moon exerts as significant an influence on our circadian rhythm as the sun. This is why the circadian cycle emulates the lunar day (24 hours and 50 minutes) rather than the solar day. It is this internal rhythm that helps to set our bodies to a biological clock, telling us when it is best to sleep and wake, and keeping us in energetic balance.

During a quest, one is brought back into contact with these natural hourly, daily, and seasonal rhythms. This is one reason why quests are such powerful pathways to wholeness and balance. Meditation is another powerful practice to achieve inner equilibrium and reach an alpha state.

## TUNING INTO EARTH SONG:
## OBTAINING ALPHA

*The Earth and myself are of one mind.*

—Chief Seattle, Nez Perce, *Bury My Heart at Wounded Knee*

Meditation has been linked to lower blood pressure, more restful sleep, and a lessening of stress, headaches, chronic muscle pain, and even skin irritations. Meditation has also been proven to be an effective treatment for depression and even coronary artery disease. For example, patients who practiced transcendental meditation for eight weeks showed an increased resistance to depression.[10]

While meditation is important to simply help reach a relaxed state of being and alpha brain waves, meditation is, of course, used for even greater energetic and spiritual purposes. Meditation is also used to obtain spiritual enlightenment. And while there are many meditation methods available, the best technique is the one that works best for you.

Kriya yoga for example, introduced to the United States in the 1950s by Paramahansa Yogananda, is an excellent meditation method. Kriya yoga seeks to "decarbonize" human blood and infuse it instead with greater amounts of oxygen. Oxygen transforms the cells of the body to higher levels of energy and light. By oxygenating the body, one awakens the energetic and spiritual centers—the brain and the spinal chord—to a higher and more delicate spiritual vibration. When the body attains a more delicate and higher level of energy vibration, it comes into attunement with the frequency of creation. At this divine frequency (the word of God or *Om*), a human being can evolve spiritually at a higher pace than one might without the help of meditation.

11

While we have come to think of meditation as an Eastern practice, meditation may have been practiced by the ancient Celts. The Celtic god of wild things, Cernunnos, is frequently depicted in a cross-legged meditation position as shown here on the Gundestrup cauldron dating to the first-century BCE. There are also references to meditation in the Bible, and some people believe that Jesus and his disciples practiced meditation. Meditation is a non denominational practice that can benefit people from all walks of life.

## CHAPTER PRACTICE

### Find a Meditation Method that Works for You

Everyone can benefit from meditation. The key to succeeding in meditation is to find one or more practices that work best for you and then to meditate daily.

You may want to ask these questions before starting a specific meditation practice:

+ Have people become enlightened using these techniques and/or is this the method that has been directly passed down to them through a line of teachers?

+ Have these techniques helped people meet the emotional, physical, and spiritual challenges in their lives?

+ Is the person or group that is offering this meditation technique interested foremost in my self-development and care, or is it more about building an institution or adding members to an organization?

+ Most important, does this specific meditation practice work for me?

Try a meditation practice diligently for at least forty days. If you are not receiving any benefits by then, assume that that practice is not for you and try a different method.

Because of the tremendous physical, psychological, and spiritual benefits of meditation, it should be a cornerstone of one's day. Even meditating for just twenty minutes once a day can be beneficial, though ideally, meditating a minimum of sixty minutes a day (every morning and evening for at least thirty minutes, or once a day for sixty) is optima for beginners.

Do not give up if you try an approach and it does not work. Try a new method until you find one that works for you. You should also note that many people move through different meditation techniques as they mature. For example, some people who start with more fire-based meditation techniques sometimes turn to more water-based meditation techniques when they are older, like the Tao water meditation method from the ancient Taoist tradition, which Lao Tzu wrote about in the *Tao Te Ching*.

Along with selecting a meditation practice that works for you, it is important to carefully choose the location that you meditate in. It is best not to meditate in an area of frequent traffic or interruptions. Choose an area in your home or outdoors that feels good to you, and where you feel safe and comfortable. Once you find a good place and start to frequently meditate there, you will enhance the energetic quality of the space through your repeated spiritual practices.

When I first started to meditate, we lived in a tiny house, which had a tiny, enclosed yard, six feet by twenty feet. I meditated every day, twice a day, on an old wooden bench in the yard that was only eighteen inches wide. Although tiny, this spot was near a wonderful tree, as well as quiet and well hidden from human traffic. I now have both an indoor meditation area in my home and many places outdoors where I also like to meditate each morning.

---

## CHAPTER PRACTICE

### Tree Meditation Practice

Find a quiet place in nature with a minimum level of distractions, human traffic, and noise. Select a tree for this practice

---

that is healthy and preferably native to the region. You may want to first determine whether a particular tree is beneficial to your energy by conducting the tree surfing practice first (see page 46).

+ Sit beneath the tree, with your back resting against the tree's trunk for support. You may want to bring a pillow or an item of clothing to serve as a soft ground cover and support for your body. This ground covering should be a natural fabric, like cotton, wool, or leather. When selecting where to sit, try to face east or north if that is practical; also consider the way the tree is positioned on the land and with the surrounding features. Ultimately, you want to be able to sit comfortably for a minimum of twenty minutes in one position.

+ Once you are sitting comfortably in the meditation position, breathe deeply for at least eight deep breathes. Once you begin to go into a relaxed state, tune into the tree, perhaps by feeling where your back touches the tree's trunk. Imagine that your back joins with the tree's trunk and that your back is as tall as the tree, lifting to the sky, and stretching below the ground to the roots in the Earth. Then, simply conduct your usual meditation practice.

You may find that meditating with a tree can bring you into a receptive state more easily or that you access insights that you may not have reached by meditating on your own; you should feel refreshed and energized. When you are

*continued on page 186*

continued on page 186

done with your tree meditation, give thanks to the tree for its help.

This practice deepens with use. For the best results, repeat the practice as often as possible—preferably with the same tree.

When we align to the Earth's greater song, the doorway to infinite possibilities opens before us. In alpha state, we can also solve problems that we may have encountered (or gotten ourselves into) in beta state. This is why it is said that one cannot solve a problem in the same consciousness from which the problem was perceived or created. When we gain greater harmony within ourselves by operating more from an Earth Song frequency, we will be better able to positively influence the Earth. The Earth is calling us back to this larger chorus of life.

# 14

## Toward a New Global Ethic

We must stop looking upon God's beautiful world as though it was given to
us so that we can devour, consume, and manipulate it without limit . . . then
and only then, when we have surrendered our idolatrous power, which is
nothing short of tyranny over God's good creation, shall we be worthy
to have that moral dominion over all which God promised us.

Andrew Linzey, *Animal Theology*

The Bering Sea is a subartic sea between Alaska and Russia that
extends to the northern Pacific Ocean through a string of small
islands in the shape of an arc. The sea supports a rich abundance of
wildlife, including 450 species of fish, 25 species of marine mammals, and 50 species of seabirds. Since prehistoric times, the Bering
Sea has supported humans and animals alike with its tremendous
biodiversity; yet, over the years, the many marine species that have
depended upon the Bering are disappearing at an alarming rate.

Dramatic changes have taken place in the Bering, most notably
the disappearance of tiny creatures called crustaceans that provide
food for many marine species. In their place, jellyfish and algae are
beginning to monopolize the Sea. These changes are due to several
factors, some of which are linked to global warming.

While protecting habitats is always a challenge, the politics of the
Bering Sea region (like many ocean habitats) make it even more of a
hurdle. The majority of the Bering Sea is "co-owned" by the United

States on one side and Russia on the other. In the middle of this arc of water lies a small, international waterway open to other countries and referred to as the doughnut hole. Since no single country claims responsibility for the Bering, there has never been effective shared management of the region. To further aggravate the situation, Russia, Britain, and the United States also share political tensions left over from years of conflict over boundary disputes and past treaties. Russia, in particular, feels that an 1893 arbitration wrongfully thwarted its right to conduct sealing operations in the region.[1]

Meanwhile, there has been a steep and steady decline in the Bering's biodiversity as each country vies for more of the natural resources in the region. In 2003, in concert with other environmental and political leaders, I launched a Bering Sea Forum to develop an international working group that would sustainably manage the sea. Representatives from Russia and the United States, along with other countries that care about or rely on the Bering for hunting and fishing, attended the forum. I was told that it was an impossible dream to bring together an international coalition for the purpose of protecting the Bering's biodiversity since so many political and economic pressures affected the region. Yet, while entrenched politics were certainly a hurdle to our efforts (representatives from the U.S. State Department refused to attend), we were able to build upon the existing efforts of individuals and organizations to bring many visionary leaders—scientists, indigenous leaders, political leaders, and nongovernmental organization (NGO) representatives—together to address the issues.

With their help and the spirit of the Bering Sea herself, we came together to share information, experiences, and stories and to discuss possible ways to provide better management on an international scale. I chose to host the forum in the Cook Inlet region, which boasts the largest population of Native Americans in the United States, to ensure Native participation in the forum. One-quarter of the people who attended were indigenous people from Russia and the United States. By bringing representatives from many walks of life, we were building not only an international community but also a multi-cultural community grounded in ancient ways of knowing as well as modern scientific and political understanding. We soon began to receive coverage for this groundbreaking initiative.

> Alarmed about over-fishing, poaching, pollution, and ecosystem shifts in the Bering Sea, an international coalition of scientists, managers, and community leaders has formed to push the United States and Russia to work together to manage what may be the most productive marine area on Earth. The International Bering Sea Forum will marry scientific data with traditional Native knowledge, while gathering reports from regular people who wrest a living from the ocean on both sides of the border.[2]

During one interview with the press, a reporter asked whether the meeting would address the thorny political boundary-line disputes between Russia and the United States. I replied that:

> Political boundaries are meaningless to the fish and mammals of the Bering Sea. They move freely from one side of the Bering to the other, so any one country's management or lack of management affects all species; this is why we need to work together. To do so, we need to apply a new perspective about how we think of the Bering Sea. It is not a resource to be used and divided up; instead, it represents a coherent, living ecosystem that supports an abundance of life.[3]

Since conference participants came from many different belief systems, our very first step was to define what the Bering Sea is. To policy makers, the Bering Sea is a place to be used, owned, and managed; to scientists, it is a place to be studied; and to the Native Americans and native Russians, the Bering is nothing less than their beloved mother—a mother whose very existence they depend on.

More than once, we needed to stop presentations by scientists and policy makers to hear out native peoples' dismay whenever resource-based terminology and concepts were bandied about. This occurrence reflected the ethical constraints of people raised in industrialized nations, who had long forgotten that a sea could be one's own mother.

## A CALL FOR A BOLD NEW ETHIC

For as long as people have inhabited the Earth, they have grappled with the ethics of decisions concerning the advancement of the human race and the protection of other species. Our existing ethical paradigm about the relationship between humankind and other species is leading to the terrible destruction of the Earth and ultimately ourselves. Should we continue to be defined by an out-of-date paradigm, or are we to achieve an ethical standard that makes sense for the world we live in today?

Many environmentalists have been at the forefront of a growing ethical vision grounded in their sense of connection and deep respect for the Earth. According to Father Thomas Berry, "It's not very acceptable anymore to think of Earth and life as being separate. What is important is to recognize the inherent value of things and how to be able to interact creatively and intimately with them."[4] The stark reality of ecological destruction lends urgency to our task. According to Berry, if we have only a short period of time in which to change our ways, we need to make clear ethical choices that enable us to regain our intimacy with the Earth. Ultimately, when we recognize the inherent sacredness of all life, we become forces for good in this world.

## THREE BOLD CHANGEMAKERS INSPIRED BY NATURE

Many people who have changed the world found their inspiration by listening to the still voice that came when they listened to nature.

Sometimes, when we simply and quietly pay attention to nature, secrets are revealed, innovative ideas are generated, and bold plans well up from our hearts.

## George Washington Carver: Plant Lover and Father of Chemurgy

> *Flower in the crannied wall,*
> *I pluck you out of the crannies*
> *I hold you here, root and all, in my hand,*
> *Little Flower—but if I could understand*
> *What you are, root and all, and all in all,*
> *I should know what God and man is.*

> —Alfred Lord Tennyson[5]

It is humbling to admit that we could possibly learn the secrets of the universe from plants. Yet George Washington Carver understood their secret language. As a child, his understanding (or perhaps "love" is a better term) brought him great joy.

> During the day [George] spent almost all of his time roving the woods and acquainting himself with every queer flower and every peculiar weed. He was also interested in studying the rocks, and different stones, and the birds. He usually played by himself, as his playmates were very few.[6]

As his love for the plants grew daily, Carver began to ask questions: "God, why did you make this plant, and for what purpose did you make it?"[7] Family, friends, and neighbors all observed Carver's uncanny "magic" with plants from the time he was a child. They would often give Carver their ailing plants to help them recover. Eventually his talent caught the notice of one of his teachers, who encouraged him to study botany. In adulthood, Carver's knowledge of plants helped him to become one of the foremost botanists of all time.

While Carver's academic work brought him national respect, he became most famous and beloved in his day by helping poor Southern farmers. Many farmers at the time did not understand that they were depleting the soil of nutrients through repeated plantings of cotton crops. Carver taught farmers to restore nitrogen to their soil by alternating cotton crops with plantings of cowpeas, sweet potatoes, peanuts, and soybeans, to name a few. Carver also developed hundreds of new uses for plants to benefit humankind. The peanut was one of his favorite plants due to its high protein content and its many other uses.[8]

Carver reported that, in spite of his impressive academic and research background and training, he made many of his astounding advances in our understanding of plants by simply listening to them.

> When I touch that flower, I am not merely touching it, I am touching infinity. That little flower existed long before there were human beings on Earth and will continue to exist for millions of years to come. Through the flower, I talk to the infinite, which is only a silent force. This is not a physical contact. It is not in the earthquake, wind, or fire. It is in the invisible world. It is that still small voice that calls up the fairies.[9]

Carver went on to discover hundreds of new and helpful uses for plants. He rarely patented his work, however, believing that God gave these innovations to him freely through nature. Carver's openness to learning from the wisdom of a plant allowed him to hear the voice of the infinite, resulting in discoveries that have been a boon for humankind.

## Paul Watson: Defender of the Whales

Some people change the world by becoming environmental and political activists because of their experiences with nature. This is certainly the case with Captain Paul Watson, founder of Sea Shepherd Conservation Society and cofounding director of Greenpeace.

Paul Watson was born in Toronto, Canada, on December 2, 1950, and his interest in animals was apparent at a very young age. One of Watson's favorite childhood friends was a beaver at a nearby pond, but one day, when Watson was just nine years old, he found that trappers had killed the beaver for its pelt. He was heartbroken and, in anger, stole and destroyed all of the leghold traps that he could find. Then, at the age of ten, Watson joined the Kindness Club, founded by Aida Flemming in New Brunswick on Dr. Albert Schweitzer's philosophy of reverence for life.[10] Watson's initial love and respect for wildlife was to later give him the strength to take a daring stand in the battle to protect whales.

As an adult, Watson became one of the cofounders of the Greenpeace Foundation, but finding Greenpeace to be too "tame" in its efforts to protect marine mammals, Watson founded his own marine conservation group called the Sea Shepard Society in 1981. The Sea Shepard Society's most recent goal is to close down illegal whaling operations. To date, the Sea Shepard (the primary vessel of the society) has conducted over two hundred voyages to stop the inhumane slaughter of whales.[11]

Paul Watson and the Sea Shepard Society were the subject of the 2008 TV documentary series *Whale Wars*, which covered their efforts to stop the Japanese government from illegally killing whales.[12] Watson's life echoes the path of many environmentalists who are driven to protect the environment because of a connection with animals forged in childhood. Sadly, since fewer and fewer children are spending time in nature today, they may not have the same opportunities to learn about nature or to shape those deep connections with other living things.

In some cases, nature inspires people to become activists who help protect and defend animals that cannot defend themselves against humankind's foibles. These activists are the warriors of the environmental movement. Other people may instead be inspired to help raise human consciousness by passing along the profound peace that they experience in nature so that others may bring that peace into their own lives.

## Peace Pilgrim: An American Prophet

*I was out walking in the early morning. All of a sudden I felt very uplifted, more uplifted than I had ever been. I remember I knew timelessness, spacelessness, and lightness. I did not seem to be walking on the Earth ... but ... every flower, every bush, every tree seemed to wear a halo. There was a light emanation around everything and flecks of gold fell like slanted rain through the air ... The most important part was not the phenomena: the important part of it was the realization of the oneness of all creation ...*

—Peace Pilgrim[13]

On January 1, 1953, the day of the Rose Parade in Pasadena, California, an extraordinary forty-five-year-old woman began her pilgrimage for peace. Already gray-haired, she wore a simple navy tunic with "Peace Pilgrim" in white. She had relinquished all her possessions and even renounced her name for the cause of peace. She later said that this was the proper timing for her message, with the war in Korea raging and the McCarthy era at its height. By the time she was seventy-three years old, Peace Pilgrim had crossed the continent seven times on foot (she had logged 25,000 miles by 1964 and then stopped counting). Her message was both simple and profound, and continues to inspire people all over the world. She understood the connection between inner and outer peace, and she was a model of living a peaceful life, bringing peace to many of the people that she met. She believed that peace was possible when people embraced peace in their lives.

All of us can work for peace. We can work right where we are, right within ourselves, because the more peace we have within our own lives, the more we can reflect into the outer situation. In fact, I believe that the wish to survive will push us into some kind of uneasy world peace, which will then need to be supported by a great inner awakening if it is to endure. I believe we entered a new age when we discovered nuclear energy, and that this new age calls for a new renaissance to lift us to a higher level of understanding so that we will be able to cope with the problems of this new age. So, primarily my subject is peace within ourselves as a step toward peace in our world.[14]

Peace Pilgrim's first spiritual awakening came in 1938. She later described this seminal moment as occurring after walking all night in the forest and then coming to a moonlit opening in the woods: "I felt a complete willingness, without any reservations, to give my life—to dedicate my life—to service."[15] Soon after this spiritual awakening, "Peace Pilgrim" was born.

Peace Pilgrim conducted many excursions into the wilderness. Her first famous pilgrimage came when she was seeking inner guidance on a five-month journey on the Appalachian Trail. She was the first woman to complete the 2,050-mile journey in one season. By the time she reached Mount Katahdin in northern Maine, she had achieved total inner peace and had discovered her calling. The idea to become a pilgrim, walking cross-country for peace, came at this time in a vision. She wrote:

> I sat high upon a hill overlooking rural New England. I then saw, in my mind's eye, myself walking along and wearing the garb of my mission ... I saw a map of the United States with the large cities marked—and it was as though someone had taken a colored crayon and marked a zigzag line across, coast to coast and border to border, from Los Angeles to New York City. I knew what I was to do. And that was the vision of my first year's pilgrimage route in 1953! I entered a new and wonderful world. My life was blessed with a meaningful purpose.[16]

Nature is a perfect place for experiencing optimal states of consciousness where harmonious and even mystical experiences can occur. Robert Wuthnow, a noted scholar, author, and expert on religious trends, conducted a survey of one thousand people in the San Francisco Bay area to define their peak life and spiritual experiences. He used three definitions to describe a peak or spiritual experience: feeling in close contact with something holy or sacred; feeling in harmony with the universe; and/or experiencing the beauty of nature in a deeply moving way.[17] An overwhelming 82 percent of the people surveyed reported being deeply moved by the beauty of nature. Of these, 49 percent found that their peak experience in nature had a lasting influence on their lives.[18]

So, while one may not become a famous botanist like George Washington Carver, a passionate activist like Paul Watson, or a pilgrim of peace like Peace Pilgrim, everyone can experience moments of meaning, peace, and joy in nature. Today, it is more important than ever for us to act from a new global ethic that promotes peace and the well-being of all living things on Earth. We cannot assume that others will do this for us or that the Earth does not need our help. The Earth and all of the animals are calling to each of us now to contribute to building a new paradigm, each in our own unique way. Whether that paradigm shift occurs in our individual lives as we seek to live and work in more sustainable ways; whether we become advocates for the protection of nature; or whether we simply witness, honoring the wisdom and beauty of the living world, the time for humankind's greatest work has come.

# 15

## REVERENCE FOR LIFE

Only by serving every kind of life do I enter the service of
that Creative Will whence all life emanates.

ALBERT SCHWEITZER, "The Ethics of Reverence for Life,"
*Christendom*

The Bering Sea conference was in its second day, and speakers from Russia and the United States had been presenting since nine that morning. By late afternoon, the air in the hotel conference room was stifling. My head felt heavy and my eyes dim as I gazed from the back of the crowded room at the scientific charts of red and black lines and dots. The charts indicated the dramatic decline of salmon populations in the Bering Sea. A bespectacled, gray-haired man—a respected Washington, DC, scientist who had been studying the Bering Sea for over a decade—pointed at the chart and droned on. "We can see that this species is in decline, as are many other species in the Bering Sea. This significantly reduces this region's usefulness as a key marine resource."

At the end of his sentence, a Native Alaskan woman of the Chugach tribe stood up quickly several rows in front of me. She rose with her back straight and tall, as if lifted smoothly upwards by an invisible rope from the sky. Her long, thick, dark hair fell around her shoulders onto a colorful jacket of red and green geometric patterns. I could not see her face, but I could see that her head was shaking slightly with agitation, her glossy hair darting slightly with each movement of her head.

I first heard about the Chugach people in 1989, soon after the Exxon Valdez struck a reef and spilled at least 10.8 million gallons of oil—the officially reported amount, but many claim that this number is low—into Prince William Sound, once prime habitat for salmon, sea otters, seals, and seabirds. The oil covered 11,000 square miles of ocean with slick, black, death-bringing substance.

On the day of our conference, almost fifteen years after the spill, the long-term impacts of the spill continued to haunt the region. According to the National Oceanic and Atmospheric Administration (NOAA), there is still heavy contamination in the region to this day, which thwarts the ability of species to survive. The Chugach tribe has been greatly affected by this accident, along with other tribes in the region. This terrible blow, while long past, indelibly shaped the experiences of many of the conference attendees that rely upon the Bering in a myriad of ways.

In a shaking voice filled with passion, the Chugach woman declared, "This is our mother we are speaking of here, and I do not care for the way that you are speaking about her." Everyone turned in the now silent room to look at her. The presenter's pointer slowly lowered toward the ground as he peered dimly through his glasses toward the woman, as if his mind was struggling to make sense of what he had just heard.

## As We Come to Be Human

### Bantu Creation Myth

Nzame was the first and supreme Creator. Nzame created the many animals in all of their variety, with fur and scales and feathers and all the colors of the rainbow, but there was no human being. One day, at a gathering of the first animals, Elephant, Leopard, and Monkey, they decided to create a new being—one that would care for all of the animals created by Nzame. After much discussion, they created the first human-like being called Fam, and bestowed a great honor by asking Fam to take care of all of the Earth and all the creatures.

Because Fam was so new to the Earth and had no claws, sharp teeth, fur, scales, or feathers, the animals helped Fam to live on the Earth, to understand the seasons of the world, and to know the ways of all living things. With the animals help, Fam grew great and strong.

But after some time had passed, Fam grew arrogant and no longer took the animals council. He began to mistreat the animals and stopped worshipping Nazme.[1]

Many believe that the human race is the most successful species on Earth, and in many ways, we are, especially if we measure success by quantity. We have, after all, increased our own population to over six billion souls. However, we need to ask ourselves if the true measure of our species' success is in the quantity of our own kind. The answer to this question largely depends upon what we believe we are here on Earth to accomplish. For thousands of years, humans' desire to control and master the Earth—to advance the wishes, not just the needs, of our singular species—has led to the diminishment and death of other forms of life, and to the soiling of the Earth. Could this really be what we are meant to do?

Humans have achieved a stunning physical mastery of the Earth that no other creature has even come close to. Our mastery is reflected in part by our astounding physical form; our brains have more neurons than any other living thing on Earth. Our closest relatives, chimpanzees, share 98 percent of the same DNA, yet the greatest difference between a human being and a chimpanzee (and all other animals for that matter) is not the size of our brains but the number of neurons that we have in our brains. The human gene wires neuron cells to continue to divide until a human brain has over 100 billion neurons. Chimpanzees' brains make only 33 billion neurons, one-third the number of a human, before they come to a stop. From the book *The Design of Life*:

> Each neuron may have tens of thousands of finger-like appendages, or dendrites, which connect with other neurons and dendrites in a bafflingly complex circuitry. No two neurons are exactly the same, with the result that the circuitry of each brain is unique. That circuitry is more complex than all of the telephone circuitry on the face of the Earth.
>
> Three decades ago, science writer Isaac Asimov was so impressed with the densely organized complexity of the human brain that he wrote: "In Man is a three-pound brain, which, as far as we know, is the most complex and orderly arrangement of matter in the universe."[2]

Yet our brains, amazing organs that they are, are entirely useless without the world around us. Studies of the effects of sensory deprivation show unequivocally that, without external stimulation, our neurons do not lay down the necessary tracks to function. People who are sensory deprived (kept in dark rooms with no light and no other sound for forty-eight hours) temporarily suffer a significant loss in cognitive ability, and can even undergo complete emotional and mental breakdown.[3] Isolation and sensory deprivation is harmful and can even lead to a complete collapse of the nervous system.

Human beings cannot exist in a vacuum. We are like living mirrors that would be empty but for the reflection when we come into contact with the world and other life forms. We hold, within the layers of our being, the immense diversity of life. When we come into contact with life in all of its manifest forms, it stirs within us an awareness that has been sleeping, and we are here to expand that awareness. Take away the world that surrounds us and we would sleep the eternal sleep of unrealized matter, with little more cognitive coherence than dust. Ultimately, without other living things, humankind would not be completely human.

We depend upon other life forms to help us survive physically. As the Fam story correctly depicts, without animals meeting our needs for food and clothing, and as companions and workmates in agriculture (oxen pulling the plow), in travel (the horse), and protection (the dog), the human race would not have survived. But more important, without other life we would not be able to develop our awareness, or our spirituality, and evolve as individuals and as a species. The physical realm once again reflects the invisible and subtle realm, that declares that all are but one.

Fortunately, a fascination with animals dates to the dawn of our species. While it may be difficult if not impossible to imagine what might have gone on when those first humans laid their feet upon the Earth, we do know that 40,000 years ago, animals were foremost in their minds. Striking images of horses, bison, and lions intermingled with geometric forms and patterns were drawn on the walls of a cave at Chauvet in 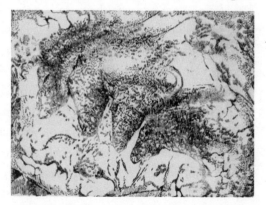 southern France. A series of animal figurines has been found at an archeological site near Ulm, Germany. One is of a horse carved out of ivory that may have been worn as a pendant by someone who walked the Earth some 34,000 years ago. In a cave nearby, another fascinating figure of a person with the head of a lion is equally ancient. So while we cannot know exactly what went on in the minds of the first humans, we can tell from their artifacts that they spent time thinking a lot about animals, depicting them in their very first artistic and spiritual expressions. In fact many archeologists now agree that these figures relate to spiritual beliefs and shamanic ceremonies. These paintings and figures indicate that animals represented more than just flesh and bone to our predecessors. The ability of the Cro-Magnons to see the animals around them from a spiritual perspective had a transformational effect on their evolving consciousness.[4]

In our species' infancy, our cognitive abilities ensured our physical survival as humanity spread far and wide across the globe. As we tuned in to the animals and plants found in each region, they helped to teach us—their younger, more physically vulnerable brothers and sisters—how to find food, what to use to make our homes, and how to migrate to different regions. We have been able to adapt to every habitat in large part because we have an incredible capacity to connect with the wide variety of life forms found around the globe. Initially, we used this innate aptitude and skill to learn from other life forms how best to survive and thrive to benefit our own kind. Having no warm fur, sharp teeth, or wings, we were at a physical disadvantage and depended upon learning from them for our survival.

So, while we believe that our greatest gift is our ability to master the world around us, what truly defines us is that human beings, more than any other living creatures, are programmed with a heightened attunement to and curiosity about the vast diversity of life on Earth. We seek expanding states of awareness perhaps more than any other creature on the Earth. We long to understand the world in the ways in which others understand and experience it. Our awareness expands greatly when we link knowledge with compassion. By forming relationships with other living beings and caring for them, we come to express the truth that we are all one.

Our ability to discern this oneness—to be wired for this—is the very way in which we are made in the likeness of the Creator. Like the Creator, we have the inclination, willingness, and capacity to know and love all life on Earth. We are equipped to experience divine union with other life and with the Creator. Our unique physicality, consisting of a spinal column and brain, supports a subtle energetic/spiritual system that no other living being possesses. This gives humans a "leg up" (or I should say a "spine and head up") over other species on the road to enlightenment. However, this does not mean that all humans take advantage of this gift. Thus, some animals achieve a higher state of enlightenment than some human beings.

We seek to understand forms of life like no other creature on Earth, and we establish relationships with more species than any other being would care to. George Archibald, founder of the International Crane Foundation in Baraboo, Wisconsin, is so "in love" with whooping cranes, an endangered species, that in order to help the species recover from the brink of extinction, he dances like a male crane for a reluctant female so that she will lay an egg, helping to ensure the species' survival. Archibald founded an innovative program to teach juvenile cranes how to migrate by following an ultra-light aircraft. It is believed that, due in large part to his efforts, the North American whooping crane, once on the verge of extinction, with only twenty-one birds counted in 1944, has now risen to over 350 in the wild.[5] One could definitely say that Archibald is "wired" for whooping cranes.

There are many other people who are similarly wired for specific species. Take for example Dian Fossey, a Kentucky woman who devoted her life to the study and protection of the rare mountain gorilla. Appalled by the killing of the gorillas by poachers in the Rwandan jungle in Africa, she led numerous anti-poaching patrols and even burned down poachers' villages. She was murdered on December 26, 1985, in the bedroom of her cabin, most likely for her anti-poaching activities. While Dian was killed, her mission was not in vain; through her work, the story of the mountain gorilla came to be told. Many misunderstandings about gorillas were also laid to rest. Her story is told in the 1988 film *Gorillas in the Mists.*

Then there is the story of Julia Butterfly Hill and her remarkable friendship with a 1,000-year-old redwood tree called Luna. Julia spent two years living in Luna's branches 180 feet above the ground. Her vigil brought the world's attention to the plight of the old-growth forests and the rampant clear-cutting that was unashamedly taking the lives of ancient trees. In spite of death threats from employees of the Pacific Lumber Company (owned by MAXXAM), Julia stayed with Luna to protect her from being cut down along with the surrounding forest.

Julia's unprecedented crusade was completely unplanned. She was on her way through northern California, after a car accident left her unable to continue managing her restaurant business. While traveling through an area where old-growth forests were being clear-cut, she wandered into the redwood forest at Grizzly Creek Redwood's State Park. This profound event changed her life forever:

> [T]he spirit of the forest just gripped me ... When I entered what I call the majestic cathedral of the redwoods, the spirituality of the holiest of holy temples, which are these forests, dropped me to my knees ... I was praying because I was thinking maybe I shouldn't leave the country right now, maybe I was led here for a purpose, and I felt completely at peace about this fact ... So I went back to Arkansas, settled a lawsuit about my wreck, sold everything I owned, bought camping gear, and used the rest of my money to finance my way back out here."[6]

Her brave and inspired action led to the signing of a conservation easement to protect Luna from clear-cutting, and to the international recognition of the importance of trees like Luna. Today, Hill is the youngest person ever elected to the Ecology Hall of Fame.

These are just three of the many people who have gone to extraordinary measures to understand and care for specific species that they have a strong bond with. Their experiences show us that, contrary to outdated societal teachings, we *are* here to have fellowship with all life and to receive fellowship from them. As the tenants of Buddhism proclaim, we are here to end not just the suffering of our own species but also the suffering of all life on Earth.

We have been perfectly crafted by the Creator to carry out this vital task. We have the spiritual, intellectual, and physical means to transform the Earth and to help shape Creation. Our role encompasses far more than the simple, physical "tending" to nature and ourselves. When we understand and fulfill not just the profane but also the sacred aspects of who we are, the human race prospers, and as we prosper, so does the rest of Creation. We have been endowed by the Creator to lead all life on Earth to a higher level of being.

Ultimately, humankind is here to continue to manifest the Creator's original intent that *all* life on Earth be fruitful and multiply. We are here to unleash the full creative and spiritual potential within us and other life forms. The Creator's purpose lies with the expanded awareness and well-being of all life, and our happiness lies with the rest of creation. Planted with the seed of potentiality to one day have dominion over all other life on Earth, humans are meant to both lead and serve. Our purpose is to help the Creator perfect creation by guiding the ascension, evolution, and transformation of all life on Earth.

We start doing this by valuing all life. In Luke 12:6 (King James Version), Jesus teaches us: "Five sparrows sell for two coins of small value, do they not? Yet not one of them goes forgotten before God." In the Bible, we are told that the plants and the animals were created before humankind, not after, which indicates that they have their own unique purpose and path beyond serving us. If we were to follow Jesus' model, instead of devaluing nonhuman creation as nothing more than a resource for our use, we would protect and care for other living things.

By developing and deepening our relationships with each other and nature, we will become wise, we will become compassionate, and ultimately, we will gain access to the sacred. When we are awakened to this truth about our sacred relationship with nature, the world will indeed be a different place—for when we become co-creators who value and care for all life on Earth, we enter the Garden of Eden, and like Noah with his ark, we bring every living thing with us.

# 16

## Singing the Animals Back to Life

When the Earth is Sick, the animals will begin to disappear.
When that happens, The Warriors of the Rainbow
will come to save them.

Chief Seattle

There was a time, not that long ago, when the possibility that humankind could dramatically alter the Earth's atmosphere was thought to be an impossibility. Yet now, we are witnessing firsthand the impact we are having on the Earth's atmosphere, as storms ravage the Earth and melting polar ice caps leave polar bears drowning in warming seas. This devastation not only affects the physical world, it takes a heavy toll on our psychic health and well-being.

I recently came across an article in *San Francisco Magazine* aptly titled "Green with Worry," which proposed that people are going from being "eco-conscious" to being "eco-neurotic," and are unable to deal emotionally with accepting our rapidly deteriorating environment.[1] The article tells the story of a forty-year-old professional woman, who suffers from this syndrome. Ever since she had heard a BBC report a few days earlier, she hadn't been able to forget the image of dozens of bears floating in the Artic waters, dead from exhaustion after trying to swim to solid ground that's disappearing as fast as ice

cubes in a hot bath. She broke down in tears in her therapist's office and sobbed, "Polar bears aren't supposed to drown. I feel so overwhelmed by what these poor animals are going through because of our incredible stupidity," she cried.[2]

Her reaction to the plight of the polar bears is similar to feelings that many people are experiencing today in subtle and not so subtle ways. Whether people suffer from underlying anxiety about the future, guilt about the extinction of so many species, or depression or anger, no one can escape the karma of our species' careless destruction of other life. Since we are connected to other living things at a deeply energetic and spiritual level, it is no wonder that people are experiencing emotional and psychic pain.

So what is one to do when faced with such overwhelming problems like global warming and species extinction? Is it too late? Can one person make a difference in light of overriding societal trends that unnecessarily harm the environment? How can we face this growing calamity? How can we face ourselves?

This past winter, as I drove down Highway 29 in Virginia with my husband and son to catch a plane to my sister's house for the holidays, I saw a sight that lays heavy on my heart. There on the side of the highway were the lifeless bodies of three deer. Their tan fur was completely tinted pink with blood and their body parts were an indistinguishable mass of flesh and fur. It was a horrendous sight, and yet people continued to drive by as if this was nothing unusual. Unfortunately, nothing was unusual because millions of animals are killed each year by cars. Merritt Clifton, editor of *Animal People* newspaper, estimated that 41 million squirrels, 5.4 million cats, 22 million rats, 8.3 million opossums, 15 million raccoons, 1.2 million dogs, and 350,000 deer are killed by motor vehicles in the United States annually.[3]

Animals killed by cars, like animals doomed by global warming, share the same fate in that their death occurs without full awareness and responsibility from their human killers. We humans bring the lives of millions of beings to an end without considering the ramifications of our actions. In most indigenous cultures, people who are responsible for taking the life of an animal are also responsible for honoring its spirit and even calling for its return to the Earth in another body. At the very least, they are certainly aware of the level of their responsibility in ending an animal's life. This is why so many cultures say prayers and express gratitude for the animal, and often handle its remains in a sacred manner. For example, the Zunis in Africa honor the animals through their guardian spirit and are careful not to destroy the bones of any animal that they have killed.[4]

When I come across a dead animal, I have a habit of saying a prayer for the animal's spirit, honoring it and asking for the Creator to look over it. If I come across an animal's remains while I am driving, I will move the body to the roadside so it is not further mutilated by cars, or I may even bury the body if I can stop safely and pull the car off the road.

One evening during a shamanic journey, I felt that my soul was pulled out of my body to a place of tremendous energetic potentiality that was literally bristling with ecstatic power. I found myself floating in a vast, dark space in a super-alert state, feeling in touch with the vast space as if it were a second skin.

From the dark, silent yet potent void, I witnessed what appeared to be an epic struggle taking place between a giant white owl and an enormous snake as large as a dragon. The beautiful, white and gold owl rhythmically flapped its powerful wings, while its claws held tightly to the dark snake writhing fiercely in its grasp. The snake seemed as strong as the bird, and neither the bird nor the snake seemed to have the upper hand. The tension between these two giant creatures was so great that the atmosphere around them seemed supernaturally charged against the silent void around them.

I felt my disembodied self, now tiny in the midst of these giants, being pulled like a magnet toward these two powerful opponents. As I came closer, I could only see the soft whiteness of the owl's breast and its delicate underwing feathers that appeared above me like a soft white sky. I longed to curl myself up in those feathers, but instead, some force continued to pull me forward toward the snake. I was soon at the edge of the snake's enormous dark eye. Staring in its eye, I saw only impenetrable darkness. I was stricken with an overwhelming fear as I realized that I was being pulled into the snake's eye.

I struggled to stay near the rim of the eye, refusing to be pulled into the depthless hole. And then, in a moment of courage, I let go, and as soon as I did, everything became still and quiet. My breathing stopped as my spirit floated silently and peacefully in gentle space. A sense of total freedom filled every cell of my being, as if nothing in the universe could hold my spirit.

Soon, floating up from beneath me and out of the darkness, came the animals. Animals of all kinds and shapes seemed to take form out of the void. As they approached, it felt like we were all from the same body. There was no difference between my spirit body and their spirit bodies. A strange recognition swept through me as I came to understand that I was meeting the spirits of all of the dead animals that I had found. Unlike the torn and broken bodies that I had seen with my physical eyes, each animal was now exquisitely formed and beautiful. As each animal passed, it became lighter and freer, as I, too, became lighter and freer.

The following Mi'kmaq poem is about "singing animals back to life."

> *Even now, there is a man somewhere singing and drumming,*
> *as he does every night, in the lodge where he lived since the*
> *world began. "I am Man singing for Animals," he explains to*
> *guests, singing for the animals, for all of the animals to come*
> *alive, to come back to life, from all those parts of them, all those*
> *wings, heads, feet, all those bones, meat, marrow, all those parts*
> *of them that have not been eaten by the people, all those*
> *parts of them that have not been eaten by other animals, all*
> *those parts of them that have not been thrown away.*[5]

> —Mi'kmaq elder

When I read that poem, I understood that I also have been "singing the animals back to life." Our spiritual bond to the animal world is great, and by acknowledging the divinity in them, we honor the eternal divinity within ourselves. By being a witness to the sacredness of life, and honoring an animal's spirit through prayer, meditation, or shamanic journeys, we not only help them become free, we free ourselves.

---

## CHAPTER PRACTICE

### Animal Altar

Creating an animal altar is one way to honor and send energy to an animal's spirit. One of the best books on how to create an altar is Denise Linn's beautiful book *Altars:*

*continued on page 212*

*continued from page 213*

The creation of an altar is a sacred act, an act of power and grace. For a few timeless minutes, you enter a dimension beyond ordinary reality, where light, sound, and energy merge into an exquisite state of being.[6]

First set a personal intent for your altar and then design the altar to best meet this intent. You can gather pictures, carvings, or some other emblem or relic of the animal(s) that you wish to honor and support. You may want to collect natural objects, such as seashells, sticks, leaves, and stones; even handmade objects, such as pictures or little statues or jewelry. You might introduce pictures of the animal's habitat, or items that it eats or uses to build its nest or burrow. You may also choose to draw or paint the animal or its spirit. An animal altar can be very elaborate or it can be very simple, comprised of just a few items.

The location of the altar is very important. I usually place my long-standing altars on small tables, out of the way of daily traffic. Occasionally, I will create a temporary altar in a more prominent place, like on a dining room table, knowing that it can be disassembled after a ceremony of prayer.

Next, gather together all of the items that you feel would be best on your altar. You may want to start with a beautiful cloth to serve as the base. The color you choose has specific qualities that you may wish to express and highlight in your altar. Creating an altar is a creative act, so feel free to go with your own intuition.

1.  Place your altar so that you face east or north when you are facing it.

2. Purify the space and items that you will be using to create the altar, and purify yourself as well. One of the best ways to do this is to purify with dried sage smoke. You can also purify and ground yourself by bathing in water infused with sea salt.

3. Assemble the items on your altar in a way that feels right and conveys a sense of harmony. You may want to also look at the altar as a *bagua* (feng shui) and treat different areas on the altar as different corners of the *bagua*.

4. After your altar is completed and you have placed all of the objects where you feel they belong, initiate the altar. When you initiate the altar you are bringing the altar to life. This can be done by simply speaking your intention, offering a prayer, and/or lighting a candle. You can also empower your altar by calling upon the four elements and representing them by lighting a candle (fire), spraying water (water), and placing dirt (earth), and possibly a feather (air) on your altar. Like your altar, the initiation ceremony should reflect your own personal style and intent.

5. You can visit your altar every day to offer a prayer, or you may wish to meditate before the altar. Even a brief visit to express an intention at the altar every day can be beneficial. A powerful way to work with your altar is to spend some time before it imagining the animal that you are honoring is healthy, and that its habitat or "home" is healthy, abundant, and peaceful. You can also say a prayer for the animal. A prayer for polar bears might go like this:

*continued on page 214*

*continued from page 213*

*Creator, help Polar Bear to survive this global storm and survive to a better day.*

*If Polar Bear needs food, let him/her find food; if Polar Bear needs shelter, let her/him find shelter; if Polar Bear is injured, help to heal him/her; if Polar Bear has died, honor his/her soul and ask for his/her spirit to be reborn.*

*Keep the polar bears and their offspring whole and forever upon this Earth.*

*Thank you, Creator, for hearing my prayer and thank you, Polar Bear, for walking upon this Earth and filling my eyes with beauty and my heart with joy.*

Keeping an altar "alive" for at least forty days will help to generate lasting effects. You can refresh your altar by cleaning the items there and/or bringing in new pieces like fresh-cut flowers, or you can even do another purification of the altar. You may feel that it is time to complete the altar and choose to start a new altar for a different animal. Or you could keep an altar year-round that has a more general spiritual purpose. To do this, just place an animal statue or picture on the altar at the times that you wish to honor a specific animal.

Human beings are capable of great healing and powerful insights. Doubt not that your intentions and prayers for other living things and the Earth will be heard. You have the ability to communicate instantaneously across vast oceans of space and time; you have the ability to change the world with your thoughts and intentions as well as with your actions.

## HEALING THE EARTH THROUGH PRAYER AND INTENTION

*He prayeth well, who loveth well*
*Both man and bird and beast.*

*He prayeth best, who loveth best*
*All things both great and small;*
*For the dear God who loveth us,*
*He made and loveth all.*[7]

—Samuel Taylor Coleridge,
"The Rime of the Ancient Mariner"

Prayer heals. Human intentions and prayers have far-reaching effects on people's well-being and ability to heal. Intent can make a difference in an individual life and in the evolution of a species. This explains why some evolutionary advances can take eons, while others just a few lifetimes. All living things have some capacity for intent. From rudimentary intent to eat and move to more advanced intentions for betterment of a species—boot-strapping an entire species forward. When we send loving, affirming thoughts and intentions to others, we are not only supporting their vitality, we also help them actualize their inner potentiality. Thoughts are energy that can influence other beings.

When we are in a loving and compassionate state, we gain greater internal coherence. From this state of coherence, we are better able to transform the world around us. This is best exhibited in the famous DNA study that proved that the rate at which DNA strands wind and unwind could be influenced by human intention.

People who could hold a loving state best, measured by a coherence in the electrical activity of the heart as measured by an electrocardiogram (EKG), had the most impact on the DNA. People trained in maintaining states of EKG coherence for long periods of time altered the DNA strands easily.[8]

While human beings can influence their own DNA and the DNA of other living things, we can also affect the primary elements (earth, air, fire, and water) and, therefore, the Earth Herself with our thoughts alone. It has already been proven that human beings can influence water crystals with their thoughts ("words of intent" specialist Masaru Emoto's controversial work shows that water's molecular structure can be altered by human thoughts and words),[9] and can heal animals and plants through long-distant healing techniques.[10]

This has far-reaching implications for the effect that our thoughts, emotions, and intentions have on the well-being of other life forms. Doubt not that holding loving and healing intentions toward the Earth and other living things can change the world. And when we become whole within ourselves, we create wholeness in the world around us.

---

## CHAPTER PRACTICE

### Sending Healing Intent to the Earth

You can send healing intentions toward animals, plants, and even the Earth Herself. Your healing intention will have the greatest impact if you feel a sense of connection to the animal or plant at the time that you are sending your intent.

1.  Find a quiet place where you can sit or stand peacefully without loud noises or distractions.

---

2.  Take several deep yogic breaths until you feel your body beginning to slow down and relax. Then, focus your attention lightly on the medulla oblongata at the back of your head, and imagine a stream of infinite light and compassionate energy entering into your body. Feel the warm energy flood your body and/or imagine a soft, golden light filling you from the inexhaustible supply available in the universe. Let this energy (and/or light) flow down through your body and fill you.

3.  Once your body is filled with warm energy and/or soft golden light (you may also feel warmth in your hands or a general feeling of well-being once you reach this state), visualize an animal or plant that you wish to send positive, life-affirming energy to. You can either imagine the recipient of your energy, or you can stand or sit before them. You can even look at a picture or visual representation. The important thing is to make this as real as you can.

4.  Let the warm energy and/or radiant, golden light flow out from your heart and fill the animal. See the animal as being bathed in the golden light or have a golden white halo. See it looking healthy and happy. If the animal has fur, try to see and/or feel the fur; if it is a fragrant plant, try to see and/or feel the texture of its petals or leaves. You can even imagine that you smell the animal or plant. If it is the Earth, imagine your warm energy and/or radiant light flowing over the surface—over forests, plains, oceans, and valleys—and bringing loving energy to all living things in its path.

*continued on page 218*

*continued from page 217*

5.  Know that this source of energy—loving intention and light—is infinite and enters your body from the infinite storehouse of the Creator. Feel/imagine the light eternally renewing itself from this universal source.

6.  The more loving/healing energy you send out, the more you renew your own energy, your own light. Hold this loving feeling for as long as you feel comfortable doing so. See the recipient of your good energy glowing with good health and happiness.

## WHAT WOLF TEACHES

*To look into the eyes of the wolf is to see your soul;*
*just be sure you want to see what is there.*

—Aldo Leopold

That evening after the Bering Sea Forum, I could not get the words of the Chugach woman out of my mind. Later, in my hotel room, I looked out at the elegant, snow-filled forest beyond the large hotel window where everything was still and peaceful. Mesmerized, I slowly sat on the edge of the hotel bed while staring into the whiteness of the newly fallen snow. I wished for a healing from this sickness that makes us destroy the Earth and ourselves. I fully felt how wrong it was to refer to the Bering Sea as an inanimate "resource" for humankind. Did the Sea not exhibit its own life force as mother for the multitude of living beings that depend upon her?

I was ashamed that I, too, had gotten caught up in that strange paradigm of viewing a living system in such a limited way. My eyes began to cloud with tears.

As soon as the first tear began to slip down my cheek, I saw what seemed to be a silver shadow move behind the trees past my window. The remaining tears froze in place as I found myself staring into the searing yellow eyes of a large gray wolf. It stood like a noble statue no more than fifteen feet from where I sat. Its eyes shone with an ancient knowledge gained from 30 million years of living on Earth, and its gaze penetrated deep into my soul. The wolf's stare pulled the sadness and shame from me until I felt nothing but serene emptiness. The stare of the wolf felt burning, like a purifying ray of white-hot light. I heard the words "with a burning fire, I will make you whole and wise."

I must have fallen asleep, as I awoke the next morning curled up on the bed. I was lying on top of the covers, chilled and fully dressed. The time was 8:00 AM, and I needed to get ready for the morning conference session. I quickly got dressed in fresh clothes and went to the bathroom to brush my hair. Looking in the bathroom mirror, I noticed that my face was slightly sun burnt and my eyes felt hot. It was then that I recalled the burning stare of the wolf. I assumed it was a dream, and began to tell myself this as I walked toward the window, but stopped short. As I looked out at the forest, shapes in the snow caught my eye. Leading to and from the woods, within a few feet of my room, were the large footprints of a wolf. I shivered, turned, and walked over to the sink, drank three tall glasses of water, and returned to the conference.

My encounter with Wolf helped me to clear away some of the limiting beliefs that many of us suffer from to one degree or another. Wolf's spirit asks much of us, and his medicine helped me come to terms with the fact that I, too, am a subject of my societal and cultural upbringing. Wolf helped me to burn through and discard some wrongful ways of thinking and being, and to connect with a powerful inner strength and commitment to change. He gave me a glimpse of a new ethic—a new way of being in the world.

Wolf leads us to care for ourselves and all life with compassion and generosity. Wolf calls for us to become "real" human beings—human beings that will care for all of creation as the Creator does. When we praise, honor, and cherish creation, we show our love and appreciation for the Creator Herself. One of the first steps toward reaching this life-affirming vision for humankind requires us to embrace the oneness of all things.

## VULTURE SAVES THE WORLD

*In the earliest of times, the sun lived very close to the Earth—
so close in fact that life upon the Earth was becoming
unbearable. The animal world got together and decided to*

*do something about it. They wanted to move the
sun further away.*

*The fox was the first to volunteer, and he grabbed the sun in
his mouth and began to run to the heavens. After a short while,
the sun became too hot, burning the fox's mouth, and he
stopped. To this day, the inside of the fox's mouth is black.
Then the opossum volunteered. He wrapped his tail around the
sun and begun running toward the heavens. Before long
though, the sun became too hot, burning its tail, and he had to
stop. To this day, the opossum has no hair upon its tail.*

*It was then that vulture stepped forward. Vulture was the
most beautiful and powerful of birds. Upon its head was a
beautiful mantle of rich feathering that all other birds envied.
Knowing that the Earth would burn up unless someone moved
the sun, the vulture placed its head against it and began to
fly to the heavens. With powerful strokes of its wings, it pushed
and pushed the sun further and further up into the heavens.
Though it could feel its crown feathers burning, the vulture
continued until the sun was set at a safe distance in the sky
away from the Earth. Unfortunately, vulture lost its
magnificent head of feathers for eternity.*

—Myth: "When Vulture Saves the World"[11]

Sometimes signs from nature can indicate larger cultural and societal shifts and trends, and certain animals often have important
teachings about these trends. This is the case with the vulture—a
creature that serves as a powerful purveyor of a new era. Vultures
are closely related to death and intimately associated with rebirth.

In the United States, there are three types of vultures: the black
vulture, the condor, and the turkey vulture, whose numbers have
increased significantly over the past few years. The turkey vulture's

Latin name is *Cathartes aura*, which means "The Golden Purifier." This name suits the vulture well since it spends its life cleaning the Earth of dead and decaying carcasses, in turn ensuring the continued health of all living things. Its dramatic increase in population speaks to a trend of purification occurring in the United States and beyond.

Vulture aids in the transition between death and rebirth by helping the dead release their physical form to become spirit. Unlike other large birds like hawks, owls, and eagles, the turkey vulture never kills. It feeds upon animals that have died a natural death or have been killed by others. Greeks placed the vulture above other birds for its laudable habit of never killing.[12] The Pueblo Indians also considered the vulture a symbol of purification. Vulture medicine restored harmony to that which had been broken; it made all things right. The Pueblo Indians also used vulture feathers for grounding during shapeshifting ceremonies to make sure that ceremonial participants returned safely to their own body and mind after their spirits' mystical flight to join the creator.

Vulture's relationship with humankind even extends much further back than the Greeks. Vultures have a most ancient relationship with Homo sapiens and a history of being revered for over ten thousand years. Hundreds of vulture wings were found in a cave 250 miles north of Baghdad along a tributary of the Tigris River called the Greater Zab, along the Turkey-Kurdistan border. According to the archeologist, Rose Solecki, who found the vulture wings at the cave site:

> The Zawi Chemi people (who lived there 10,000 years ago) must have endowed these great raptorial birds with special powers, and the faunal remains we have described for the site must represent special ritual paraphernalia. Certainly, the remains represent a concerted effort by a goodly number of people just to hunt down and capture such a large number of birds. Either the wings were saved to pluck out the feathers or they were used as part of a

costume for a ritual. One of the murals from a Catal Hayuk shrine … depicts just such a ritual scene; i.e., a human figure dressed in a vulture skin.[13]

It is no accident that vultures are increasing in numbers in western society along with a rise in spirituality and disillusionment with material comforts.

At a spiritual and energetic level, vulture power is about the ability to clean and purify consciousness and spirit. This is why Vulture medicine is so important for our times. We are fortunate that vultures are here to deal with the physical and spiritual aspects of death and transformation. Yet, in India the population of old world vultures is declining, leading to unwanted events.

In India, the Paris descendants of the Persians and the prophet Zoroaster share a strange and unique relationship and ritual with vultures. Paris pallbearers carry the dead up Malabar Hill to the aptly named Tower of Silence. In this large stone amphitheater, corpses are laid out in the open, awaiting purification. The actors of purification, oddly enough, are not human but teeming flocks of hungry vultures. The vultures are physically empowered with unique digestive enzymes to clean the Earth of dead and diseased bodies without harm to themselves, a chore that would kill most other animals. Like Psychopompos, they escort beings from one world to the next, from body to spirit, from death to rebirth. When there are perhaps a hundred or more vultures gathered, a common number in the past, the corpses are picked clean in an hour, leaving only a skeleton. To the Paris people, vultures play a critical role in the human transition from death to rebirth. The Paris people believe that the vulture's actually help their deceased to let go of their body and release their spirit.[14]

In many ways, vultures play the role of angels on Earth, taking in the unwanted, the discarded, and the nonliving, and assisting them on their journey to the divine realms. It is fitting that vultures, specifically condors, have one of the largest wing spans, up to ten feet wide, and that angels are most commonly indicated by their large wings capable of carrying souls heavenwards.

The lesson of the vulture is to purify one's thoughts, attitudes, and actions toward all living things and to honor the sacred around us. The purifying effect of the vulture on our society is helping us come to terms with the destruction that our exorbitant lifestyle leads to.

## THE LESSON OF PHOENIX: BEYOND DUALITY

The vulture is the closest living bird to the great, legendary phoenix. The Chinese believe that the phoenix has been sent to Earth to help the development of humankind: Phoenix is the keeper of the fires of creation, and represents continual transformation and regeneration. This is why it is immortal. In some accounts, the phoenix is either immortal, like the Chinese version of *fenghuang* (birds that reign over all other birds), or it has a one-thousand-year life cycle, as in the Greek myth. Near the end of its life, the phoenix bursts into flames and is reduced to ashes, from which a new, young phoenix or phoenix egg arises, reborn. I particularly like the Chinese version of the phoenix, *fenghuang*, which is actually two birds: *feng*, the male bird, and *huang*, the female bird. The male is yang and represents the solar cycle, while the female is yin, the lunar cycle. That these two forces come together in perfect balance is why the phoenix is such an auspicious bird. It has the unique ability to go beyond duality and find unity in all things.

Everything in the manifest world is ruled by duality, sometimes expressed as yin/yang, good/evil, and hot/cold. This is why all of our technological and biological systems use a dual system, such as

224

negatively or positively charged electrons for living systems and the binary heart of all computers—based on simply 1 or 0. (The status 0 means that there is no charge, and 1 means the opposite: that there is a charge.)

When we are born into the world as manifest beings, we enter a world based on duality. The Bible story of Adam and Eve also speaks to the human experience of duality. When we "eat of the tree of knowledge," humankind "falls" from unity or "Paradise" and enters the dualistic realm of illusion and manifestation. In duality, everything appears separate and opposite, like good and evil, and life and death. In addition, the manifest world is a place of continual changes, since it is the dance between yin and yang, action and rest, 0 and 1. When we move from spirit and "manifest" as human beings, we are born into a world of changes and become mortal. The Bible speaks to this, "But of the tree of the knowledge of good and evil, thou shalt not eat of it: for in the day that thou eatest thereof thou shalt surely die (Isaiah 11:6–9, King James Version)." When we enter duality and leave Eden, we then experience duality like good and evil when these are but illusions of a manifest world.

Phoenix medicine is about overcoming duality by balancing the contrasting energies within us. For most of our present history, masculine energy has dominated in Western cultures, leading to an imbalance (overabundance) in the yang energy. An overabundance of either yin or yang energy is destructive. This yang imbalance appears to be shifting, slowly but surely, to incorporate more yin energy, which brings greater balance to our society.

Fortunately, today we are experiencing a growing liberality of beliefs and spiritual expression that has not existed since the days of religious tolerance of the pre-Christian era. Rising Vulture and Phoenix energy indicate that we are entering a time of new awakenings—a time when we can see beyond duality to the unity within.

When we burn through the impurities of thought and delusion of duality, we awaken to the truth that "All is One."

# 17

# THE BIGGEST LOVE

Nature is the unseen intelligence that loved us into being.

ELBERT HUBBARD

I sat cross-legged on the ground, among blue-eyed grass and coyote bushes, and clasped the sweet-smelling earth in my hands. A silvery mist ascended gently from the dew-covered grasses as the sun's rays warmed the cool night air from the land. The subdued blue-gray shadows of early dawn enfolded the small valley in a peaceful innocence. It felt like the first morning on Earth, long before history or remembrance. I watched the shadows of early morning vanish before the new day. As I sat on the ground, I felt a compassionate presence communing with my soul. I wondered if the loving feeling that I had for this place, the place that Turkey showed me in a vision, could love me back. I uncurled my fingers and let the earth slide tenderly from my hands.

Around me, each blade of grass was imbued with a potent vibrancy, as messages from the land filled my consciousness. These subtle but powerful messages were about Love—love of the Earth for Her people, and the calling for the love of the people to return to the Earth. The Earth and all of the creatures are waiting for us to return to them—to return to a love that will make our own hearts greater.

Love is the most powerful, transformative force in the universe. To be in love is to be in harmony with oneself and the world. The power of love can alter people's lives forever and change the course of history. Love uplifts people above what even they themselves believed possible. When we participate in what is referred to as unlimited love—a love of all human beings without exception—we experience a love that has the power to create world peace. When we further expand our love to all living things, we experience the biggest love of all.

D. H. Lawrence believed that humankind's greatest mistake was turning away from nature, the great wilds, and the vast love that exists there. He wrote about this in his masterpiece, *Lady Chatterly's Lover*:

> Oh what a catastrophe for man when he cut himself off from the rhythm of the year, from his unison with the sun and the Earth. Oh what a catastrophe, what a maiming of love when it made a personal, merely personal feeling, taken away from the rising and setting of the sun, and cut off from the magical connection of the solstice and the equinox. This is what is the matter with us.[1]

D. H. Lawrence believed that a loving relationship with the Earth was central to being fully human and alive. While most people's experience of love is limited to family and friends, it has not always been this way. For our ancestors and people that practice an Earth-based spirituality, love includes all creation.

When we see the world as the Creator sees it, we open ourselves to experiencing the greatest love of all. As a young child of six, Opal Whiteley expressed how we might come to see the world in this way:

> I lay my ear close to the Earth, where the grasses grew close together; I did listen. The wind made ripples on the grass as it went over. There were voices from out the Earth. And the things of their saying were things of gladness of growing. And there was music. And in the music, there was sky-twinkles and Earth-twinkles that was come of the joy of living. I have thinks all the grasses growing did feel glad feels from the tips of their green arms to their toe roots in the ground.[2]

Love is sometimes measured by self-sacrifice because love can lead us to care about another as much as we care for ourselves. One of the most dramatic stories of self-sacrifice is the story of Buddha's sacrifice of his own life for a tigress and her cubs. This act—the final act in a series of Buddha's lifetimes—led to his ultimate rebirth as the Buddha, in a state of complete spiritual liberation. Prior to his life as Buddha, at the tender age of five years old, he came across a wounded female tiger with five cubs. The mother tiger was very weak and was unable to provide food for her babies. He provided his own body as food for the tigers, saying: "Right now I am only able to give temporary help to these starving beings, just removing their hunger. May these tigers who are enjoying my flesh, blood, and bones be reborn to a higher realm, and may I be able to teach them and lead them out of cyclic existence."[3] The tiger and her cubs survived, and the five cubs were reborn in their next lives as human beings. It is these cubs that became Buddha's first human disciples.

While stories of people giving their life to save animals are rare, stories about animals saving human lives are commonplace. For example, Omar Eduardo Rivera, a blind computer technician, can attest to the unconditional love of his guide dog, Dorado. Dorado saved his life on the day of the 9/11 attacks on the Twin Towers. Rivera was working on the 71st floor of the north tower when the hijacked airliner struck the building twenty-five floors above his office. According to Rivera:

> I stood up and could hear how pieces of glass were flying around and falling. I could feel the smoke filling up my lungs, and the heat was just unbearable. Not having any sight, I knew I wouldn't be able to run down the stairs and through all the obstacles like other people. I was resigned to dying and decided to free Dorado to give him a chance of escape. So I undid his lead and ordered him to go. I hoped he would be able to quickly run down the stairs without me and get to safety. I thought he'd be so scared he'd run. Everything was in chaos. Yet Dorado returned to my side and, over the next hour, guided me down seventy flights of stairs and out into the street, amid terrorized and panicking people. It was amazing. It was then I knew for certain he loved me just as much as I loved him. He was prepared to die in the hope he might save my life.[4]

## LOVING LEADS TO KNOWING

In a state of love and intimacy, we are in a heightened state of openness and awareness. When we love someone or something, we can see and know things about that being or thing that someone who is uncaring or indifferent cannot see. When we love something, we gain greater understanding and knowledge about it. Many visionaries have expressed the importance of the relationship between knowledge and love.

*Anything will give up its secrets if you love it enough. Not only have I found that when I talk to the little flower or to the little*

*peanut, they will give up their secrets, but I have found that*
*when I silently commune with people, they give up*
*their secrets also—if you love them enough.*

—George Washington Carver

We can learn the secrets of other living things—and even the universe—if we simply love enough. Given that love is the highest expression of intimacy, love and caring love also presents the highest path to gaining greater knowledge. Scientists who seek to remain objective at all times are deeply passionate about what they study. Many discover "secrets" intuitively before proving them through scientific testing. For example, while Newton has been depicted as inventing a "mechanistic" view of the universe, he actually believed just the opposite. Newton's astounding discoveries—the laws of light and the theory of gravity—were not obtained from pure scientific or rational reasoning alone. Newton's true inspiration came from his spiritually driven and, at the time, heretical belief in an all-encompassing, intelligent universe.

Newton was an alchemist at heart, whose true beliefs were unearthed in the twentieth century when his many papers were found hidden in the archives of the Royal Society. Newton wrote over a million words on the subject of alchemy. Yet, in 1727, after Newton's death, the Royal Society deemed that his manuscripts were not fit to be printed and hid their existence from the public. Notably, the Royal Society was concerned that Newton's fascination with light came from his heretical belief that light embodied the very word of God.

Newton was not the first of the age of reason ... He was the last of the magicians, the last of the Babylonians and Sumerians, the last great mind that looked out on the visible and intellectual world with the same eyes as those who began to build our intellectual inheritance rather less than 10,000 years ago. Newton opened a door to our world, sure. But he belonged to the world we have left behind.[5]

Today, over four hundred years after his death, we are not only rediscovering Newton's "fanciful ideas," science is now proving that there may be some merit to these beliefs. Quantum physics shows us a magical world, where seemingly solid objects shift and change. Depending upon the perspective of an observer, an electron will behave and appear, either as a wave or a solid object. In other words, the electron behavior depends upon the observer's preference or predisposition. Electrons can act like matter or they can act like energy. They will behave like matter when the observer intends for them to be matter, or like a wave when an observer influences the outcome by presupposing that they are energy.[6]

Thus, it is the relationship of an observer to that which is being observed—in this case an electron—that influences what the electron is and does. The relationship makes what it is. Without the relationship to someone or something else, there is no electron as we know it. If relationships shape what something is and does, then relationships shape our very reality. When we infuse our relationships with love, we gain not just deep wisdom about the beloved, but our love actually changes the beloved.

---

## CHAPTER PRACTICE

### Loving and Appreciating Nature

One of the best ways to express your love and appreciation for nature is through acts of thanksgiving. Appreciating even little things like the flowers in your garden, a tree that provides shade for your home, or a bird that brings a beautiful song can expand your heart.

It was the Native Americans who first saved the pilgrims from dying of starvation and introduced them to the ritual of thanksgiving. Giving thanks was a celebration that

---

Indians practiced long before the pilgrims came to America. Thus, it is fitting to offer this example of a Native American thanksgiving prayer that you may want to use.

> *Great and Eternal Mystery of Life, Creator of All Things, I give thanks for the beauty You put in every single one of Your creations.*
>
> *I am grateful that You did not fail in making every stone, plant, creature, and human being a perfect and whole part of the Sacred Hoop.*
>
> *I am grateful that You have allowed me to see the strength and beauty of All My Relations.*
>
> *My humble request is that all of the Children of Earth will learn to see the same perfection in themselves.*
>
> *May none of Your human children doubt or question Your wisdom, grace, and sense of wholeness in giving all of Creation a right to be living extensions of Your perfect love.*
>
> —NATIVE AMERICAN THANKSGIVING PRAYER[7]

# 18

## HUMANITY AND PURPOSE

*If we want children to flourish, to become truly empowered,*
*let us allow them to love the Earth before we ask them to save it.*
*Perhaps this is what Thoreau had in mind when he said,*
*"the more slowly trees grow at first, the sounder they are at the core,"*
*and I think the same is true of human beings.*

DAVID SOBEL, *Beyond Ecophobia*

Indigenous people provide their children with education about their environment on a daily basis. Children learn how to find food and how to build shelter, and in doing so they come to know and understand everything that walks, crawls, or grows. They gain a "naturalist intelligence," a term coined by psychologist Howard Gardner,[1] which is the ability to recognize everyday natural objects and living things, like insects, branches, plants, rocks, and animals. Today, as the planet becomes more industrialized and computerized, "civilized" societies are losing their naturalist intelligence. This is because we spend so little time in nature, and there is little being offered to children to make up for this lack of contact and nature-based experiences.

## Learning About the Earth as if It Were Our Home

David Brower, one of the world's greatest environmentalists, said that he learned some of the most important lessons in life from nature. In an interview that I conducted with Brower years before he died, he told me how, as a young boy, he had watched a butterfly struggling to escape from its cocoon. He said that he wanted to help the butterfly out of its cocoon, so he removed the cocoon from the struggling butterfly with his fingers. To his great dismay, his "help" turned out to be too fast and harmful for this delicate process. The butterfly's wings were damaged beyond repair, leaving the butterfly unable to fly. He told me that he learned deeply from this experience that some things must happen in their own time and way. This was a simple lesson but one that became profoundly meaningful to him. Today, with 90 percent of Americans spending less than one hour a week outdoors, there are fewer opportunities to have these types of learning experiences.

This is one reason why I began offering Youth Quests to provide youth ages 9–16 the opportunity to spend time in nature. Studies conducted across the world have conclusively shown that engaging children in natural settings and providing them with hands-on learning experiences accelerates creative imagination, self-confidence, active play, and exploration. In addition, Youth Quests offer coaching and scholarship application opportunities to help youth focus in on their unique skills and interests. These scholarships have helped youth advance their individual interests, ranging from art, dance, singing, sports, and marine biology, to name just a few.

Youth Quests are held at beautiful outdoor locations (often at state or county parks) near where the children live so that they can see local plants and animal. Children learn about the natural history of the area and the species that reside there. During Youth Quest outings, they are allowed to simply spend time in nature to experience it firsthand, through their own exploration and observation.

Many years ago, when I was the executive director of the Texas Audubon Society, I helped support and shape another wonderful youth education program, at Sabal Palm Sanctuary. Sabal Palm lies on the border between the United States and Mexico, seven miles from Brownsville, Texas, and twelve miles from Matamoros, Mexico, in the Rio Grande valley. The sanctuary sits on the bend of the Rio Grande River where the state's largest and oldest native sabal palm forest exists. The sanctuary is a tiny piece of preserved wilderness no bigger than a postage stamp within the surrounding expanse of northern Mexico and southern Texas. It's proximity to two major cities and many schools provides locals and tourists with easy access. Its native palms and rare wildlife connect people to nature in a way that textbooks cannot. The area used to be called *Rio de Las Palmas*—River of Palms—because the river used to be surrounded by a palm forest that extended for over three hundred miles along the length of the Rio Grande. Due to development, habitation, and agricultural clearing, only thirty-five acres of the original sabal palm forest still exists.

The Rio Grande used to be wide and deep enough to accommodate large ships moving goods. Today, it is a shadow of its former self due to increasing water withdrawals. In fact, the habitat loss in this area of the world is staggering. Ninety-five percent of the original native brushland in the lower Rio Grande Valley has been cut down since the 1920s. While the forest is now only a fraction of its original size, the native palm trees still catch the wind in their topmost fronds as they did over ten thousand years ago. The sanctuary provides a home and resting place for many rare species of plants, animals, and insects, like the bobcat, the buff-bellied hummingbird, and the blue sailor butterfly.

The lower Rio Grande Valley is a volatile mixture of economic depression (Brownsville is the poorest city of its size in the country), rapid growth, and environmental devastation. With the pressing economic issues facing the region, one would imagine that a nature sanctuary would fall at the bottom of a list of priorities in the region. However, under the leadership of Jimmy Paz, a native-born resident and the manager of Sabal Palm, the sanctuary has become a vibrant center for local communities on both sides of the border. Tourists, families, and local schoolchildren all come to Sabal Palm to see a piece of natural resource history brought to life. Recently, interest in the sanctuary has expanded, as the region's residents now recognize the site's value to nature tourism and have come to appreciate its ability to bring economic benefits to the area. Another equally important factor to rising interest for the sanctuary is Paz's concerted efforts to encourage local people to take a personal interest in the sanctuary and learn about conservation.

Children from Brownsville area schools and scouting groups are now coming to Sabal Palm in increasing numbers. Sabal Palm is also seeking to extend its conservation message beyond the Sanctuary— all the way into the schools and community of Matamoros, Mexico, on the other side of the river.

During visits to Sabal Palm, children learn how the native plants can be used as food, medicine, weaving baskets, and shelter. The Rio Grande retains only a small measure of its former grandeur, with many of the area species vanishing. Gone also are the routine floodings that used to ensure the health of the forest and vegetation surrounding the river by bringing not just water but nutrient-rich soil from the river bottom.

"The . . . thing I want them to realize," says Paz, "is how, without that intention, people destroy the habitat." To make this comprehensible to children, Paz told me the story of the cycle of caterpillars and butterflies.

When the worm is eating the plant, we stop and say, "Hold it. Look at that," and the kids say, "Ohhh, gusanos [worms]." That's what the people say when they see the worms eating their leaves. They go get their sprayers, . . . fill them with pesticides, . . . spray the leaves, and unknowingly kill future butterflies. Not only that, but what happens to the poison when it gets into the soil? When the children leave here, I want them to be aware that what goes into the ground eventually goes into the river— our only water source.

Like Sabal Palm's education program, the primary goal of similar education programs is to connect people to nature in a meaningful way so that they learn from direct experience. An important part of making that connection is getting youth outdoors to observe nature firsthand. This is why programs like Youth Quest and the education program at Sabal Palm Sanctuary are so important. According to psychotherapist Harold Searles,

The well-being of individuals and the world depend upon the degree to which people can integrate their ability to think abstractly with secure bonds of affection for particular people, animals, places, and things. [We] must define development paths that are optimal, not just for the individual or for society, but for local habitats and the Earth's eco-system as a whole.[2]

There is a pressing need to close the growing knowledge gap about the natural world. For ten years, the National Environmental Education and Training Foundation, NEETF, has teamed with the nation's largest survey company, Roper Reports, to measure Americans' environmental IQs. What they found is that most Americans believe they know more about the environment than they really do. This is why 45 million Americans think the ocean is a source of fresh water; 120 million think spray cans still have CFCs in them even though CFCs were banned in 1978; another 120 million people think disposable diapers are the leading problem with landfills when they actually represent about 1 percent of the problem; and 130 million believe that hydropower is America's top energy source, when it accounts for just 10 percent of the total. They also discovered that very few people understand the leading causes of air and water pollution, or how they should be addressed.

Years of data from Roper surveys show a persistent pattern of environmental ignorance, even among the most educated and influential members of society. At a time when Americans are confronted with increasingly challenging environmental choices, we learn that our citizenry is both uninformed and misinformed.[3]

In some cases, people understand the primary cause of an environmental problem but do not know how to address it effectively. For example, over 70 percent of people understand that habitat loss is the leading cause of species extinction, yet most do not understand the leading causes of habitat loss. And a majority of Americans have misperceptions about how the Endangered Species Act (ESA) works, and are unaware that, in an overwhelming number of ESA cases, projects that do damage habitats and threaten species are allowed to go forward, even if there are endangered species in the area. Misperceptions inappropriately lull people into a state of compliance when they need to be taking action to address environmental problems. Global warming is a significant problem, and yet, we are just now coming to terms with it.

Al Gore's film *An Inconvenient Truth* points out that public misinformation campaigns spearheaded by the oil industry have purposely provided misinformation about global warming and its causes in order to confuse the American public and protect their oil-dependent practices. The result is that for too long, many people in America questioned whether global warming was real when they should have been taking remediative action decades ago. Since people are out of touch with nature, they are themselves unable to see the telltale signs of climate change. This leaves them prey to politically manipulated half-truths. If people do not have a clue about the environment, we will not be able to guide our actions to conserve and protect life on Earth for future generations.

In the twenty-first century, knowledge about the environment will be essential not only for conserving the planet but also for ensuring our very survival. Unlike Icarus, we must learn to fly with natural limits and laws. The United Nations Tbilisi Declaration aptly speaks to this need:

> Environmental education is a learning process that increases people's knowledge and awareness about the environment and associated challenges, develops the necessary skills and expertise to address the challenges, and fosters attitudes, motivations, and commitments to make informed decisions and take responsible action.[4]

## EARTH AS TEACHER:
## INNOVATION INSPIRED BY NATURE

*The world is a vast repository of unappreciated or unknown biological strategies that have immense importance for humans if we can develop a science of integrating the stories embedded in nature in the basic systems that sustain us.*

—John Todd, *Ecological Engineering, Living Machines, and the Visionary Landscape*

Humankind has an ingenious way of developing new technologies, yet many of these technologies are incredibly wasteful and clumsy compared to nature's ways. For example, the Centre for Biomimetics & Natural Technologies at the University of Bath has estimated that up to 70 percent of manmade technologies often use far more energy than needed in order to resolve the problems addressed. In comparison, nature overcomes similar problems through energy-sustainable and non-polluting approaches.

According to Professor Julian Vincent, who led the research at the University of Bath:

> Evolution has sculpted animals, insects, and plants to produce incredibly efficient machines that carry out a range of impressive engineering feats. From the way desert cockroaches gather water to the way wasps bore a hole into a tree, nature has developed a myriad of ways of solving difficult problems. By better understanding the way in which biology defines and solves technical problems, we can develop new approaches that could significantly reduce our dependence on energy.[5]

Janine Benyus, the author of *Biomimicry: Innovation Inspired by Nature*, first compared the striking difference between the human manufactured Kevlar used in bulletproof vests and the silken cocoon that protects a spider's eggs. Kevlar is one of the strongest and toughest materials that we know how to make. It is made through an intensive, energy extensive and polluting process that includes pouring petroleum-derived molecules into a pressurized vat of concentrated sulfuric acid and boiling them at several hundred degrees Fahrenheit. The material is then subjected to intense high pressure to force the fibers into alignment for greater strength. Once finished, this super material can protect a person's body from shrapnel. Yet, creating Kevlar is a very expensive process, which creates hazardous byproducts that then have to be disposed of.[6]

Kevlar is an embarrassment (especially when one looks at the huge expense and energy expended to make a single vest) when compared to spider's silk. Spider's silk is five times stronger than steel, highly elastic, and waterproof! If we could re-create the silk that a spider uses, we would have one of the most miraculous materials on Earth at our command. Most important, however, the spider makes silk without polluting the environment or relying on petroleum from a foreign country. Clearly, there is something to be learned here from this tiny being, whose ancestors have been on Earth for 380 million years.

Fortunately, an increasing number of people around the world are recognizing that there are innovative and sustain-able ways to do things. In fact, over the recent two decades, there has been a veritable flowering of advances in sustainable technologies.

For example, Iceland leads the pack in sustainable energy technology. For more than fifty years, Iceland has been tapping the natural power of waterfalls, volcanoes, geysers, and hot springs to harness renewable energy. As nature writer Harold Sears notes,

> Iceland is the only country in the world that can claim to obtain 100 percent of its electricity and heat from renewable sources. Glaciers and rivers are harnessed to generate 80 percent of this energy, while geothermal fields provide the remaining 20 percent of the country's electricity needs ... Geothermal water from the fields is used to heat 90 percent of Iceland's homes, and keeps pavements and car parks snow-free in the winter.[7]

Fifty years ago, Iceland was as dependent as most countries in the world are on unsustainable and polluting energy technologies, but the country completely turned around its energy system, saving $100 million in imported fossil fuels each year. Today, Iceland has reduced its greenhouse gas emissions by 40 percent.[8]

While the majority of the world does not have access to the abundant geothermal and hydro potential in Iceland, everyone on the planet has access to sunlight. In one hour, enough sunlight strikes the Earth to provide the entire planet's energy needs for one year! Yet, our existing solar technology does not allow us to capture and store the sun's energy. This gap in existing solar technology has held the energy industry back immensely, though it is likely that the energy storage problem will be solved in our lifetime.

Inspired by photosynthesis, MIT scientists have recently developed a process where the sun's energy can be "stored." By duplicating a reaction that occurs during photosynthesis, they are able to "unlock the most potent, carbon-free energy source of all: the sun." According to MIT's Daniel Nocera, the Henry Dreyfus Professor of Energy at MIT and senior author of a paper describing the discovery in the July 31, 2008, issue of *Forbes*:

> This is the nirvana of what we've been talking about for years . . . Solar power has always been a limited, far-off solution. Now we can seriously think about solar power as unlimited and soon.[9]

Through the invention of smarter ways to use energy, we can wean ourselves off of the dinosaur technologies that are expensive and polluting. Natural-sciences writer Janine Benyus was the first to coin the term "biomimicry," which is a new field of science that studies nature's best ideas and replicates them in technology. Benyus states:

> The core idea is that nature, imaginative by necessity, has already solved many of the problems we are grappling with. Animals, plants, and microbes are the consummate engineers . . . and what surrounds us in nature is the secret to survival.[10]

Solar cells, which were inspired by how plants use energy directly from the sun, are an excellent example of biomimicry. If we develop and adopt technologies by following examples found in nature, we will be able to quickly turn around many of our environmental woes.

We do need to recognize, however, that there are limits to our human-made technology. I believe that we will not be able to successfully address global warming without the help of nature. Some scientists and policy makers are relying too much on dramatic, technological solutions that create more problems than they solve. The suggestion that a huge "mirror" be launched into space to block the sun's rays from the Earth is one such total technology cure-all. Yet, the possible hazards of this type of technology are obviously immense.

A more promising "total technologically" idea, but one which also has limits, is the synthetic tree. Inventor and professor Klaus Lackner has designed a synthetic tree that mimics the function of natural trees by pulling carbon dioxide out of the air.[11] Each synthetic tree could potentially remove ninety thousand tons of carbon dioxide a year from our atmosphere. While carbon sink machines like this could prevent catastrophe and be put into commission short term, the use of synthetic trees as a long-term solution is not wise. These trees are far less sophisticated than natural trees, and while they can remove carbon dioxide, they cannot store it or change its composition. This means that once captured and stored, the carbon would need to be disposed of somewhere. Most important though, there are many other things that trees and plants do that are now on the frontier of discovery.

More plausible solutions to global problems lie in working with natural processes. One of my favorite examples of biotechnology being used to clean water is John Todd's amazing Living Machine. One of these Living Machines can be found at Corkscrew Swamp Sanctuary in Florida.

## THE LIVING MACHINE AT CORKSCREW SWAMP SANCTUARY

The Corkscrew Swamp Sanctuary is unique because of its intricate system of boardwalks and its beautiful cypress underwater forests. By the late 1990s, the sanctuary became a favorite tourist destination, but when the visitor level rose to over one hundred thousand people a year, the sanctuary was faced with having to build a sewage system to handle the waste.

Sanctuary officials were stunned by the cost of building a sewage treatment plant. They were also concerned about the effect of the sewage treatment chemicals on the sanctuary's wildlife as well as the large amount of acreage needed to build the plant.

Then they learned about John Todd's Living Machine, which purifies wastewater by using sunlight, bacteria, and green plants. Today, the Living Machine is taking 90 percent of the dirty wastewater and turning it into near-drinkable water. In addition, the Living Machine is only 70 × 70 feet and can purify waste without additives. Astonishingly, the Living Machine "restored water" is cleaner than water from a nearby municipal water treatment plant!

Sanctuary staff soon discovered that a bonus of the Living Machine is that it has become a popular attraction and educational opportunity for the many sanctuary visitors. According to Ed Carlson, Sanctuary and South Florida Audubon manager, "We've already booked tours that have come specifically to see the system in action. We feel this attractive yet functional wastewater treatment plant is the ideal setting to teach water chemistry, purification, and recycling lessons."[12]

## LEAVING THE STATUS QUO BEHIND

While Corkscrew's Living Machine is an innovative model of transforming waste, the Environmental Protection Agency (EPA), which permits waste treatment plants, was initially unable to "deal" with this new technology. Since the Living Machine did not fit within the EPA's narrow definition of what a waste treatment plant could be, the agency initially refused to permit the facility. Fortunately, after considerable time and discussion, the EPA recognized this new technology and provided the needed permit.

Many new and wonderful innovative technologies have already been created but face similar hurdles to implementation. Changes in systems, technologies, habits, and people are needed to support these great new methods, and training in green technology and green jobs is as important as creating the new technology itself. Also, providing training in mastering these new biotechnologies is key. Hopefully, manning an oil rig will be a skill set of the past, while installing solar technology and other renewable energy systems will become the jobs of the future.

In addition, people who make a profit from old technologies apply political and economic pressure to keep outdated methods in place and money in their pockets. Today, huge subsidies are given to large industrial agricultural companies and to the oil industry, which use both old and polluting technologies. These funds—from taxpayer dollars—support large farms that use unsustainable technologies and pesticides, and grow genetically engineered crops. These methods are used because they are often touted as the fastest way to get the most out of the land or an animal, but they keep us dependent on unhealthy food and practices that are inhumane.

As mentioned above, the oil industry is also highly subsidized—according to some estimates receiving up to $35 billion per year![13] Just imagine how quickly our energy system could be completely revamped if we were investing $35 billion a year to do so! Like Iceland, we could be creating 100 percent of our electricity from renewable technology. Politicians are finally beginning to try to address these enormous inequities in how we apportion our taxpayer dollars.

Ultimately, we must discontinue our financial backing of dinosaur technologies and businesses, and invest in more efficient, sustainable, and healthful methods. We owe this to our children, to other living things, and to the Earth Herself. By integrating sustainable agriculture, solar technology, and processes like the Living Machine, we will have resolved many of humankind's greatest challenges, and we will begin to experience the world in ways that we are just now beginning to grasp.

# A Yup'ik Teaching Story:
# A Story of Redemption

I first learned of the Yup'ik's story of Amik in the traditional oral manner from a Russian orthodox priest who was married to a Yup'ik woman. The Yup'ik people (*Yup'ik* meaning "real people") are native to Alaska. Their culture depends upon cooperation and working with natural laws in the delicate ecosystem in which they live. One of their most famous teaching stories is the story of Amik, which is sometimes called "Through the Eye of the Needle." While this story has ancient roots, its moral is aptly suited for this generation. I relate this story below from memory.

Little Amik, a nine-year-old Yup'ik youth, lived with his grandmother in a tiny sod hut several miles away from the shore of the Bering Sea in Alaska. Amik's grandmother, a wise woman of her people, spent her days sewing with a beautiful needle carved from whale bone. While her eyes were old, "the open eye of her needle helped her see many things."

As spring slowly came upon the land, melting the ice and warming the Earth, Grandmother tells Amik that he is now big enough to go out alone on his first hunting expedition to bring food back home to the tribe. Filled with great anticipation, Amik leaves his grandmother's house and walks west toward the sea.

Along the way Amik soon comes upon a nest with three bird eggs. He eats one and considers taking back two to Grandmother, but he feels hungry and knows he will find more food, so he eats the other two. A little while later, Amik comes upon a ptarmigan [grouse] and catches it. As he holds its still-warm body in his hands, he feels very hungry and decides to eat it rather than put it in his skin pouch. A while later, as Amik walks farther from home, he comes upon a stream and catches a salmon. He is proud of what he will be able to show Grandmother when he brings it home, but he finds that he feels so ravenously hungry he eats the entire salmon. He then realizes he has nothing to show for his hunting excursion, so Amik continues walking to the sea.

Once by the ocean shore, he notices a large, dark shape moving in the water. It is a walrus. Amik runs into the water toward the walrus and is able to capture it. Amik no longer thinks he will be able to bring some back home. Instead, he quickly eats it all himself. As Amik consumes more and more, he gets bigger and bigger. By the time he is finished eating the entire walrus, he has become so large he is not able to see his toes, and he feels very strange. Yet then he sees the flap of a tail of a small whale out in the water. Amik manages to hunt and catch the whale and remarkably eats the entire animal!

As darkness begins to overtake the sky, Amik's homesickness overcomes his hunger. He begins his journey back toward his grandmother and his village empty-handed. Halfway home, he crosses the river that flows by the village and leans over it to quench his thirst. In his amazement, he soon sees that he has consumed the entire river until the fish flap helplessly on the dry riverbed. He eats these too.

Meanwhile, his grandmother, who has been sewing with her needle, senses that all has not gone well with Amik. She soon feels the Earth tremble, and hears a large crashing noise in the dark that sounds like an earthquake coming closer and closer to their little sod home. She runs outside, and in the distance, above the tops of the trees, she sees a frightening sight: a gigantic monster, over two hundred feet high, that was once Amik, coming home.

In a few giant steps, Amik finds himself standing above the tiny home, with his grandmother peering up toward him from the ground. Amik then begins to feel remorse and shame since he realizes that he can no longer fit through the door of his house.

His grandmother, a great shaman, divines a cure for Amik's terrible condition. She reaches her arm high in the air, holding in her fingers her tiny bone needle. His grandmother calls out loudly to Amik that he must go through the eye of the needle. Amik is so large and the needle is so tiny that he cannot see it from his great height. Amik hesitates as his eyes fill with tears and block his sight, but he trusts in the wisdom of his grandmother. Grandmother ties her thread around Amik and soon finds himself magically transported through the needle's eye, transforming back into a little boy. As he transforms, he disgorges a great flood of animals (still living) and the entire river. Everything is restored to wholeness. Amik hugs his grandmother with great appreciation and joy. He can once again return home.

In some ways, we, too, have become monstrous, like Amik, in how we overconsume the bounty of the Earth. By causing the destruction of the environment and the extinction of species, we also cannot return to that home that we once knew. Our children and future generations face a world dramatically changed by environmental destruction and loss of species. Yet, what I love most about Amik's teaching story is that it is a story of redemption. Ultimately, Amik recognizes his mistakes, regrets his actions, listens to Grandmother, and is able to right the wrongs he has done. Because of this, he is able to return home once again, and everything is restored. Similarly, while we need to take action to remedy the environmental degradation we have caused, we also need to believe that it is possible to restore the Earth. If we cannot consider redemption a possibility, we will not be empowered to make the sweeping changes that need to take place.

The tiny eye of the needle ended up being the passage through which Amik's transformation and thus, the restoration of the animals took place. Similarly, it may be that our own redemption will come through a seemingly unique way. As we gain greater energetic and spiritual knowledge and experience, we will be better equipped to shift the underlying energetic imbalances that are occurring in the world. Today, the external energy crisis and resultant global warming speaks to our own inner energy crisis of misusing our internal life-giving energy. We restlessly seek new things and outward experiences, expanding our houses, businesses, and accumulating many belongings, when true happiness and peace can be found by doing less, acquiring less, and enjoying the simpler things in life.

When we gain mastery over our own energetic and spiritual being, we will simultaneously gain mastery over the manifested mechanical energy that turns the external world. As we spend more time building our inner strength, listening to the still, quiet voice inside of us, we will get in touch with our inner light and joy and feel less inclined to have to "conquer" the external world around us. At the same time, we will be able to bring this inner light to guide our everyday actions. With greater inner peace, we will have less drive to consume and accumulate things, and will no longer be driven to "improve" upon creation through covering every inch of the Earth with manmade constructions.

The better we become at tapping into our own energetic and spiritual core, the better we will be able to tap into the infinite storehouse of energy that surrounds us. When we join scientific inquiry to heightened spiritual experience, we will discover the holy grail of energy that exists around us in every moment. We will come to understand that there is ample energy to support every living thing that is or will be. Like Grandmother, we will learn how to use the power of the small and/or invisible realm to create significant and beneficial changes.

## A VISION OF THE EARTH

*"The wolf will reside for awhile with the male lamb,*
*and with the kid, the leopard itself will lie down,*

*and the calf and the maned young lion and*
*the well-fed animal all together."*

—Isaiah 11:6–9 (King James Version)

The stories we choose to tell ourselves and others are powerful and might come true simply because we thought it so. Doubt not that stories and thoughts can powerfully affect the world. This is why it is so important to envision and think about how our lives can be—and how the Earth will be—in the future. Our thoughts and stories lay down energetic "vision paths" or songlines that have the potential within them to create our future. Like Grandmother's needle, they may be invisible to our eyes, but they contain world-changing power.

The stories that I choose to share are stories of hope. How might the Earth look as we come to partner with nature? I envision a future where we honor nature and ourselves, and where even the humblest form of life is seen for what it truly is: no less than a miracle.

By seeing an empowering future for the human race and the Earth, we will have greater commitment and energy to tackle challenging problems like global warming. No matter how overwhelming our environmental problems may appear, there is always a possibility for redemption. There is even a possibility that our best dreams, our most hopeful and beautiful visions, will come to pass.

Please join me in applying your dreams and imagination to thinking about what the world could be like for the next generation. Here are a few possibilities that I would like to share with you:

+ People spend an appreciable part of each day outside in nature. Schools and communities have more open spaces, natural playgrounds, and gardens where children can spend time learning about ecosystems through hands-on projects and observation. People have more access to nature in public open spaces, and parks are found in increasing numbers in and around urban areas.

+ Vast tracts of wilderness, where wild animals can roam and plants and animals thrive, are spread around the globe. These wild places protect critical habitat areas, like key breeding grounds. Because their habitat is protected, even large species like elephants, lions, and bears have room to roam and thrive.

+ National and international work project campaigns (reminiscent of Roosevelt's public works program) employ people to restore and conserve the Earth. These projects provide gainful employment for people who replant forests, restore native habitats, and create sustainable buildings.

+ We work with plants to unleash their powerful healing to heal humankind, other species, and the Earth and protect them through massive planting protection programs.

+ Biomimicry-based technology soars as new inventions are created that provide sustainable, economical, and healthful products for the Earth.

+ Ugly, cracked concrete parking lots, walls, and buildings make way for buildings made from natural materials like living walls and roofs made of plants. Inner cities and suburbia are transformed into places of beauty and health.

+ Global warming is a thing of the past, as we meet all of our energy needs through sustainable sources. We create an inexhaustible clean supply of energy from photons streaming from the sun. (While today, solar power accounts for less than 0.1 percent of current U.S. electricity, in the future it will not only meet 100 percent of our needed energy supply, it will exceed it!) Photovoltaics become a major contributor to the energy grid, when nano-sized quantum dots[14] generate multiple electrons per photon, greatly increasing electrical output over traditional solar technology. We work with nature to absorb harmful carbon dioxide, reducing carbon in the atmosphere by helping forests to grow, and planting trees on a massive scale.

+ More people seek and find places on the land for energetic and spiritual renewal for healing and Earth balancing. There is a rise in the existence of labyrinths and altars in nature. These special places of healing are protected in much the same way that critical habitat areas are protected today.

+ People spend time each day in a state of prayer and gratitude. People come together in groups to send healing prayers and intentions to other people, other life forms, and the Earth. There are many more global actions like Fire the Grid,[15] an international effort to have people around the world send a bioelectric surge of love to the Great Unity (referred to as the Grid). Through our cohesive energetic and spiritual efforts we collectively help to heal the Earth and the animals.

+ People lead lives in greater rythym with natural cycles which leads to greater human health. We also discover the meaning of larger universal rythmyc cycles. We pickup where the Aztecs left off tracking cosmic cycles well beyond 2012 and gain great wisdom by doing so.

+ As we come into full awareness of the sacredness of all life, we serve as examples to all life by giving up our predatory ways. We end war and adopt a vegetarian diet

By giving up predation and meat eating, we solve major global problems, such as the cutting of rain forests to make grazing land and the overload of methane into our atmosphere—a primary global-warming gas from livestock. We also "purify" our bodies and increase the amount of oxygen that our bodies can hold within their cells, readying ourselves for greater health.

+ We put an end to the suffering of many thousands of people and millions of animals. A huge karmic chain of suffering is removed from the Earth, causing wide-scale beneficial changes that benefits all beings.

---

## CHAPTER PRACTICE

### Create Your Vision for the Future

If one person imagines a positive future for themselves, there is a greater likelihood that that future will unfold. If many people create and hold a paradigm of a positive future, we create powerful pathways, or songlines, moving us toward that destiny.

What is your vision for the future? What would the world look like—be like—if we partnered with nature? If you can imagine it, it is possible. Write down your vision of the future, date it, and save it. Pull it out five or ten years later and see if there has been any progress toward your vision. You may even want to create a Vision Seed Collage for what your vision of the world would look like. Share your vision with others.

---

# Epilogue
## Discovering Joy in Nature

When you walk across the fields with your mind pure and holy,
then from all the stones, and all the growing things, and all animals,
the sparks of their souls come out and cling to you, and then they
are purified and become a holy fire in you.

Ancient Hasidic prayer

*T*here is an eternal flowing source of joy that exists near us at every moment. Even in the darkest hours of the night, when your heart feels empty and alone, joy flows on right next to you, awaiting your arrival, calling to your heart to be filled with humble gratitude and for your mind to be filled with sweet thoughts like nectar.

It is in nature that our cup of joy fills to the brim. Joy is there in the yellow halo of a new morning sky; joy is there in the animated movements of a gray squirrel leaping from branch to branch; joy is there in the deep purple of a wild iris; joy is there in the still, glasslike surface of the lake. We feel such happiness and joy in nature because we belong in nature. We belong to nature because the Creator planted this joy seed in our heart that blooms in nature.

I remember one of these joyous moments, when my heart shone as brightly as the harvest moon. I was walking quietly in the early morning along a narrow trail in northern California. The trail, more fit for delicate deer hooves than human feet, wound along the southern slope of Mount Tamalpais. The brown dirt trail was lined with foot-high yellow-green grasses, which leaned toward its center and brushed delicately against my calves as I walked. Three hundred feet below me was a small narrow valley, where the sunlight gave way to the gray-green shade below. A California buckeye tree had dropped amber-brown nuts closely together in a tiny rivulet alongside the path. The morning spring air felt cool on my skin, and the sun was just beginning to rise over the closest ridgeline. A veil of fog was slowly lifting from the tips of the surrounding hillsides.

Up ahead, thirty feet or so, was my dog, Lia, cheerfully waving her golden flag of a tail. My steps had been slowing and I was beginning to fall behind, so Lia was now alternating her quick steps with glances over her shoulders to check on my progress. Her head turned, and her smiling eyes encouraged me to "come along, come along." Lia's "come along" was good advice, not just to match her pace but also to move along as well from my thoughts. In spite of the surrounding beauty and the serenity of the trail, for the past few minutes, my thoughts had been far away and of the past. I was having a flashback, recalling a time of past unhappiness that was clouding my present experience. How is it that our bodies can inhabit a place of beauty, and yet our thoughts and minds imprison us in a place we would not choose to go?

Mark Twain once jokingly said, "I've lived through some terrible things in my life, some of which actually happened."[1] Here, Twain pokes fun at one of humankind's greatest foible and most terrible burden. All of us, now and then, and some of us more often than others, imagine "terrible things" coming to pass in our minds that never actually occur. The more stressed and anxious we are, the more we tend to do this. So, on that beautiful morning, I found myself for a few minutes in that predicament that plagues the human race: my mind filled with unwanted thoughts, my brow slightly furrowed, eyes cast slightly downward. Then, Lia's tail disappeared beyond a sharp bend to the east and the newly rising sun. As I rounded the bend a few minutes later, a sight opened before me that completely shifted my consciousness.

On the northern incline of the trail, in the sheltered blue-gray shade of live oak trees draped with Spanish moss, over one hundred of the most exquisite wild white lilies sprang from the ground. Narrow beams of soft, golden light from the sun illuminated each delicate flower. Each flower's six pristine white petals appeared to be communing with the sun as the light streamed softly between the upper branches of the trees. It seemed as if I had innocently come upon a mysterious gathering of angels lighting upon the Earth as flowers.

Elevated in that shimmering moment, every cell of my body was infused with ecstatic grace and joy. Inhaling deeply, my lungs filled fully with the morning air that was still touched with the memory of the cool starry night. The sacredness of the place brought me fully into a moment of oneness with all of creation—a moment that seemed to span an eternity of time and space. I was beyond myself, clear of my own small cares and filled with a greatness that seemed as far-reaching as the universe itself. I was the saintly white irises; I was the soft light of the sun; I was the powdery blue Spanish moss that hung gracefully from the branches.

When that moment had passed, I could hear with great clarity the delicate singing of the small stream below and the sweet morning songs of the birds. I felt lighter and immeasurably freer. With my spirit lifted beyond my previously limited thinking, I whispered thanks to the Creator. Simply writing about this experience fills me once again with great joy.

Eckhart Tolle, the bestselling author of *The Power of Now*, describes being awakened one morning to find himself in this joyful state of being fully alive:

I was awakened by the chirping of a bird outside the window. I had never heard such a sound before. My eyes were still closed, and I saw the image of a precious diamond. Yes, if a diamond could make a sound, this is what it would be like. I opened my eyes. The first light of dawn was filtering through the curtains. Without any thought, I felt, I knew, that there is infinitely more to light than we realize. That soft luminosity filtering through the curtains was love itself. Tears came into my eyes ... That day I walked around the city in utter amazement at the miracle of life on Earth, as if I had just been born into this world.[2]

Tolle's experience is available to everyone when we enter the time of NOW, which is being present in each and every moment. This is what I meant when I said that we have the potential to escape time altogether. Because we are energetic, spiritual beings, we can break free of the limits of linear time. As aptly explained by Itzhak Bentov in his brilliant book *Stalking the Wild Pendulum: On the Mechanics of Consciousness*, in expanded or altered states of consciousness—like theta state for example—we become more space-like and less time-like, in our being. We become less bound by structured realities of time as we move into the timelessness of Indra's web and beyond.[3]

In this timeless place, we can experience qualities that reflect eternity and enjoy the omnipresent aspects of the larger unity. As Tolle discovers in his breathtaking journey to the NOW, nature is the perfect portal to these sacred moments.

It is no coincidence that Tolle's experience of oneness occurred as he listened to the song of a bird. By tuning into the truth of other living things, we step outside of ourselves and experience the world from other ways of being. We embrace the wisdom and power of the wind, the sky, and the sea. We experience beauty, multiplied many times over, and with the combined senses of many. By joining our single note with notes from the greater song of creation, we experience a place where there is no end and no beginning; there exists only unity and continuity.

Eden is here now. We inherently know this and have experienced this already. If we have forgotten it as an adult, the child within us knows it. We can reignite the experience of those childhood days when the world seemed brighter, the stars more brilliant, and the grass a deeper hue of green. We all have the ability to become something new when we are filled with the elixir of nature.

Just go outside and lie in the grass, look up at the trees and the sky. Take the time to walk over to the flowers to smell their fragrance; look deep inside their petals to see the subtle colors. Do not fool yourself that these acts are less important than spending tedious, long hours working. What kind of person will you be when you are filled with the warm rays of the sun, the clarity of the blue sky, or the freedom of a soaring hawk? Let these things grow inside you, and from this your soul will be much richer and fuller than it will ever be from a thousand promotions. Doubt not that the world reflects your very soul or that that the light of your spirit can change the world.

My hope for you, dear reader, is that your life is filled with moments of great joy and, from that joy, your heart opens to a greater appreciation, honoring, and care of nature and the Earth.

It is evening now as I finish writing at my desk in my living room. Beyond the living room, the land flows out from our small garden, past the fragrant roses, and rolls in smooth, undulating hills twelve miles west to the Pacific. The ocean's fluid surface, with waves gently cresting and falling, shimmers under the same rainbow-haloed moon that shines upon us all tonight.

*Deep peace*
*of the running wave to you*
*Deep peace*
*of the flowing air to you*

261

*Deep peace*
*of the quiet earth to you*
*Deep peace*
*of the shining stars to you*
*Deep peace*
*of the spirit of peace to you.*

—A Celtic blessing

# ACKNOWLEDGMENTS

Books never come about on their own; they reflect the efforts of many people. While I cannot acknowledge all who are a part of this book, I am grateful to Cynthia Black and Richard Cohn for having faith in this book and to their wonderful team at Beyond Words. I particularly want to thank Marie Hix, who has been a guiding light throughout the process; Lindsay Brown, who has ably led the editorial and design process; as well as Julie Clayton, Ali McCart, and Gretchen Stelter for their editing support. Many thanks as well to Isis Design, Devon Smith, and Sara Blum for their inspiring design work.

I also want to thank Dawson Church, publisher of Elite Books, and Jeanne House for encouraging me to put words on paper, for the anthology *Healing the Heart of the World*, and for providing initial feedback on the *Partnering with Nature* manuscript.

Several brave friends read the first ungainly draft of the manuscript and offered their heartfelt advice, including Allison Frost, Amy Racina (author of the wonderful book *Angels in the Wilderness*), and Rosaleen Bertolino. Rosaleen, a beautiful writer in her own right, went above and beyond by providing detailed editing advice on several of the chapters. I cannot thank her enough. I also wish to thank the many people who have participated in my vision quests and youth quests over the years.

In addition, I want to remember my parents, Irene and Joseph: while their lives were short in years, their lives were full measured by the number of people they loved and inspired. I want to acknowledge my beautiful sisters Ann, Jane, and Jo, and my godparents, Gillian Kyles and Marge and Dick Delano, for helping to raise me—no easy chore. I want to recognize my grandfather, Ian MacGregor, in whose footsteps I follow when it comes to writing. I recently found a letter from him to my mother, sending her some poems he wrote and published in Scotland. Thank you, Grandfather, for reaching beyond your lifetime to bring words of encouragement. I also want to acknowledge the MacGregors of royal descent who lost their ancestral home, and who became the "Children of the Mists."

I am indebted to the many wonderful teachers, mentors, colleagues, and friends who have shaped my life. I am especially grateful for Denise Linn, a modern day shaman and wise woman. I cannot thank her enough for her wisdom, guidance, and love. I also want to acknowledge Sandra Cohen, Nancy Rakela, Jim Gilkeson, Master Wang Hong of the Medicine Buddha Temple, Hidy Hiraoka, and Vimala Rodgers. What a blessing it has been to know each of you. Last but certainly not least, I wish to express my appreciation for my husband—for encouraging me to write and for being there, with humor, love and grace. For my son, Joseph, I can only say what I have said since the day you were born: "I love you as big as the sky."

# Notes

## PART 1

### Chapter 1

1. Wikipedia contributors, "Songlines," *Wikipedia: The Free Encyclopedia,* http://en.wikipedia.org/wiki/Songlines (accessed November 2009).

Songlines (or "Dreaming tracks") are native to indigenous Australians, who use them as a navigation device through life's physical and spiritual journey alike. Passed down from generation to generation, these ancient oral traditions deliver messages from the spirit world through song, dance, and other cultural outlets. The "Dreaming" or "Dreamtime" is believed to be the time when the world was created, and it was during this time that spirits of all kinds manifested into beings of the landscape, leaving important messages throughout the world via animals, plants, rocks, and other natural phenomena. Sharing songlines maintains the maps to these messages, preserving Aboriginal tradition while keeping their sacred spaces alive.

2. Benjamin Hoff, *The Singing Creek Where the Willows Grow: The Mystical Nature Diary of Opal Whiteley* (New York: Penguin Books, 1995), 273.

## Chapter 2

1. Denise Linn, *Quest: A Guide for Creating Your Own Vision Quest* (New York: Ballantine Books, 1997), 2.

2. Konstantin Klokov, "Reindeer Husbandtry in Russia," *International Journal of Entrepreneurship and Small Business* 4, no. 6 (2007): 23–72.

In recent times, in large part due to pressure from the Russian government, the Evenk have domesticated reindeer and rarely make the long migrations of their ancestors. Russia's domesticated reindeer make up about two-thirds of the world's population within this industry, creating a viable economic resource for the nation. Reindeer husbandry has decreased significantly in the last decade, however, creating a difficult situation for the indigenous cultures that adjusted to meet the economic pressures of the initial legislation. Now, the government is trying to creat a balance that recognizes the needs and rights of the Evenk while establishing the best solution for wild and domesticated herds alike.

3. Piers Vitebsky, *The Reindeer People: Living with Animals and Spirits in Siberia* (New York: Mariner Books, 2006), 268.

## Chapter 3

1. Internet Medieval Sourcebook, "Gildas (c. 504–570): Works" (New York: Fordam University Center for Medieval Studies, 1999), part 2, chap. 4, http://www.fordham.edu/halsall/basis/gildas-full.html; and Wikipedia contributors, "Gildas," *Wikipedia: The Free Encyclopedia*, http://en.wikipedia.org/wiki/Gildas (accessed November 2009).

Gildas, St. Gildas, or Gildas Sapiens ("Gildas the Wise") was a British monk from the sixth century whose strongly worded work *De Excidio et Conquestu Britanniae*, or *On the Ruin and Conquest of Britain*, condemned church and government alike for the intolerable, unjust conditions of the time.

2. Brother Azarias, *Aristotle and the Christian Church: An Essay* (London: Kegan Paul, Trench & Co., 1888), 21.

3. Wicasta Lovelace, trans., *The Malleus Maleficarum of Heinrich Institoris* (Kramer) and James Sprenger, unabridged online republication of the 1928 edition, Summers, Montague, trans. and ed. (1928/1948: rpt. New York: Dover, 1971), http://malleusmalefi carum.org (accessed October 2009).

4. Elaine Pagels, *Beyond Belief: The Secret Gospel of Thomas* (New York: Random House, 2001), 52.

5. Kahlil Gibran, *The Prophet* (New York: Alfred A. Knopf, Inc., 1923), 62.

6. William H. Prescott, *History of the Conquest of Mexico, with a Preliminary View of Ancient Mexican Civilization, and the Life of the Conqueror, Hernando Cortes*, Electronic Text Center website (Charlottesville, VA: University of Virginia Library, 2000), http://etext .lib.virginia.edu/toc/modeng/public/PreConq.html (accessed July 21, 2009); and Anonymous informants of Sahagún, *Florentine Codex*, book XII, chapter XVI, translation from Nahuatl by Angel Ma. Garibay.

7. Simon Martin and Nikolai Grube, *Chronicle of the Maya Kings and Queens: Deciphering the Dynasties of the Ancient Maya* (London and New York: Thames & Hudson, 2000).

8. R. Wilhelm and C. F. Baynes, Foreword to *The I-Ching or Book of Changes* by Carl Gustav Jung (Princeton, NJ: Princeton University Press, 1967), xxiv.

9. Mara Freeman, *Kindling the Celtic Spirit: Ancient Traditions to Illumine Your Life Through the Seasons* (New York: HarperOne, 2000), 138.

10. Anthony Aveni, *The Book of the Year: A Brief History of Our Seasonal Holidays* (New York: Oxford University Press, 2004), 11–28.

# PART 2

## Chapter 4

1. William E. Stein et al., "Giant Cladoxylopsid Trees Resolve the Enigma of the Earth's Earliest Forest Stumps at Gilboa," *Nature* 446 (April 19, 2007): 904–907.

2. "Stromatolite Pictures," SeaPics Marine Wildlife Photography website (Hawaii: 2008), http://seapics.com/feature-subject/marine-invertebrates/stromatolite-pictures.html (accessed November 2009).

This site displays pictures of hard, rock-like structures called stromatolite, which first created oxygen in the atmosphere over 3.5 billion years ago. They are living, ancient organisms made by a buildup of photosynthesizing cyanobacteria, also mistakenly called blue-green algae. They survive today in highly rich salt waters, where predators like snails cannot feed on them.

3. Michael Pollan, *The Botany of Desire: A Plant's-Eye View of the World* (New York: Random House, 2002), xiii.

4. Melvin Calvin & J. A. Bassham, *The Photosynthesis of Carbon Compounds* (New York: W. A. Benjamin, Inc., 1962), 3.

5. John Flinn, "World's Tallest in Arboreal Witness Protection," *San Francisco Chronicle* (August 17, 2008), section F-1.

6. Jennifer Emick, "Ogham—the Celtic Oracular Alphabet," About.com (January 19, 2007), http://altreligion.about.com/library/weekly/aa022203a.htm (accessed July 21, 2009).

7. Ed Collins and The Celtic Connection, "Sacred Celtic Trees and Woods," The Celtic Connection website (1997–1999), http://wicca.com/celtic/celtic/sactrees.htm (accessed April 18, 2009).

8. Marcel Vogel, as quoted by Peter Tompkins and Christopher Bird in *The Secret Life of Plants* (New York: Harper & Row, 1973), 23.

9. H. A. Harper, V. W. Rodwell, P. A. Mayes, *Review of Physiological Chemistry*, 16th ed. (Los Altos, CA: Lange Medical Publications, 1977), 102.

10. Tony Edwards, "Cancer's Achilles' Heel," *Ode Magazine*, June 2008, 62.

11. Otto Warburg, "The Prime Cause and Prevention of Cancer with Two Prefaces on Prevention," revised lecture at the meeting of the Nobel Laureates at Lindau, Lake Constance, Germany (June 30, 1966), Life Enthusiast Co-op website (2008), http://www .life-enthusiast.com/index/Articles/Warburg (accessed November 2009).

12. Paramahansa Yogananda, *Autobiography of a Yogi*, 1st ed. (New York: The Philosophical Society, 1946; repr., Nevada City, CA: Crystal Clarity Publishers, 1995).

13. Paramahansa Yogananda, *Scientific Healing Affirmations* (Los Angeles: Self-Realization Fellowship, 1981), endnotes.

14. Paul Rothemund, "Hemin and Chlorophyll: The Two Most Important Pigments for Life on Earth," *The Ohio Journal of Science* LVI, no. 4 (July 1956): 198.

15. Yogananda, *Autobiography of a Yogi*, 353.

16. James Lovelock, *Gaia: A New Look at Life on Earth* (New York: Oxford University Press, 2000), 10.

17. Jurriaan Kamp, "They're All Ears," *Ode Magazine* (December 2007), 17.

18. Yogananda, *Autobiography of a Yogi*, 66.

19. Time-Life Books Editors, *Earth Energies* (Alexandria, VA: Time-Life Books, 1991), 132–133.

20. Peter Tompkins and Christopher Bird, *The Secret Life of Plants*, 10.

21. Ibid., 11.

22. Ibid., 7.

23. Terry Robson, *An Introduction to Complementary Medicine* (Crows Nest, Australia: Allen & Unwin, 2003), 174.

24. U.S. Environmental Protection Agency, "Indoor Air Facts No. 4 (revised) Sick Building Syndrome," fact sheet (Washington, DC: February 1991), 1.

25. David Steinman, "The Architecture of Illness: Millions of Workers Are 'Sick of Work,'" *Update* newsletter (Environmental Health Association of Nova Scotia, Fall 1993), http://www .environmentalhealth.ca/fall93sick.html (accessed April 22, 2009).

26. Martina Giese et al., "Detoxification of Formaldehyde by the Spider Plant (Chlorophytum comosum)," *Plant Physiology* 104, no. 6 (1994): 1301–1309.

27. Belinda Hawkins, Suzanne Sharrock, and Kay Havens, *Plants and Climate Change: Which Future?* (Richmond, U.K.: Botanic Gardens Conservation International, 2008).

28. Stefan Lovgren, "Costa Rica Aims to Be 1st Carbon-Neutral Country," *National Geographic News* online publication (March 7, 2008), http://news.nationalgeographic.com/news/2008/03/080307-costa-rica.html (accessed November 2009).

29. Convention on Biological Diversity, "The Global Strategy for Plant Conservation: GSPC 2002," Convention on Biological Diversity website (Montreal, Canada: November 11, 2006), http://www.cbd.int/gspc/intro.shtml (accessed June 22, 2009).

30. Greenbelt Movement website, http://greenbeltmovement .org/index.php (accessed November 2009).

**Chapter 5**

1. Terry L. Root et al., "Fingerprints of Global Warming on Wild Animals and Plants," *Nature* 421 (January 2, 2003): 57–60.

2. Maryann Mott, "Can Animals Sense Earthquakes?" *National Geographic News* online publication (November 11, 2003), http://news.nationalgeographic.com/news/2003/11/1111_031111_earth quakeanimals.html (accessed February 21, 2009).

3. Rupert Sheldrake, "Listen to the Animals: Why Did So Many Animals Escape December's Tsunami?" as printed in *The Ecologist* (March 2005), http://www.sheldrake.org/papers/Animals/animals _tsunami.html (accessed June 15, 2008).

4. Ibid.

5. Mott, "Can Animals Sense Earthquakes?"

6. Ranjit Devraj, "Tsunami Impact: Andaman Tribes Have Lessons to Teach Survivors," Inter Press Service News Agency website (January 6, 2005), http://ipsnews.net/africa/interna.asp?idnews= 26926 (accessed November 2009).

7. Plutarch, *Parallel Lives, VII: Demosthenes and Cicero, Alexander and Caesar*, Bernadotte Perrin trans., Loeb Classical Library ed. (New York: Harvard University Press, 1919).

Caesar was warned by Spurinna to be on his guard on March 15, which the Romans call the "ides." (Ides refers to the fifteenth day of several months on the Roman calendar.) When Caesar was on his way to the senate house that very day—the day he was murdered— it is said that he passed and greeted Spurinna with a confident boast, saying, "See, the Ides of March has come," while the Seer is said to have replied, "Aye, Caesar, but not gone."

8. Ron Peterson, "Learning as Leadership Reflection" paper (unpublished essay, 2007).

## Chapter 6

1. J. B. Holroyd, *Historical Sketches of Christianity in England, from the Earliest Records to the Passing of the Roman Catholic Relief Bill, in 1829* (London: John Mason, 1834; electronic ed., Google Books), 276–279, http://books.google.com/books?id=fUmuNgP5 dq4C&printsec=frontcover&source=gbs_navlinks_s#v=onepage& q=&f=false (accessed November 2009).

2. Ibid.

3. Terri Jean, *365 Days Walking the Red Road: The Native American Path to Leading Spiritual Life Every Day* (Avon, MA: Adams Media, 2003), 15.

4. M. Balser and C. A. Wagner, "Observations of Earth-Ionosphere Cavity Resonances," *Nature* 188, no. 4751 (1960): 638–641.

5. Robert Burns, "To a Mouse," *Poems, Chiefly in the Scottish Dialect* (Kilmarnock, Scotland, 1870), 138. See Robert Burns World Federation for the Standard English Translation, http://www.worldburnsclub.com/poems/translation/554.htm (accessed January 2010).

6. John Broomfield, *Other Ways of Knowing: Re-charting Our Future with Ageless Wisdom* (Rochester, Vermont: Inner Traditions International, 1997), 2.

7. Stith Thompson, *The Seafarer, From Old English Poems Translated Into the Original Meter Together with Short Selections from Old English Prose*, trans. Cosette Faust (Chicago: Scott Foresman and Co., 1918), 68–71.

## Chapter 7

1. Sharon O'Brien, *American Indian Tribal Governments* (Norman: University of Oklahoma Press, 1989), 147.

2. A thrust fault is a break in the Earth's crust where two of earth's tectonic plates move and push against each other. With their compressed power, one side thrusts up and over the other, creating steep mountainous formations in the land. In the case of a blind thrust fault, the break occurs below the surface of the earth leaving little physical evidence of its presence.

3. Keay Davidson, "Sinister Quake Hazard May Lurk Beneath Mount Tam/Scientist Believe 'Blind' Fault Could Induce 6.5 Tremblor," *San Francisco Chronicle* (December 16, 2004), http://articles .sfgate.com/2004-12-16/bay-area/17456666_1_blind-thrust-fault-slip-faults-big-quake (accessed December 30, 2009).

4. Matthew Davis and Michael Farrell Scott, *Opening the Mountain: Circumambulating Mount Tamalpais, A Ritual Walk* (Emeryville, CA: Shoemaker & Hoard, 2006), 9.

5. Richard L. Burger and Lucy C. Salazar, eds., *Machu Picchu: Unveiling the Mystery of the Incas* (New Haven: Yale University Press, 2004), 36.

6. Philip Coppens, "Chartres: The Virgin Mary's Seat on Earth," Philip Coppens website, http://www.philipcoppens.com/chartres.html (accessed July 22, 2009).

7. Caitlín Matthews and John Matthews, *Walkers Between the Worlds: The Western Mysteries from Shaman to Magus* (Rochester, VT: Inner Traditions International, 2003), 33.

8. Paul Devereux, "Leys / 'Ley Lines'," abridged paper presented at "*Wege des Geistes—Wege der Kraft* (Ways of Spirit—Ways of Power)" conference in Germany (October 1996), http://www.pauldevereux.co.uk/new/html/body_leylines.html (accessed June 23, 2009).

9. Ibid.

10. Martin Gray, "Stonehenge Facts," SacredSites.com, http://www.sacredsites.com/europe/england/stonehenge-facts.html (accessed October 6, 2008); and Geoffrey of Monmouth, *Histories of the Kings of Britain*, Sebastian Evans, trans. (London: J. M. Dent & Sons, 1911), 203.

Stonehenge is made of two types of stone: sarsen and bluestone. The bluestones, weighing up to four tons and revered for their healing properties, were erected in the center of the site to form two concentric circles. The sarsen stones are an enormous eighteen feet in height and weigh twenty-five tons. They were probably brought to the site from the Marlborough Downs, about 30 kilometers to the north.

11. Gray, "Stonehenge Facts."

12. Ibid.

13. Devereux, "Leys / 'Ley Lines'."

14. Ibid.

# PART 3

## Chapter 8

1. Theodore Andrea Cook, *The Curves of Life* (London: Constable and Company, 1914; unabridged repr., New York: Dover Publications, 1979), 44.

2. Robert Olby, *The Path to The Double Helix: The Discovery of DNA* (London: MacMillan, 1974), 110.

3. James L. Pearson, *Shamanism and the Ancient Mind: A Cognitive Approach to Archaeology* (Walnut Creek, CA: Altamira Press, 202), 61, 87–88.

4. Don Edward Beck and Christopher C. Cowan, *Spiral Dynamics: Mastering Values, Leadership, and Change* (Oxford, England: Blackwell Publishing, 1996), 27, 29.

5. Ken Wilber, *A Brief History of Everything* (Boston and London: Shambhala, 1996), 42–43.

6. Wikipedia contributors, "Indra's net," *Wikipedia: The Free Encyclopedia*, http://en.wikipedia.org/wiki/Indra%27s_net (accessed November 2009).

The Mahayana Buddhist school developed the concept of Indra's net in the third century. Among the spiritual/philosophical concepts (or "jewels") it demonstrates are emptiness, dependent origination, and interpenetration.

7. Francis H. Cook, *Hua-yen Buddhism: The Jewel Net of Indra* (University Park: Pennsylvania State University Press, 1977), 67.

8. Lynne McTaggart, *The Field: The Quest for the Secret Force in the Universe* (New York: HarperCollins, 2002), xxvii.

## Chapter 9

1. Arnold Krupat, editor, *Native American Autobiography: An Anthology* (Madison: University of Wisconsin Press, 1994) 250–253.

2. Ibid., 256.

However, in the end, the Crow's land was reduced from 38.3 million acres to only 2.2 million, and the undignified restraints of reservation life were seen as a terrible failure by some of the Crow people.

3. M. Balser and C. A. Wagner, "Observations of Earth-Ionosphere Cavity Resonances," *Nature* 188, no. 4751 (1960): 638–641.

4. Mara Freeman, *Kindling the Celtic Spirit: Ancient Traditions to Illumine Your Life Through the Seasons* (New York: HarperOne, 2000), 111.

## Chapter 10

1. Louise Carus Mahdi, Nancy Geyer Christopher, and Michel Meade, eds., *Crossroads: The Quest for Contemporary Rites of Passage* (Chicago: Open Court Publishing Company, 1996), 32.

2. Paolo Mazzarello, "What Dreams May Come," *Nature* 108, no. 523 (November 30, 2000): 23.

3. Kneaded Dreams website, http://kneadedreams.com/famous-dreams.php (accessed July 12, 2009).

4. Patricia Garfield, *Creative Dreaming* (New York: Simon & Schuster, 1974), 80.

5. Paramahansa Yogananda, *Autobiography of a Yogi*, 1st ed. (New York: The Philosophical Society, 1946; repr., Nevada City, CA: Crystal Clarity Publishers, 1995), 395–411.

In this book, Yogananda recounts the insights of his guru Sri Yukteswar Giri on the existence of astral worlds and how they are reflected in our sleep. During the process of reincarnation, we may go back and forth between astral worlds and the Earth realm over a series of lifetimes.

## Chapter 11

1. ACS News Center, "Tap Into the Healing Power of Mother Nature: Contact with Nature is Good Medicine," American Cancer Society website (March 29, 2001): 23, http://www.cancer.org/docroot/NWS/content/NWS_2_1x_Tap_into_the_Healing_Power_of_Mother_Nature.asp (accessed November 2009).

2. Hippocrates, *On Airs, Waters, and Places*, Francis Adams, trans. (Whitefish, MT: Kessinger Publishing, 2004), 1.

3. Jim Karnstedt, "Ions and Consciousness," *Whole Self* magazine (Spring 1991; cited in "Archives," Cerebrex website), http://cerebrex.com/archives.htm#ion (accessed May 15, 2009).

4. Ibid.

5. Fred Soyka with Alan Edmonds, *The Ion Effect: How Air Electricity Rules Your Life and Health* (New York: E. P. Dutton & Co., 1977), 91.

6. Visit New York website, "Niagara Falls, New York," http://www.visit-newyork-online.com/niagara_falls_ny.htm (accessed December 2009).

7. Jim Karnstedt and Don Strachan, "Negative Ions, Vitamins of the Air?" Portal Market website, http://portalmarket.com/negion.html (accessed on July 23, 2009).

8. Michael Terman and Jiuan Su Terman, "Treatment of Seasonal Affective Disorder with a High-Output Negative Ion Generator," *Journal of Alternative and Complementary Medicine* 39, no. 3 (1995): 87–92.

9. Theodore A. David, John R. Minehart, and Igho H. Kornbleuh, "Polarized Air as an Adjunct on the Treatment of Burns," *American Journal of Physical Medicine and Rehabilitation* 39, no. 111–3 (June 1960).

10. Emil J. Bardana, Jr. and Anthony Montanaro, eds., *Indoor Air Pollution and Health* (New York: Marcel Dekker, Inc., 1996), 76.

11. B. K. Frantzis, *Relaxing Into Your Being: The Water Meditation Method of Taoist Meditation Series, Volume 1* (Fairfax, CA: Clarity Press, 1998), 50–53.

12. Fritz-Albert Popp and ZHANG Jinzhu, "Mechanism of Interaction between Electromagnetic Fields and Living Organisms," *Science in China* 43, no. 5 (October 2000): 507–518.

13. S. Cohen and F. A. Popp, "Biophoton Emission of the Human Body," *Journal of Photochemistry and Photobiology* 40, no. 2 (1997): 187–189; and R. O. Becker and G. Selden, *The Body Electric:*

*Electromagnetism and the Foundation of Life* (New York: Quill, William Morrow, 1985).

## Chapter 12

1. Elaine Pagels, *Beyond Belief: The Secret Gospel of Thomas* (New York: Vintage Books, 2004), 70.

This refers as well to the need to release negative energy from our being.

2. For additional information, see Walpola Rahula, *What the Buddha Taught* (New York: Grove Press, 1974).

3. Denise Linn, *Soul Coaching: 28 Days to Discover the Real You* (New York: Random House, 2003), 4.

4. Lynne McTaggart, *The Field: The Quest for the Secret Force in the Universe* (New York: Harper, 1987), 6.

5. Examples of major traditions and philosophies with strong elements of mysticism are: Bahá'í Faith, Rontian mysticism, Kabbalah (Judaism, Christianity, occult), mystery religions, the Rosicrucian Cosmo-Conception (Rosicrucian), Sufism (Islam), Taoism, Tibetan Buddhism, Transcendentalism (Unitarianism), Unity, Vedanta (Hinduism), Wicca, Yoga (Hinduism), and Zen (Buddhism).

6. Joseph Campbell, *Primitive Mythology: The Masks of God* (New York and London: Penguin Books, 1976), 112.

7. Thomas Pater, *Miraculous Abstinence: A Study of the Extraordinary Mystical Phenomena* (Washington, DC: Catholic University of America Press, 1946), 10.

8. Terri Jean, *365 Days Walking the Red Road: The Native American Path to Leading Spiritual Life Every Day* (Avon, MA: Adams Media, 2003), 15.

9. Bethe Hagens, "Plato's Cosmic Container," *Parabola* 31, no. 3 (Fall 2006): 30, presented on Bethe Hagens's website, http://missionignition.net/bethe/platos.php (accessed November 2009).

10. Carl Gustav Jung, *Collected Works of C. G. Jung*, vol. 6, *Psychological Types*, Gerhard Adler and R. F. C. Hull, trans. (Princeton: Princeton University Press, 1971), 29.

11. G. S. Kirk, J. E. Raven, and M. Schofield, *The Presocratic Philosophers: A Critical History*, second ed. (Cambridge, United Kingdom: Cambridge University Press, 1983), 56.

12. Refer to Denise Linn's website to learn more about her work: http://www.deniselinn.com/index.htm (accessed November 2009).

13. Some people like to be very precise in discerning where the center of the circle is by measuring with rope. Other people seek the center of the circle intuitively by sensing the spot where the energy feels strongest. This spot may not be the actual measured center of the circle.

14. Acknowledging a spiritual boundary of the sacred circle as if it were a physical boundary helps to maintain the power and protection of the sacred circle.

15. David Greene and Frank O'Connor, eds. and trans., *A Golden Treasury of Irish Poetry, AD 600–1200* (London: Macmillan, 1967; repr. 1990), 32.

## PART 4

### Chapter 13

1. Kristian Schlegel and Martin Füllekrug, "Fifty Years of Schumann Resonance," Catarina Geoghan, trans. (*Physik in unserer Zeit* 33, no. 6, 2002: 256-26; trans. 2007, presented at h.e.s.e. project website), http://www.hese-project.org/hese-uk/en/niemr/natural.php?content_type=R (accessed November 2009).

2. M. Balser and C. A. Wagner, "Observations of Earth-Ionosphere Cavity Resonances," *Nature* 188, no. 4751 (1960): 638–641.

The Earth sings a polyphonic song of at least eight frequencies (this is what we have been able to measure with our instruments to date). As human beings, we experience the waves of 7.83 hertz along with higher frequencies that fall within the gamma state and the lower waves of the delta state.

3. Ibid.

4. Richard Alan Miller and Iona Miller, "The Schumann Resonances and Human Psychobiology," *Nexus Magazine* 10, no. 3 (April–May 2003), http://twm.co.nz/schumann.html (accessed December 2009).

5. John Douillard, *Perfect Health for Kids: Ten Ayurvedic Health Secrets Every Parent Must Know* (Berkeley, CA: North Atlantic Books, 2004), 309.

6. Ibid., Richard Alan Miller and Iona Miller, quoting Lewis B. Hainsworth.

7. World Health Organization, "The 10 Leading Causes of Death by Broad Income Group," fact sheet no. 310 (Geneva, Switzerland: 2004; updated 2008), http://www.who.int/mediacentre/factsheets/fs310/en/index.html (accessed November 2009).

8. Alzheimer's Research & Prevention Foundation, "The 4 Pillars of Alzheimer's Prevention; Pillar 3—Exercise: Physical, Mental, and Mind/Body" (ARPF website, 2008), http://www.alzheimersprevention.org/pillar_3.htm (accessed July 29, 2009).

A recent study found that middle-age people suffering from early-onset Alzheimer's symptoms reversed their symptoms by practicing a Kirtan Kriya singing exercise (a type of meditation) for twelve minutes a day. Single Photon Emission Computerized Tomography (SPECT) scans proved that the majority of the group participants had increased the blood flow and oxygenation of their brains.

9. Balser and Wagner, "Observations of Earth-Ionosphere Cavity Resonances."

Note that there are +/-0.5 Hz variations caused when the sun changes during the day and night (see diagram on page 180).

The lunar cycle (approximately twenty-eight days) and sunspots also impact the frequency.

10. Andy Fincuane and Stewart W. Mercer, "An Exploratory Mixed-Methods Study of the Acceptability and Effectiveness of Mindfulness-based Cognitive Therapy for Patients with Active Depression and Anxiety in Primary Care," *BMC Psychiatry* 6, no. 14 (2006), http://www.biomedcentral.com/content/pdf/1471-244X-6-14.pdf (accessed July 2, 2009).

11. This drawing depicts the Gundestrup cauldron, which was found in 1891 in a peat bog near the hamlet of Gundestrup in Himmerland, Denmark. This singularly beautiful silver cauldron depicts Celtic deities and rituals. It was likely created for conducting rituals for the Druidic religion.

## Chapter 14

1. E. O. S. Scholefield and F. W. Howay, *British Columbia: From the Earliest Times to the Present* (Vancouver, BC: S. J. Clarke Publishing Company, 1914), 2:233.

2. Doug O'Hara, "Coalition Seeks to Protect Bering Sea," *Anchorage Daily News*, national ed. (August 6, 2003), 6.

3. Catriona MacGregor, interview notes from meeting with Doug O'Hara, a reporter with the *Anchorage Daily News*, for his article "Coalition Seeks to Protect Bering Sea" (August 5, 2003; article published August 6, 2003).

4. Catriona Glazebrook, "Father Thomas Berry: A Reverence for Life," *Whole Terrain* 3 (Antioch University New England journal, 1994), 4.

5. Alfred Lord Tennyson, *Poems of Tennyson*, ed. Henry Van Dyke and D. Laurance Chambers (Boston: Ginn & Co., 1903), 270.

6. Raleigh Howard Merritt, *From Captivity to Fame: The Life of George Washington Carver* (Boston: Meador Publishing Company, 1929; electronic ed., University of North Carolina at Chapel Hill,

2000), 14, http://docsouth.unc.edu/neh/merritt/merritt.html (accessed July 23, 2009).

7. Ibid.

8. Ibid., 33–34.

9. Glenn Clark, *The Man Who Talks With the Flowers: The Intimate Life Story of Dr. George Washington Carver* (Whitefish, MT: Kessing Publishing, 2007), 39.

10. Dr. Schweitzer served as the Kindness Club's first honorary president.

11. Learn more about episodes of *Whale Wars* at Animal Planet's website, http://animal.discovery.com/tv/whale-wars/ (accessed February 18, 2009).

12. Ibid. (accessed July 12, 2009).

13. Peace Pilgrim, *Peace Pilgrim: Her Life and Work in Her Own Words* (Santa Fe, New Mexico: Ocean Tree Books, 1982), 42.

14. Ibid., 8.

15. Ibid., 23.

16. Ibid., 21.

17. Robert Wuthnow, *Experimentation in American Religion: The New Mysticisms and Their Implications for the Churches* (Berkeley: University of California Press, 1978), 52.

18. Ibid.

## Chapter 15

1. Catriona MacGregor, paraphrased from a creation myth told in oral form; and Matt Alsdorf, "Which Creation Theory?" *Slate* magazine website, "Explainer: Answers to Your Questions About the News" (September 10, 1999), http://www.slate.com/id/1003588/ (accessed January 12, 2008).

2. William A. Dembski and Jonathan Wells, *The Design of Life: Discovering Signs of Intelligence in Biological Systems* (Dallas, Texas: Foundation for Thought & Ethics, 2008), 11.

3. Simon Crompton, "Sensory Deprivation: The Story Behind Horizon's TV Experiment; What Happens to the Brain When It's Deprived of Sensory Input?" *The Times*, January 19, 2008, http://women.timesonline.co.uk/tol/life_and_style/women/body_and_soul/article3209803.ece (accessed January 2010).

4. David Lewis-Williams and David Pearce, *Inside the Neolithic Mind: Consciousness, Cosmos, and the Realm of the Gods* (London, England: Thames & Hudson, 2005), XXX.

5. International Crane Foundation website, http://www.savingcranes.org/(accessed November 2009).

6. Julia Butterfly Hill, "Butterfly's Tale," Circle of Life website, http://www.circleoflife.org/tale.php (accessed November 2009).

## Chapter 16

1. Leslie Crawford, "Green with Worry," *San Francisco Magazine* (February 2008), 27.

2. Ibid., 29.

3. Merrit Clifton, "Roadkill Avoidance Tips from *Animal People*," *Animal People* newspaper website, http://www.animalpeoplenews.org/IMPORTANT_MATS/roadkillTips1104.htm, (accessed April 13, 2009).

4. Byron H. Earhart, ed., *Religious Traditions of the World: A Journey through Africa, Mesoamerica, North America, Judaism, Christianity, Islam, Hinduism, Buddhism, China, and Japan* (New York: HarperCollins, 2001), 36.

5. Calvin Luther Martin, *The Way of the Human Being* (New Haven, CT: Yale University Press, 1999), 71.

The Mi'kmaq were the dominant tribe in the Canadian Maritimes. They were the first Native Americans to come into contact with Europeans, and three-fourths of their population was wiped out by diseases from the Europeans.

6. Denise Linn, *Altars*, (New York: Rider & Co, 1999), 3.

7. Helen Gardner, ed., *The New Oxford Book of English Verse: 1250–1950* (New York & Oxford: Oxford University Press, 1972), 544.

8. Glen Rein and Rollin McCraty, "Structural Changes in Water and DNA Associated with New Physiologically Measurable States," *Journal of Scientific Exploration* 8, no. 12 (1995): 438–439.

9. Masaru Emoto, *The True Power of Water: Healing and Discovering Ourselves* (Hillsboro, OR: Beyond Words, 2005).

10. C. Nicholas, "The Effects of Loving Attention on Plant Growth," *New England Journal of Parapsychology* 1, no. 11 (1977): 19–24.

11. Ted Andrews, *Animal Speak: The Spiritual and Magical Powers of Creatures Great and Small* (St. Paul, MN: Llewelyn, 1993), 201.

12. The common turkey vulture rarely kills other animals and usually forages for carcasses, although its cousins the black vulture and condor may sometimes kill small- to medium-size animals.

13. Rose L. Solecki, "'Predatory Bird Rituals at Zawi Chemi Shanidar," *Sumer* 33 (1977): 42–47.

14. Celia W. Dugger, "Bombay Journal; In Death, the Unlovely Vulture Is Sorely Missed," *The New York Times* (March 1, 2001), 1.

**Chapter 17**

1. D. H. Lawrence, *Lady Chatterly's Lover* (New York: Penguin Classics, 1994), 323.

2. Benjamin Hoff, *The Singing Creek Where the Willows Grow: The Nature Diaries of Opal Whiteley* (London, England: Penguin Books, 1994), 240.

3. Stanley Frye, *Sutra of the Wise and Foolish* (Dharamsala, India: Library of Tibetan Works and Archives, 1981), 60.

4. DogsInTheNews.com, "Faithful Dog Leads Blind Man 70 Floors Down WTC Just before Tower Collapses" (September 14,

2001), http://dogsinthenews.com/issues/0109/articles/010914a
.htm (accessed November 2009).

5. James Gleick, "Isaac Newton's Gravity: How a Major New
Exhibition Gets the Scientist Wrong," *Slate* magazine website
(October 21, 2004), http://www.slate.com/id/97498/year/2004/
landing/1/ (accessed July 1, 2008); and Tim Radford, "Newton the
Alchemist Revealed in Lost Papers," *The Guardian* (July 2, 2005),
http://www.guardian.co.uk/uk/2005/jul/02/science.research,
(accessed July 2, 2008).

In 1936 some of Newton's manuscripts were sent from the
old Royal Society archives to Sotheby's in London to be sold at auc-
tion. Economist John Maynard Keynes purchased some of them.

6. Brian Greene, *The Elegant Universe: Superstrings, Hidden
Dimensions, and the Quest for the Ultimate Theory* (New York:
Random House, 2000), 104.

7. Bill P. and Lisa D., eds., *The 12 Step Prayer Book: A Collection
of Favorite Twelve Step Prayers and Inspirational Readings* (Center
City, Minnesota: Hazelden Foundation, 2007), 3.

**Chapter 18**

1. Howard Gardner, *Intelligence Reframed: Multiple Intelligences
for the 21st Century* (New York: Basic Books, 1999), 47–49.

2. Harold Sears, as quoted by Louise Chawla, "Children's
Concern for the Natural Environment," *Children's Environments
Quarterly* 5 no. 3 (Boulder, CO: University of Colorado, 1988):
13–20.

3. National Environmental Education & Training Foundation,
"Environmental Literacy in America: What 10 Years of NEETF/
Roper Research and Related Studies Say About Environmental Literacy in the U.S." (September 2005), http://www.neefusa.org/
resources/publications.htm#neetfpubs.

4. UNESCO, Tbilisi Declaration (1978), based on recommendations of the Intergovernmental Conference on Environmental Education, Tbilisi, USSR (1977).

5. Julian Vincent, as quoted by Vlad Tarko, "Learning from Nature: How to Save Energy? Nature Has Solutions Built in Structure and Behaviors Unlike Manmade Technology," *Sci-Tech News* (May 10, 2006), http://news.softpedia.com/news/Learning-from-Nature-How-to-Save-Energy-23169.shtml (accessed January 2, 2010).

6. Janine Benyus, *Biomimicry: Innovation Inspired by Nature* (New York: Perennial, 2002); and Peter Hesseldahl, "Biomimetics, an Interview with Janine Benyus," Peter Hesseldahl blog (August 2002), http://www.nynatur.dk/english/janine_benyus_eng.html (accessed August 30, 2009).

7. Jessica Aldred, "Iceland's Energy Answer Comes Naturally," *The Guardian* (April 22, 2008), http://www.guardian.co.uk/environment/2008/apr/22/renewableenergy.alternativeenergy (accessed on June 1, 2008).

8. Iceland is now exploring how to take its fishing fleet, cars, and buses to the next level by weaning them off fuel oil. Hydrogen fuel cells are one alternative solution that could become a reality within just the next twenty to thirty years. See Ólafur Ragnar Grímsson, President of Iceland, "Iceland: A Laboratory for Green Driving" (speech made on May 15, 2009), http://english_forsetti.is/media/files/09_05_15_Stavanger.pdf (accessed January 2, 2010).

9. Johnathan Fahey, "Solar Energy, All Night Long," Forbes.com (July 2008), http://www.forbes.com/2008/07/30/nocera-solar-power-biz-energy-cz_jf_0731solar_print.html (accessed August 20, 2008).

10. Janine Benyus, *Biomimicry: Innovation Inspired by Nature* (New York: Perennial, 2002); "What is Biomimicry?", Ask Nature: A Project of the Biomimicry Institute, website, http://asknature.org/article/view/what_is_biomimicry (accessed January 2, 2010).

11. Klaus S. Lackner et al., "Carbon Dioxide Disposal in Carbonate Minerals," *Energy* 20 (1995): 1153–1170.

12. Ed Carlson, as quoted on the National Audubon Society website, http://www.audubon.org/Local/Sanctuary/Corkscrew/Information/LivingMachine.html (accessed November 2009).

13. Dalias Kachan, "Oil Industry Subsidies for Dummies," Clean Tech (January 5, 2007), http://www.cleantech.com/news/node/554 (accessed July 23, 2009).

14. Los Alamos National Laboratory, Fact Sheet, "Renewable Energy Innovations," www.lanl.gov/news/factsheets/renewable_energy.shtml (accessed November 2009).

Nano-scale crystals, called "quantum dots," generate multiple charge carriers from the absorption of a single photon of light. This phenomenon, called "carrier multiplication," arises from the unique physics of nanomaterials and could dramatically improve the conversion efficiency of solar energy.

15. Shelley Yates, Fire the Grid website, http://www.firethegrid.com/ (accessed November 2009).

**Epilogue**

1. Mark Twain, as quoted on GoodReads.com, http://www.goodreads.com/author/quotes/1655 (accessed July 20, 2009).

2. Eckhart Tolle, *The Power of Now: A Guide to Spiritual Enlightenment* (New York: New World Library, 1999), 4.

3. Itzhak Bentov, *Stalking the Wild Pendulum* (Rochester, VT: Destiny Books, 1988), 64.

# Resources

## ENVIRONMENT/ENVIRONMENTAL STUDIES

+ **Antioch New England Graduate School:** antiochne.edu
    This is one of the oldest and best graduate programs for environmental studies, providing "transformative education through scholarship, innovation, and community action for a just and sustainable society."

+ **Children Nature Network:** childrenandnature.org
    Founded by bestselling author of *Last Child in the Woods*, Richard Louv.

+ **National Association for Environmental Educators:** naaee.org
+ **Sharing Nature with Children:** sharingnature.com
    Founded by Joseph Cornell, highly regarded international expert on environmental education.

## PERSONAL/SPIRITUAL DEVELOPMENT

+ **Animal wisdom:** *Animals as Teachers and Healers*, by Susan Chernak McElroy (Ballantine Books, 1998).
    In addition to being a *New York Times* bestselling author, Susan is also a teacher and a storyteller.

- **Catriona's vision quests, nature quests, and shamanic journeys:** naturalpathfinder.org, info@naturalpathfinder.com (Workshops and one-on-one training are available.)

- **Denise Linn's soul coaching seminars and books:** deniselinn.com

- **Energy healing:** *Energy Healing,* by Jim Gilkeson (Marlowe & Co., 2000), jimgilkeson.com
  Jim's site also offers classes to develop energy sensitivity for healing.

- **Kriya yoga, Paramahansa Yogananda:** ananda.org

- **Medicine Buddha Temple:** medicinebuddha.us
  Founded by Master Wang Hong, supports people in vegetarian diets and offers life saving healing therapies.

- **Spirit In Nature Tours:** eagle-tours.co.nz
  Take a guided tour with John Broomfield to visit aboriginal elders in Australia or sacred sites in India and New Zealand.

- **Tairona Heritage Trust:** tairona.myzen.co.uk
  Teaches about the descendants of the Tairona civilization, which includes the Kogi Indians.

## VISIONARY ACTIVIST AND WORLD CHANGE

- **Eyak Preservation Council:** redzone.org
  Founded by visionary Dune Lankard, working to protect the Copper River Delta in Alaska.

- **Friends of Peace Pilgrim:** peacepilgrim.com
  Learn more here about Peace Pilgrim, the incredible woman who walked across the North American continent numerous times for peace.

- **Green Belt Movement (Kenya):** gbmna.org
  This great initiative gathers rural populations to restore empowerment by planting trees throughout Africa. Its website

also offers updates on its amazing female founder (and Nobel Peace Prize–winner), Wangari Maathai.

+ **Julia Butterfly Hill:** http://juliabutterflyhill.wordpress.com/
Since her time living in Luna the redwood, Julia continues her important, loving work with environmental advocacy.

+ **Women's Earth Alliance:** womensearthalliance.org
This global organization, founded by Melinda Karmer, unites women on the front of environmental causes, coordinating training, technology, and financial support for thriving women, communities, and the Earth.

## YOUTH/EDUCATION

+ **Nature activities and practices:** *Sharing Nature with Children*, by Joseph Bharat Cornell (Dawn Publications, 1998).

+ **Nature-deficit syndrome:** *Last Child in the Woods*, by Richard Louv (Algonquin Books, 2008), richardlouv.com
Richard's site and bestselling book discuss how a lack of contact to nature is negatively affecting our children while offering solutions to this widespread problem.

+ **Opal Whiteley:** *The Singing Creek Where the Willows Grow: The Diary of Opal Whiteley*, afterword by Benjamin Hoff (*The Tao of Pooh*) (Penguin Books, 1994).
Read one of the most beautiful accounts of nature from the eyes of a child genius, and learn the heartwarming story of Benjamin Hoff's herculean efforts to bring this masterpiece to the eyes of the public.

+ **Youth Quest:** www.awengrove.org, info@awengrove.org
Youth Quest provides natural history education, experiential learning, coaching, and team building for youth, ages 9–16. In addition, this program seeks to encourage at-risk youth to pursue meaningful life choices by providing scholarships to assist them

in gaining skills and knowledge in their area of interest. Since the program is conducted outdoors in beautiful natural settings, youth also learn basic ecological principles while gaining a simple appreciation for the outdoors.

## BIOMIMICRY/NEW TECHNOLOGY

+ **Biomimicry:** biomimicryguild.com

    Biomimicry is the term/field created by Janine Benyus in which natural systems are studied to generate environmentally friendly solutions for modern-world / human problems.

+ **Ocean Arks International:** oceanarks.org

    Visit the website of visionary ecological designer Dr. John Todd, who invented the Living Machine.

+ **Total Environment Systems (TES):** Awen Grove (California): awengrove.org, info@awengrove.org

    A TES analysis will provide you with an analysis on the health of your indoor space. This includes a review of any harmful EMFs and ley lines, as well as any recommendations for enhancing your indoor space.

# About the Author

*A* visionary bridge builder between nature and humankind, Catriona helps people connect to nature and their own spirit through vision quests, shamanic journeys, spirit animal discovery, and nature-based coaching. She is a wise woman who weaves her many life experiences, spirituality, and intuition into a tapestry of hope.

A catalyst for positive change, Catriona is an authority on environmental trends in the United States and internationally, and over the past twenty years, she has led conservation initiatives and environmental education programs in Latin America, Eastern Europe, Asia, and the United States. She has been a voice for animals and wild places all of her life.

Catriona is also contributing author of *Healing the Heart of the World: Harnessing the Power of Intention to Change Your Life and the Planet*, along with Carolyn Myss, Jean Shinoda Bolen, Masaru Emoto, Fritjof Capra, Thich Nhat Hanh, and others.

She lives in northern California with her husband, Paul, her seventeen-year-old son, Joe, and many animal friends, domestic and wild.